Sun Lust
to
Sun Plus

Sun Lust to Sun Plus

NICHE TOURISM IN THE CARIBBEAN

Edited by
Acolla Lewis-Cameron
Leslie-Ann Jordan

The University of the West Indies Press
7A Gibraltar Hall Road, Mona
Kingston 7, Jamaica
www.uwipress.com

© 2023, Acolla Lewis-Cameron, Leslie-Ann Jordan

All rights reserved. Published 2023

A catalogue record of this book is available from the National Library of Jamaica.

ISBN: 978-976-640-941-8 (print)
ISBN: 978-976-640-942-5 (epub)

Cover and text design by Christina Moore Fuller

The University of the West Indies Press has no responsibility for the persistence or accuracy of URLs for external or third-party internet websites referred to in this publication and does not guarantee that any content on such websites is, or will remain, accurate or appropriate.

Printed in the United States of America

CONTENTS

List of Figures vii

List of Tables ix

Foreword xi

Acknowledgements xiii

1. Introduction: Caribbean Realities from Past to Present 1
   Leslie-Ann Jordan

2. Niche Tourism Development 22
   Acolla Lewis-Cameron

3. The Development of a Framework for Educational Tourism 33
   Elizabeth Ince-Peters

4. Accessible Tourism: A Case Study of Two of Grenada's Main Tourist Attractions 53
   Jovari Hagley

5. Stop Making Noise, Make Image – Unleashing the Possibilities of Music Tourism in Trinidad through Participation 77
   Leandra Simon-Richards

6. Festival Tourism in the Caribbean: A Comparative Analysis of the Barbados and St Lucia Jazz Festivals 101
   Leslie-Ann Jordan

7. Food Tourism in the Caribbean: The Case for Slow Food and Slowness in Travel 121
   Therez B. Walker

8. Examining the Case of Volcano Tourism in Montserrat, British West Indies 146
   Ineta R. West-Gerald

9. Unlocking the Potential of Diaspora Tourism in Trinidad and Tobago 167
   Andre Phillips

10. Medical Tourism: An Examination of Caymankind 187
    Belinda Blessitt Vincent

11. Cruise Tourism in the Caribbean Island of Cozumel: Challenges and Opportunities for Sustainability in the Post-COVID-19 Era 211
    Kennedy Obombo Magio

12. Resident Attitude to Domestic Tourism in a Core-Periphery Island Context 231
    Sherma Roberts

13. Niche Marketing in the Caribbean: A Call for a Scorecard Approach in Tourism-Intensive SIDS 254
    Narendra Ramgulam and Acolla Lewis-Cameron

Concluding Remarks 276
Acolla Lewis-Cameron

About the Contributors 279

Index 283

List of Figures

Figure 1.1:	International Tourism Receipts as a Percentage of GDP: The Top 25	6
Figure 1.2:	Map of the Caribbean	7
Figure 1.3:	Caribbean Tourism Economic Impacts	11
Figure 2.1:	Framework of Tourism Product Development Options	28
Figure 3.1:	The Framework for the Development and Management of ET	48
Figure 4.1:	Conceptual Framework for Barrier-Free Tourism Sites and Attractions	70
Figure 5.1:	Interactive Music Activities	80
Figure 5.2:	Participatory Framework for Music Tourism Development	90
Figure 5.3:	Music Tourism Participation Push Strategies towards Active Interest	92
Figure 5.4:	Music Tourism Participation Pull Strategies – Towards Sharing Benefits	94
Figure 7.1:	Slow Food and Slowness in Travel	127
Figure 7.2:	Impact of Scalable Community Initiatives on Small Island Destinations	134
Figure 7.3:	Slow Food and Food Tourism Relationship	137
Figure 8.1:	Volcanic Hazard Zones – Montserrat, 2014	154
Figure 8.2:	Volcanic Eruption	155
Figure 13.1:	Product/Market Growth Matrix	255
Figure 13.2:	Factors Shaping Market Competitiveness	257
Figure 13.3:	Sample of a Scorecard Model	267

List of Tables

Table 1.1:	Vulnerability Factors for SIDS	3
Table 4.1:	Amenities Provided at the Sites for People with Disabilities	65
Table 5.1:	Community Participation in Tourism	82
Table 5.2:	Willingness to Participate in Music Tourism	86
Table 5.3:	Examples of Music Movements in Trinidad	87
Table 5.4:	Ability to Participate in Music Tourism Development (Empowerment)	88
Table 5.5:	Participation Typologies as a Construct of Behavioural Intention – Interest	91
Table 5.6:	Participation Typologies as a Construct of Behavioural Intention – Empowerment	91
Table 5.7:	PTD Strategy Selection	92
Table 6.1:	List of Jazz Festivals in Caribbean Region	103
Table 8.1:	Montserrat Tourism Data – 2010–20	161
Table 9.1:	Trinidad and Tobago International Stayover Annual Arrivals	170
Table 9.2:	Comparison of US-Born and Trinidad and Tobago-Born Stayover Visitors for the Period 2013–17	170
Table 9.3:	Breakdown of Migrant Participation in Transnational Activities in the US	179
Table 11.1:	High-Risk Topics and Recommendations Based on Stakeholder Views	224

Foreword

Tourism is a significant change agent for many of the Caribbean's small island developing states and territories. It is therefore essential that it be continually examined through a critical lens. *Sun Lust to Sun Plus: Niche Tourism in the Caribbean*, conceived and edited by Dr Acolla Lewis-Cameron and Dr Leslie-Ann Jordan, seeks to do just that. Lewis-Cameron and Jordan, two of the Caribbean's foremost tourism scholars, recognize that while there are many books written about tourism, not many have specifically interrogated Caribbean tourism. Fewer still have focused on niche tourism in the region, and none encompass the specific niches that are presented in this volume.

In *Sun Lust to Sun Plus*, the authors aim to examine existing and potential tourism niches for the Caribbean, at a time when a unique selling position for the destinations in the region is critical to securing their competitive advantage in a saturated market. They accomplish this through a curation of contributions that both look at current niches and ways in which they can be enhanced and explore potential niches that are yet to be fully tapped by tourism entrepreneurs. For example, while educational tourism has existed for as long as tourism has, which Caribbean destination has made a deliberate effort to develop this niche rather than watching it occur through happenstance? Similarly, is this an opportune time to develop tourism that is centred on visiting the various dormant volcanoes around the region, like the US state of Hawai'i has done?

Sun Lust to Sun Plus is being published at a time when Caribbean tourism needs to be more strategic than ever before to strengthen and rebuild in ways that reflect the global social, environmental and economic changes that have emerged in the few years prior to its publication. I view *Sun Lust to Sun Plus* as a timely intervention. Tourism stakeholders from industry practitioners to government agencies would do well to heed its recommendations to create a more resilient and sustainable industry. Students, educators and researchers also stand to benefit from using this book as a launchpad for their work. The Caribbean tourism industry can no longer play "catch up" but must proactively foster small- and large-scale local entrepreneurship; promote best practices in employment; and create physical spaces and service standards that are welcoming to guests of all abilities. The case study on accessible tourism in Grenada is particularly insightful on the latter.

Since the late 1970s and early 1980s, writers about Caribbean tourism and other stakeholders have highlighted opportunities within niche tourism. There has been much conversation, but not the same amount of action. Now is the time for action. Fortunately, the cases offered in *Sun Lust to Sun Plus* provide guidance and exemplars of how to put decades of words into action. As such, *Sun Lust to Sun Plus* is a significant contribution to tourism in general and Caribbean tourism in particular. Moreover, it is a valuable addition to the body of knowledge about tourism. It is imperative that Caribbean scholars lead the way in studying the peculiarities of the Caribbean, ensuring that space is carved out in the body of tourism research for the Caribbean context because the region has much to offer the rest of the world.

I congratulate my colleagues and friends, Dr Acolla Lewis-Cameron and Dr Leslie-Ann Jordan, for recognizing the need for this work and stepping up to bring their case authors together to present the important volume. I hope you will find it as timely and useful as I have.

Mechelle N. Best, PhD
Dean
College of Health and Human Development
California State University – Northridge
mechelle.best@csun.edu

Acknowledgements

We wish to acknowledge and thank all the contributors in this volume for their patience and cooperation in bringing this publication to fruition. This book is unique in that contributions were received from academics, practitioners and research students. We are especially excited to provide an avenue to celebrate some of the valuable research that our young Caribbean scholars are producing during their graduate tourism degree programme at the University of the West Indies. We hope that this was an insightful and educational exercise that will hopefully spur additional research on niche tourism in the Caribbean.

We are sincerely grateful to the staff at UWI Press for willingly taking on this project and for their kind assistance and guidance during the preparation and submission of this manuscript.

We are also eternally grateful to our families for their continued love, support, encouragement and assistance. Last, but not least, thanks to the Lord Jesus Christ for His love, grace and patience. In Him, we live and move and have our being.

1.
Introduction: Caribbean Realities from Past to Present

Leslie-Ann Jordan

Small Island Developing States (SIDS)

Small island developing states (SIDS) have long attracted the attention and fascination of scholars and researchers from a wide range of disciplines such as geography, biology, history, politics, ecology, anthropology and economics. For many researchers, islands function as small-scale spatial laboratories where theories can be tested and processes observed in the setting of a semi-closed system (Alexander 1980; King 1993; Baum 1997). SIDS vary dramatically in their physical size and their total land area; in their location, either in favourable and hospitable situations or in truly challenging ones where they cope with natural hardships such as hurricanes and cyclones; in their natural resource bases, both on land and offshore; and in their prospects for self-reliant economic development (Wood 1967; King 1993; Bartmann 2001). They also differ in the nature of their political cultures, in their particular historical experiences, in their vulnerability to external intervention and in their ecological fragility (Bartmann 2001; Payne and Sutton 2001). As a result of such diversity, many scholars have become fascinated by SIDS and their commonalties and differences.

In fact, some authors acknowledge that SIDS possess strengths that are necessary for the development of a competitive and sustainable tourism industry (Roberts 2010). For example, many SIDS have relatively strong democratic systems, having transitioned from colonial rule to independence. Their political stability is evident in the existence of political freedom, civil liberties and political rights (Roberts 2010; Ott 2000; Hadenius 1992, cited in Sutton, 2007). As Roberts (2010, 4) noted, this foundation of safety and security "are critical factors when choosing a tourism destination, and so democracy and certain civil liberties cannot be discounted".

Additionally, SIDS possess a rich and diverse cultural and natural heritage and, in many cases, strong intellectual and social capital. According to Roberts (2010, 5), "the coral reefs, rivers, sea and landscape, biodiversity, intangible and tangible heritage all attest to the high capital resident in many SIDS." These resources serve as the pull factor for the new tourists who Poon (1993) described as looking for an experience beyond the traditional sun, sea and sand.

Despite these strengths, the economies of most SIDS are shaped by forces outside their control due to their openness and high dependence on a narrow range of exported products, and this makes their economies vulnerable to external shocks (Briguglio 2007; Turvey 2007; Briguglio 2003). Apart from global external shocks, Turvey (2007) outlines other vulnerability factors for SIDS (table 1.1).

The characteristics of SIDS clearly indicate the challenges they face and signal the importance of the diversification of these economies. The UNCTD (2010, 18) aptly describes their predicament by stating "SIDS are inherently economically vulnerable due to their remoteness and insularity, susceptibility to natural disasters, fragile ecology, limited institutional capacity, limited ability to diversify, strong dependence on a narrow range of exports, and high import content, particularly of strategic goods such as food and fuel, whose prices have exhibited high volatility".

Despite their 'locational advantage' (Brookfield 1990; UNEP 1996), many small islands have few natural resources that can be exploited. Those that do exist, such as fish, minerals, timber and, for the Caribbean, bananas and sugar, have dwindled significantly due to the lack of economic alternatives and development options (Holder 1980; Pantin 1995; Baum 1997). For example, some three decades ago, Holder (1980) described the low potential for alternative forms of economic development in the Caribbean and cited factors such as underdeveloped agriculture and fishing sectors; reliance on export crops such as sugar and bananas; some possibilities for the development of light industries and agro-industries; few possibilities for heavy industry and escalating energy bills. Undoubtedly, the role of agriculture in small states has been declining due to the continuous decline in prime commodity prices. At the same time, some of these countries cannot develop a heavy manufacturing sector because of the smallness of their local market and the lack of capital and technology (Holder 1980; Connell 1988; UNEP 1996). As a result, neither primary nor secondary sector exports are able to

Table 1.1: Vulnerability Factors for SIDS

Economic factors	• Vulnerability to external economic shocks • Fragility due to intrinsic factors • Susceptibility of domestic economy to extreme events • Vulnerability to routine risks in 'everyday life'
Geographic factors	• Vulnerability to natural disasters • Vulnerability from locational disadvantages – peripheries, ghettos, slums • Endangered zones and impaired habitats – typhoon and hurricane bells, polluted areas • Vulnerability to structural weakness – dependence, food insecurity, powerlessness, poverty and lack of response capabilities • Fragility of ecosystems and physical environment • Rural, urban, sectoral and communal space of vulnerability
Socio-political factors	• Enforced vulnerability of population – forced labour, forced resettlement and uprooting, economic sanctions, ethnic cleansing and regions of misrule • Vulnerability to interpersonal forces – population factors, economic, cultural and environmental conflicts

Source: Turvey (2007, 247)

provide the market share needed to generate employment and foreign exchange (Amara 1994).

Additionally, small island states have had to contend with the forces of globalization and economic restructuring, which has brought with it the emergence and dominance of market-driven economies, underpinned by the impulse of technological change (Ritchie 1993; Pantin 1995). Pantin (1995) further explained that globalization is "more a geographically dispersed manifestation of the pressures which more competitive firms place on competitors within their home market given the absence of any protectionist barriers". This new political and economic order has inevitably brought greater hardship to small island states, which were heavily dependent on preferential trade agreements and foreign aid.

Why Tourism Development?

In light of the many challenges facing island states in the twenty-first century, many of them have been motivated, or in some cases compelled, to identify policy alternatives which are not only effective and efficient but which also provide the greatest potential to realize the desired economic and social outcomes. Consequently, many of them have identified tourism as an engine of growth with the promise to help them generate foreign exchange, reduce unemployment, augment government revenue, positively impact their balance of trade and diversify their economic base (Butler 1993; Mather and Todd 1993; Conlin and Baum 1995; Craig-Smith 1996). Tourism was a natural choice given the fact that many small islands were already very popular tourist destinations and, for many people, island tourism conjured images of sun-drenched, palm-fringed white sandy beaches that epitomized paradise, rest and relaxation. In today's fast-paced, commercial environment, islands seem to be the ideal holiday destination to get away from it all, to escape, recharge overworked batteries and generally appreciate the benefits of peace and tranquillity (Butler 1993; Baum 1997; Harrison 2001b). However, the range of tourism issues facing small island states and the impact of tourism upon their economy and environment is diverse.

According to UNWTO (2017) tourism has been a major contributor to economic growth and the number of international tourists visiting SIDS increased from US$28 million in 2000 to US$41 million in 2013. During that same period, exports from tourism grew from US$26 billion to US$53 billion. This represents significant growth for these SIDS. Tourism also accounts for over 20 per cent of gross domestic product (GDP) in two fifths of the SIDS where data is available. While this is noteworthy, it does leave these tourism-intensive SIDS vulnerable to external shocks, particularly if their source markets are impacted by volatile financial and economic conditions. This in turn affects visitor numbers, revenue, employment (both direct and indirect), foreign exchange, the government's social spending, and the inability to balance national budgets.

In terms of positive impacts, tourism has many linkages with other economic sectors. If properly integrated into national development plans with adequate provisions for intersectoral linkages, it can contribute to the growth of all tourism-related activities in all major economic sectors, such as agriculture, fisheries, industry, and services and transportation. Some of the socio-economic and cultural benefits of tourism that have been documented in the literature include:

- positive contribution to foreign exchange earnings and the balance of payments;
- generation of employment, income and government revenue;
- improvement of economic structures and the encouragement of entrepreneurial activity; and
- contribution to the conservation of the destination's cultural, archaeological and natural resources (Mathieson and Wall 1992; Pattullo 1996; UNEP 1996).

It is important to note that the extent of tourism activities in small island states varies widely between geographical regions, as well as between countries within regions, and that the economic benefits derived from tourism are diverse. For example, at the regional level, the development of the tourism industry is generally more advanced in the Mediterranean and Caribbean SIDS than those in the Asia-Pacific and African regions (UNEP 1996). And even in the Caribbean region, there is disparity in terms of the role that tourism plays in national development. For example, Jamaica and Trinidad and Tobago view tourism as a tool to help them diversify their economy instead of as a major source of export earnings, whereas in countries like Antigua and Barbuda, St Lucia and Grenada, tourism receipts account for 60.49 per cent, 47.87 per cent and 46.89 per cent of GNP, respectively (The Global Economy 2021) (see figure 1.1).

However, the influx of large numbers of tourists is more likely to have a profound cultural, social and environmental effect on SIDS destinations than on larger mainland resort destinations because of the small scale at which SIDS operate (Conlin and Baum 1995). The literature documents some possible negative impacts:

- dominance of foreign ownership and the lack of linkages with other sectors of the economy and as a result the substantial leakage of foreign exchange earnings;
- increased inflation and higher land values;
- seasonality of production and a low rate of return on investment;
- over-dependence on tourism;
- destruction of local culture and displacement of residents; and damage to environmental resources (Burkart and Medlik 1981; Mathieson and Wall 1992; Pattullo 1996).

Figure 1.1: International Tourism Receipts as a Percentage of GDP: The Top 25

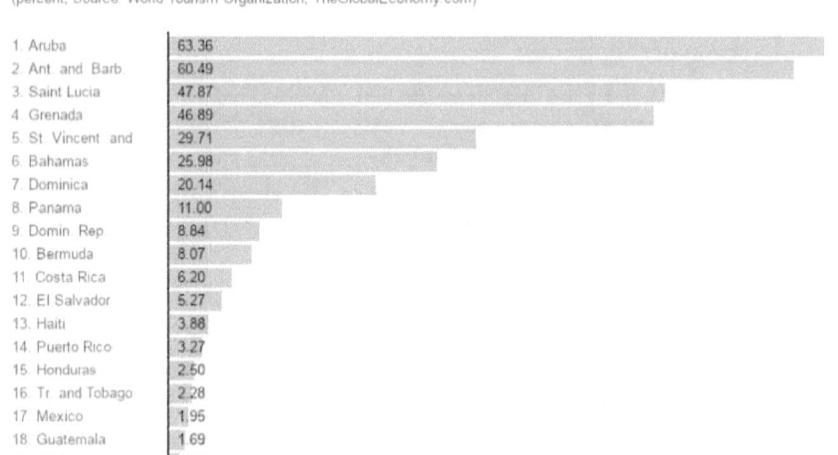

Source: The Global Economy 2021

In light of both the positive and negative impacts of the tourism industry and the development constraints facing small island states, many island governments have recognized that tourism affects and is affected by all other sectors of the economy. As a consequence, they have acknowledged the need for integrated planning in order to protect the environment; to minimize leakages from the economy; to maintain flexibility and adaptability in the face of changing market conditions; to provide sustainability for the economy over the long run; and to develop and maintain some level of self-reliance within the regional economy (Duval 1998; Tosun and Jenkins 1998; Roberts 2021).

Overview of Tourism Development in the Caribbean

According to the United Nations Economic Commission for Africa (2017), out of the fifty-two SIDS recognized by the United Nations, twenty-three are located in the Caribbean. Most of these countries depend heavily on tourism, with their major source markets being the United States of America, Canada and Europe. The Caribbean consists of several hundreds of islands grouped politically in some thirty island states. Mackay and Spencer (2017, 46) define the Caribbean as "large and small countries (in terms of both land mass and population); island states and countries on mainland continents; Spanish, Dutch, French and English-speaking countries; and independent and dependent territories". Figure 1.2 shows a map of the Caribbean islands.

According to Lewis-Cameron (2021, 9), "the majority of these islands rely upon a very limited range of economic activities, and concomitant vulnerability to fluctuations in these sectors". The region's colonial history saw the introduction of and specialization in a few plantation crops such as sugar, coffee, copra and bananas. However, climate and soil conditions restrict the variety of agricultural products (Lockhart and Smith 1997) and, consequently, many islands have historically relied on a few of these agricultural cash crops for foreign exchange.

As early as the 1940s, the tourism sector was seen as potentially important for Caribbean economic growth, but it was only with the advent of mass tourism in the late 1950s and inexpensive jet air travel in the early 1960s that tourism became a major economic activity in the region (Holder 1993; Wilkinson 1997; Grassl 1999). The tourism industry attained a more prominent place in the region's economy during the 1980s, against a backdrop of depressed oil and bauxite prices on the international market (Holder 1993). This situation was

Figure 1.2: Map of the Caribbean

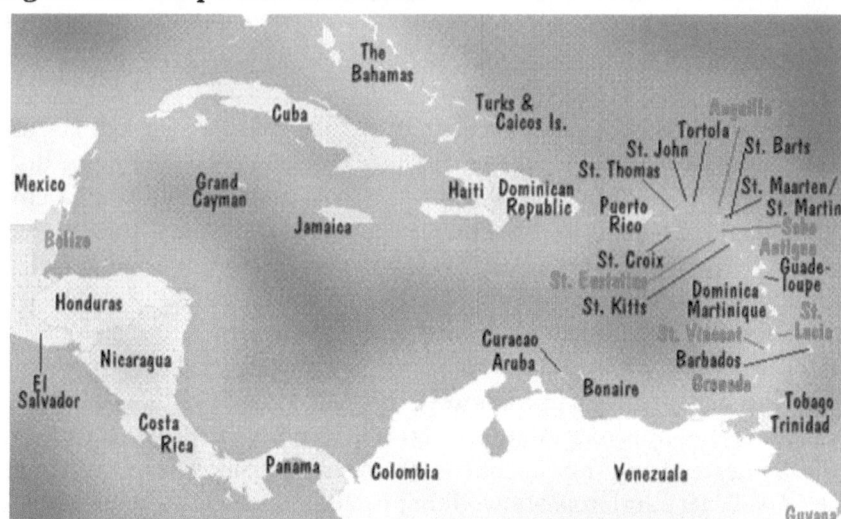

Source: http://www.turq.com/caribbeanandcentralamerica/map.php

compounded by the fact that Caribbean sugar and banana exports were threatened, both by loss of preferential status in the US and European markets and by increased competition from larger and cheaper producers (Girvan 1999; Bonnick 2000). Additionally, other Caribbean manufacturing sectors also continued to shrink in the face of the deep recession in Europe and North America (Pantin 1995). In the light of these factors, during the second half of the 1980s, many Caribbean governments placed greater dependence on the tourism industry to help them increase their foreign exchange earnings, which was much needed to pay for imported goods and services (Gayle and Goodrich 1993a; Holder 1993).

There appeared to be an almost universal view that many island states, particularly those that are tropical islands in the periphery, had little economic choice but to accept traditional tourism development, which has been characterized by mass tourism, control by multinational companies and large-scale facilities (Wilkinson 1989; Gayle and Goodrich 1993b; UNEP 1996; Weaver 1998). The literature suggested that while island economies should seriously search for alternative forms of economic development, tourism was seen as almost inevitable, assuming that international tourism continued to grow (Carter 1987; Wilkinson 1989). Many Caribbean governments have identified tourism as an economic tool to help them achieve national objectives such as creating sustainable employment; increasing foreign exchange earnings; forging linkages with other economic sectors such as agriculture, manufacturing and retail; creating an income base on which to levy taxation; and diversification of the economy (Wilkinson 1989; Mather and Todd 1993; Harrison 2001).

Governments in the Caribbean have recognized tourism as an export industry that generates foreign exchange, creates jobs and encourages economic diversification. To this end, the Caribbean currently leads all other regions worldwide as having the largest relative dependency on travel and tourism in its national output, employment and investment. For the majority of the Caribbean, there has been an overdependence on tourism, which is viewed as a panacea for growth and development. On average, the tourism sector is said to account for approximately 30 per cent of GDP for all SIDS and generates approximately US$30 billion per year (Coke-Hamilton 2020). Figures from the Caribbean Tourism Organization from before the COVID-19 pandemic showed that in 2019 Caribbean destinations received an estimated 32.0 million international tourist arrivals, 4.4

per cent or approximately 1.3 million more than the 30.7 million of 2018 (CTO 2021). Although total visitor spending declined slightly, approximately by 1 per cent to US$38.3 billion, tourists spent slightly more per trip than they did in 2017 – US$1,177 per trip compared to US$1,171 in 2017.

Among the destinations, tourist arrivals showed uneven growth. Several countries reported double-digit increases in 2018 such as Guyana (15.9 per cent), Belize (14.6 per cent), the Cayman Islands (10.7 per cent), the Bahamas (10.5 per cent) and Grenada (10.0 per cent), while the hurricane-impacted countries recorded double-digit declines. In 2018, the cruise sector had its best performance, demonstrating a rapid recovery from the 2017 hurricanes. The number of cruise passenger visits reached an estimated 28.9 million, up by 6.7 per cent (CTO 2019).

It is therefore not surprising that the governments and leaders of the Caribbean have finally and almost unanimously realized that tourism is anything from "an important" to "the most important" to "the only" means of economic survival for their states (Pattullo 1996, 10). Tourism in the Caribbean is now advanced and dominates the landscape (McElroy and de Albuquerque 1998). According to Mather and Todd (1993, 11), "tourism is both the glue that holds the region's economies together and a vital source of employment for the growing population". As an economic activity, tourism in the Caribbean is of an importance scarcely matched by any other region in the world (Mather and Todd 1993; Wilkinson 1997; McElroy and de Albuquerque 1998).

However, research has emphasized the socio-environmental damage of over-rapid mass tourism development and the fact that much of this growth has been unplanned and intrusive and has damaged insular eco-systems. For example, the scarring of mountains with condominium developments and road networks has caused widespread erosion and wildlife extinction. Additionally, the concentration of large infrastructure and resort complexes along delicate coastlines has destroyed mangroves and beaches and caused lagoon pollution from sand mining, dredging and sewage dumping (Wilkinson 1989).

Tourism Current Reality

According to the World Travel and Tourism Council (WTTC 2021), prior to the COVID-19 pandemic, travel and tourism (including their direct, indirect and induced impacts) accounted for one in every four new jobs created across the world, 10.6 per cent of all jobs (334 million), and 10.4 per cent of global GDP (US$9.2 trillion). Meanwhile, international visitor spending amounted to US$1.7 trillion in 2019 (6.8 per cent of total exports, 27.4 per cent of global services exports). However, the United Nations World Tourism Organization reported that almost all countries had implemented travel restrictions of one sort or another, such as travel bans, visa controls and quarantines, in order to stop the spread of the virus (UNWTO 2020). As a result, international tourism was almost totally suspended in April and May of 2020.

The post-pandemic figures for the tourism industry are dismal. WTTC's (2021, np) latest annual research showed:

- The Travel & Tourism sector suffered a loss of almost US$4.5 trillion to reach US$4.7 trillion in 2020, with the contribution to GDP dropping by a staggering 49.1 per cent compared to 2019; relative to a 3.7 per cent GDP decline of the global economy in 2020.

- In 2019, the Travel and Tourism sector contributed 10.4 per cent to global GDP; a share which decreased to 5.5 per cent in 2020 due to ongoing restrictions to mobility.

- In 2020, 62 million jobs were lost, representing a drop of 18.5 per cent, leaving just 272 million employed across the sector globally, compared to 334 million in 2019. The threat of job losses persists as many jobs are currently supported by government retention schemes and reduced hours, which without a full recovery of Travel and Tourism could be lost.

- Domestic visitor spending decreased by 45 per cent, while international visitor spending declined by an unprecedented 69.4 per cent.

Unfortunately, the UNWTO (2021) reported that tourism experts do not expect a return to pre-COVID-19 arrival levels until 2023 or later. As figure 1.3 shows, the picture is not much brighter for the Caribbean region. Caribbean economies were among the most affected by the pandemic. According to the International Monetary Fund (IMF 2021), "with annual hotel stays plummeting by 70 per cent and cruise ship travel completely halted, tourism-dependent countries contracted by 9.8 per cent in 2020". Commodity exporters in the region like Trinidad and Tobago, Suriname and Guyana were less affected and saw a mild contraction of 0.2 per cent.

In a period of much instability in the global tourism arena, many destinations are considering more sustainable types of tourism

Figure 1.3: Caribbean Tourism Economic Impacts

Caribbean Key Data	2019	2020	
Total contribution of Travel & Tourism to GDP:	**14.1%** of Total Economy Total T&T GDP = USD58.4BN	**6.4%** of Total Economy Total T&T GDP = USD24.5BN	**-58.0%** Change in Travel & Tourism GDP vs -9.0% real economy GDP change
Total contribution of Travel & Tourism to Employment:	**2.76** Jobs (MNs) (15.4% of total employment)	**2.08** Jobs (MNs) (12.2% of total employment)	Change in jobs: **-24.7%** -0.7 (MNs)
Visitor Impact International:	USD **35.4** BN Visitor spend 21.2% of total exports	USD **11.4** BN Visitor spend 8.1% of total exports	Change in international visitor spend: **-68.0%** -USD 24.1 BN
Domestic:	USD **12.6** BN Visitor spend	USD **6.3** BN Visitor spend	Change in domestic visitor spend: **-49.6%** -USD 6.2 BN

Source: WTTC 2021

activities, ones that impact communities and the environment positively while bringing economic benefits. The effects of mass tourism prior to COVID-19 are more apparent than ever as movement came to an absolute halt in 2020. Due to near eradication of travel, many destinations experienced a rebirth in their tourism assets, with some reporting cleaner waterways, crisper air and spotless surroundings. At the same time, travellers experienced many restrictions that prohibited their movement, fostering a greater appreciation for the natural environment that would facilitate social distancing and improve their health. Furthermore, the recovery period is expected to be quite long, with predictions of pre-pandemic travel patterns emerging in 2024. This simply means that destinations are now competing for the attention of travellers in a leaner marketplace. These travellers are more discerning and demand greater value and more authentic and safer experiences. It is therefore no surprise that the development and implementation of niche tourism products have become of paramount importance to destinations and their planning agencies.

Organization of Book

This book offers rich content that will bridge the gap between theoretical and practical perspectives in a Caribbean context regarding the niche tourism approach. The cases examined in this book are set against an opening discussion by Jordan in chapter 1 on the Caribbean realities of vulnerability and a historical overdependence on tourism. This is followed by an interrogation of the concept of niche tourism and its applicability in a Caribbean context, presented by Lewis-Cameron in chapter 2.

Each case study illustrates either the development of or the potential to develop a niche product alongside the Caribbean's traditional sun, sea and sand product offering. In chapter 3, Ince-Peters highlights that educational tourism has become a staple in higher education institutions and presents several advantages for host destinations. However, for such a niche to sustainably develop, she argues that six key stakeholders should be involved in its planning and management, namely: the tourists, industry, local community, government, special interest groups and educational institutions. In this vein, this chapter addresses the question "how can educational tourism be developed in order to effectively contribute to tourism diversification?" Using Grenada as a case study, Ince-Peters discovered that the core requirements of the stakeholder groups for the development and management of educational tourism included: support for the initiative, effective identification of and response to demand, safety within the destination, and collaboration among stakeholders. The Grenada case presents a good example of educational tourism in SIDS as stakeholders facilitated, and continue to facilitate, its development, continually seeking to satisfy the desires of the target market and create a safe destination. However, she concludes that collaboration amongst stakeholders is still fairly ad hoc and that there was a need to formalize collaborative initiatives through institutional arrangements, including memorandums of understanding and the creation of an Educational Tourism Stakeholders Board.

Accessible tourism is the niche discussed by Hagley in chapter 4. He argues that despite the increase in international tourist arrivals, there is a lack of facilities and services that cater to people with disabilities, people with special needs and seniors. This presents a potential missed opportunity for SIDS as the World Health Organization highlighted that over a billion people, or approximately 15 per cent of the world population, are people with disabilities (WHO

Media Centre 2013). This chapter seeks to determine to what extent Grenada should develop two of its main tourist attractions towards achieving universal accessibility for all visitors. Hagley discusses the benefits of accessible tourism, the rights of persons with disabilities and the importance of creating a universal design. Additionally, the chapter discusses the importance of tourism to the island of Grenada and the need for accessible tourism resource development in Grenada.

In chapter 5 Simon-Richards explores the socio-spatial configurations which both mirror and favour the development of dense creative networks and the attendant forms of conflict, diversity and collaboration that enable music tourism interactions to flourish in local communities. The chapter explores the concept of participatory tourism development as a strategy for increased tourism benefits for local communities wanting to develop music tourism as a viable niche market. The participation framework for music tourism development is presented as a tool for critically analysing the strategy for music tourism development in Trinidad. This model implies that an interest in music can trigger a movement from passive to active participation where stakeholder willingness is concerned. It also implies that high levels of conflict and other inhibitive factors, which impede opportunities to share benefits, suppress or frustrate participatory tourism development. The case also explores the development of music tourism as a contributor to place identity and a destination promoter and adopts the view that developing Trinidad as a music destination will motivate residents and tourists alike to travel to spaces of music creation to engage in place-based social interactions that facilitate the creation and extraction of formal and substantive value. Simmons argues that music tourism can enable a more meaningful set of experiences to be created in Trinidad as it widens the focus of niche tourism from a narrow set of highly specialized, seasonal and disjointed products to one that appeals to a more mainstream audience in a cohesive, permanent, year-round setting.

In chapter 6, Jordan uses the St Lucia Jazz Festival and the Barbados Jazz Festival to explore festival tourism in the Caribbean. St Lucia and Barbados are the pioneers of jazz festivals within the Caribbean and have used festivals as a tourism strategy to increase tourist arrivals in their off-peak seasons. However, there have been significant financial challenges to the management and organization of these festivals, so much so that in 2010, the organizers of the

Barbados Jazz Festival were forced to cancel the event. One of the main aims of the research was to identify some of the critical success factors for managing music events and the challenges associated with such events. This chapter analyses the management of the Barbados and the St Lucia Jazz festivals by means of a comparative analysis using a qualitative case study approach. Based on the analysis, Jordan recommends that countries seeking to host jazz festivals employ public-private partnerships in their development and management. Furthermore, focus should be placed on increasing community participation and engagement to ensure economic and socio-cultural sustainability of the festival. This research provides a unique perspective as it compares jazz festivals in the Caribbean region and addresses the paucity of literature on festival management in the Caribbean.

In chapter 7, Walker presents another variation on the food tourism niche, that of slow food tourism. She discusses the fact that food and the unique culinary aspects of a destination are becoming important travel motivators. Moreover, the relationship between food and tourism can serve as a catalyst for sustainability in local communities. Given this reality, food tourism can be seen as a practical approach to sustainable tourism for Caribbean SIDS, where the 3 Es of sustainability, economy, ecology and equity, are holistically realized. By highlighting the abundance of cultural diversity, together with authenticity in local cuisine, this chapter highlights the value of encouraging sectoral linkages and developing food tourism as an important niche that responds to changing consumer dynamics. She argues that tourism in the Caribbean can benefit from focusing on the social economy through agri-tourism and enable a symbiotic relationship that extends to food tourism. The slow food movement is currently present in several Caribbean islands and sets a supportive framework for food tourism in the region. Here, food tourism presents pertinent considerations for ways in which the tourism industry can be extended to offer an enhanced experience, reduce environmental impact, empower communities and stimulate the local economy. This chapter examines the attractiveness of food tourism in the Caribbean as a niche tourism product and presents a framework for its development. The role of slow food is conceptualized, and this chapter also considers the current realities of Caribbean destinations before presenting a future outlook for becoming sustainable gastronomic destinations that integrate tourism with sustainable food production that benefits local communities.

Montserrat is the focus of chapter 8, as West-Gerald examines the case of volcano tourism. She argues that although volcanic eruptions can be deadly and can cause distress to countries – socially, economically, culturally, physically and environment – on the other hand, these eruptions provide numerous opportunities for countries to make them rewarding. The success of volcano tourism, however, requires management of the risks associated with these natural phenomena. This chapter examines how one tiny island in the Caribbean has been using its volcano to its advantage since it roared back to life more than twenty-six years ago.

In chapter 9, Phillips explores diaspora tourism as a panacea for the poor results of the pursuit of more conventional tourism built around leisure and business tourist arrivals and spending in the Caribbean. This chapter introduces the nature, characteristics and potential benefits of a form of tourism that is rooted in travel by migrants and their descendants to homeland Trinidad and Tobago. It outlines how diaspora tourism can be a gamechanger in strengthening the tourism sector and enabling sustainable tourism in Trinidad and Tobago.

In chapter 10, Blessitt Vincent examines the evolution of medical tourism in the Cayman Islands and the island's trajectory to become the medical tourism capital of the Western Hemisphere. There are four major hospitals and several state-of-the-art medical services available in the islands, offering various medical treatments to locals and visitors. The government has also encouraged investment in medical tourism projects in an effort to diversify the economy and provide employment and new opportunities for its residents. The intent of this new tourism product is not only to attract visitors from its current marketplace in the United States, United Kingdom and Canada but also to seek new visitors from Latin America and the Caribbean. There is also the potential of wellness tourism. According to the Department of Tourism, the Cayman Islands boasts first-world infrastructure, accommodations and communication systems, a wide array of leisure activities and the beautiful Caribbean Sea at its doorstep. Therefore, medical tourism is combined with wellness tourism to allow for recuperation and rehabilitation in an island-resort setting. Additionally, since "Caymankind" (the island's mantra) is the heart and hospitality of the Caymanian people that turns first-time guests into lifetime visitors, the various stakeholders see this connection as a positive multiplier effect for the industry.

Focusing on Cozumel, in chapter 11, Magio examines some of the key issues facing cruise tourism on the island and how the destination is trying to manage change, both positive and negative. Cruise tourism in the Mexican Caribbean is experiencing major challenges as a result of the COVID-19 pandemic: cancellations or temporary suspension of cruise tourism activities by cruise lines and port destinations and loss of jobs and income for host communities (many small island nations rely heavily on the jobs and cash flow from the industry). Other issues like climate change, increasing concerns about socio-economic and environmental impacts and insecurity existed before the pandemic. Therefore, it is important to analyse and understand the depth of these issues in each port destination and identify the potential opportunities for cruise lines to have a positive effect on the host communities, especially as it relates to the local culture, environment and sustainable on-shore excursions. Magio found that stakeholders in both public and private sectors (residents, opinion leaders and tourism operators, among others) were supportive of cruise tourism. However, there were issues related to the excessive number of cruise tourists (before the pandemic) and diminishing recreational opportunities for the locals.

The focus of chapter 12 is domestic tourism, which Roberts argues is seldom given any attention (and if so, almost always in a national or international economic crisis) as the assumption is that it does not produce sufficiently significant economic multipliers to warrant any serious interest (Scheycker 2014). While the economic argument is privileged in the government discourse, relatively little is known about the socio-cultural sustainability of both domestic and international tourism. This question becomes even more significant within the context of island states with systemic inequalities by virtue of, inter alia, size and history. This chapter examines the extent to which domestic tourism can create strong socio-cultural sustainability contributions in destinations and, if this is the case, whether domestic tourism needs an institutional champion, like a Destination Management Organization. The study was conducted in the twin-island state of Trinidad and Tobago, where over the last ten years there has been an increase in tourism flowing to Tobago from the bigger island of Trinidad (Tobago Tourism Agency 2019).The findings reveal a very complex picture where residents are in favour of tourism development in Tobago and have a clear understanding of the economic benefits and opportunities the industry presents for self-reliance and empowerment. However, they are also of the view that local identity and pride decreased as a result of the influx of Trinidadians as domestic tourists, and that crime, feelings of domination and traffic congestion have increased. This dialectic presents a challenge to socio-cultural sustainability in an island space and requires urgent and sensitive interventions at all levels of governance and civil society.

These case studies present strategic considerations to public and private sector practitioners in implementing measures to strengthen the competitive positioning of their destinations as they contend with the enhanced dynamism of the tourism sector. Most significantly, the penultimate chapter provides destination management organizations with a practical, user-friendly approach to identifying, selecting and developing the most appropriate niche tourism products based on the peculiarities of their destination.

The final chapter, chapter 13, by Lewis-Cameron and Ramgulam, addresses the issue of what niche products SIDS should diversify into. This research makes a call for a scorecard approach to be considered. The scorecard model assesses SIDS' potential niche market options across a range of variables found in the literature. These variables were selected by using the methodological approach of applying content analysis to existing literature on global tourism case studies and filtering those variables through the Sustainable Development Goals outlined by the United Nations (2017). The completed scorecard model then rates and ranks the most viable niche products that these SIDS can diversify into and therefore spread development into other areas. This is a unique contribution of this chapter as it proposes a model that adds a strategic approach to niche product development which is new to the literature and to the practice of niche tourism product development.

References

Alexander, L.M. 1980. "Centre and Periphery: The Case of Island Systems." In *Centre and Periphery: Spatial Variations in Politics*, edited by J. Gottmann, 135–47. London: Sage.

Amara, Y.A. 1994. "Externally Traded Services and the Development of Small Economies." In *External Linkages and Growth in Small Economies*, edited by D.L. McKee, 7–16. Connecticut: Praeger Publishers.

Bartmann, B. 2001. "Island Studies as an Emerging Discipline." http://www.upei.ca/~iis/iiswhaum.htm.

Baum, T. 1997. "Island Tourism as an Emerging Field of Study." *Islander Magazine* 11 (3): 37–53.

Bonnick, G. 2000. *Toward a Caribbean Vision 2020: A Regional Perspective on Development Challenges, Opportunities and Strategies for the Next Two Decades.* Washington, DC: Caribbean Group for Cooperation in Economic Development.

Briguglio, L. 1995. Small Island Developing States and Their Economic Vulnerabilities. *World Development,* 23 (9): 1615–32.

———, and W. Galea. 2003. "Updating and Augmenting the Economic Vulnerability Index." Occasional paper, Islands and Small States Institute of the University of Malta, 4, 1–15.

Brookfield, H.C. 1990. "An Approach to Islands." In *Sustainable Development and Environmental Management of Small Islands,* Man and the Biosphere Series, edited by W. Beller, P. d'Ayala and P. Hein, 23–33. Paris: UNESCO; Carnforth, UK: Parthenon Publishing Group.

Butler, R.W. 1993. "Tourism Development in Small Islands: Past Influences and Future Directions." In *The Development Process in Small Island States,* edited by D. Lockart, D. Drakakis-Smith and J. Schembri, 71–91. London: Routledge.

Burkart, A.J., and S. Medlik. 1981. *Tourism: Past, Present and Future.* 2nd ed. London: Heinemann.

Caribbean Tourism Organization (CTO). 2019. *CTO Caribbean Tourism Performance Report 2018 & Outlook for 2019.*

———. 2021. *CTO Annual Statistical Report 2019.* https://www.onecaribbean.org/buy-cto-tourism-statistics/annual-statistical-report/.

Carter, E.A. 1987. "Tourism in the Least Developed Countries." *Annals of Tourism Research* 14 (2): 202–26.

Coke-Hamilton, P. 2020. "Impact of COVID-19 on Tourism in Small Island Developing States." *UNCTAD,* 24 April 2020. https://unctad.org/news/impact-covid-19-tourism-small-island-developing-states.

Conlin, M.V., and T. Baum, eds. 1995. *Island Tourism: Management Principles and Practice.* Chichester, UK: John Wiley and Sons.

Connell, J. 1988. *Sovereignty and Survival: Island Microstates in the Third World.* Research Monograph No. 3. Sydney: Department of Geography, University of Sydney.

Craig-Smith, S. 1996. "Economic Impact of Tourism in the Pacific." In *Tourism in the Pacific: Issues and Cases,* edited by C.M. Hall and S.J. Page, 36–48. London: International Thomson Business Press.

Duval, D.T. 1998. "Alternative Tourism on St. Vincent." *Caribbean Geography* 9 (1): 44–57.

Gayle, D.J., and J.N. Goodrich. 1993a. "Caribbean Tourism Marketing, Management and Development Strategies." In *Tourism Marketing and Management in the Caribbean,* edited by D.J. Gayle and J.N. Goodrich, 1–19. London: Routledge Publishers.

———. 1993b. *Tourism Marketing and Management in the Caribbean.* London: Routledge Publishers.

Girvan, N. 1999. *Globalisation, Fragmentation and Integration: A Caribbean Perspective.* https://www.geocities.ws/CollegePark/Library/3954/girvan.pdf.

Grassl, W. 1999. "Tourism and Economic Growth in the Caribbean." Unpublished thesis, Mona School of Business and Management, University of the West Indies, Jamaica.

Harrison, D. 2001. "Islands, Image and Tourism." *Tourism Recreation Research* 26 (3): 9–14.
Holder, J.S. 1980. "Buying Time with Tourism in the Caribbean." *Tourism Management* 1 (2): 76–83.
———. 1993. "The Caribbean Tourism Organization's Role in Caribbean Tourism Development towards the Year 2000." In *Tourism Marketing and Management in the Caribbean*, edited by D.J. Gayle and J.N. Goodrich, 205–19. London: Routledge Publishers.
International Monetary Fund (IMF). 2021. "How the Caribbean Can Avoid Becoming a COVID-19 Long-Hauler." https://www.imf.org/en/News/Articles/2021/03/11/na031221-how-the-caribbean-can-avoid-becoming-a-covid-19-long-hauler.
King, R. 1993. "The Geographical Fascination of Islands." In *The Development Process in Small Island States*, edited by D. Lockart, D. Drakakis-Smith and J. Schembri, 13–37. London: Routledge.
Lewis-Cameron, A. 2021. "Introduction." In *Managing Crises in Tourism*, edited by A. Lewis-Cameron, L.A. Jordan and S. Roberts. London: Palgrave Macmillan, Cham. https://doi.org/10.1007/978-3-030-80238-7_1.
Lockhart, D.G., and D. Smith, eds. 1997. *Island Tourism: Trends and Prospects.* London: Cassell.
Mackay, E.A., and A. Spencer. 2017. "The Future of Caribbean Tourism: Competition and Climate Change Implications." *Worldwide Hospitality and Tourism Themes* 9 (1): 44–59. https://doi.org/10.1108/WHATT-11-2016-0069.
Mather, S., and G. Todd. 1993. *Tourism in the Caribbean: Special Report No. 455.* London: Economist Intelligence Unit.
Mathieson, A., and G. Wall. 1992. *Tourism: Economic, Physical and Social Impacts.* Harlow, UK: Longman.
McElroy, J.L., and K. de Albuquerque. 1998. "Tourism Penetration Index in Small Caribbean Islands." Annals of Tourism Research 25 (1): 145–68.
Ott, D. 2000. *Small is Democratic: An Examination of State Size and Democratic Development.* New York: Garland Publishing.
Pantin, D.A. 1995. Finding the "Safe Havens" for Sustainable Caribbean Development in the 21st Century. http://www.tidco.co.tt/local/seduweb/research/dennisp/martniq.htm.
Pattullo, P. 1996. *Last Resorts: The Cost of Tourism in the Caribbean.* London: Cassell.
Payne, A., and P. Sutton. 2001. Charting Caribbean Development. London: Macmillan Education.
Poon, A. 1993. *Tourism, Technology and Competitive Strategies.* Oxfordshire, UK: CABI Publishing.
Ritchie, J.R.B. 1993. "Issues in Price-Value Competitiveness of Island Tourism Destinations." In *World Travel and Tourism Review: Indicators, Trends and Issues*, Vol. 3, Special Report: Island Tourism: Price-Value Issues in the 1990s, edited by J.R.B. Ritchie, D.E. Hawkins, F. Go and D. Frechtling, 299–305. Oxfordshire, UK: CAB International.

Roberts, S. 2021. "Conceptualizing Resilience in Small Island States." In *Managing Crises in Tourism*, edited by A. Lewis-Cameron, L.A. Jordan and S. Roberts. London: Palgrave Macmillan, Cham. https://doi.org/10.1007/978-3-030-80238-7_3.

———, and A. Lewis-Cameron. 2010. "Small Island Developing States: Issues and Prospects." In *Marketing Island Destinations*, 1–10. London: Routledge.

Scheyvens, R. 2007. "Poor Cousins No More: Valuing the Development Potential of Domestic and Diaspora Tourism." *Progress in Development Studies* 7 (4): 307–25.

Sutton, P. 2007. "Democracy and Good Governance in Small States." In *Commonwealth Small States: Issues and Prospects*, edited by E. Kisanga and S. Danchie, 201–17. London: Commonwealth Secretariat.

Tosun, C., and C.L. Jenkins. 1998. "The Evolution of Tourism Planning in Third-World Countries: A Critique." *Progress in Tourism & Hospitality Research* 4:101–14.

The Global Economy. 2021. "International Tourism Revenue, Percent of GDP in North America." https://www.theglobaleconomy.com/rankings/international_tourism_revenue_to_GDP/North-America/.

Turvey, R. 2007. "Vulnerability Assessment of Developing Countries: The Case of Small-Island Developing States." *Development Policy Review* 25 (2): 243–64.

United Nations. 2015. "Sustainable Development Goals." Accessed on 14 April 2017. http://www.un.org/sustainabledevelopment/blog/2015/12/sustainable-development-goals-kick-off-with-start-of-new-year/.

United Nations Conference on Trade and Development (UNCTD). 2010. "Promoting Foreign Investment in Tourism." In *Investment Advisory Series*. Series A, number 5. Geneva: United Nations Publications. Accessed on 10 January 2017. http://unctad.org/en/docs/diaepcb200916_en.pdf.

United Nations Economic Commission for Africa. 2017. Economic Report on Africa 2017. Economic Report on Africa 2017 | United Nations Economic Commission for Africa (uneca.org).

United Nations Environment Programme (UNEP). 1996. "Progress in the Implementation of the Programme of Action for the Sustainable Development of Small Island Developing States: Sustainable Tourism Development in Small Island Developing States." http://www.umep.ch/islands/d96-20a3.htm.

United Nations World Tourism Organization (UNWTO). 2020. "100% of Global Destinations Now Have Covid-19 Travel Restrictions." *UNWTO Reports*. https://www.unwto.org/news/covid-19-travel-restrictions.

———. 2021. "Tourist Numbers Down 83 Per Cent but Confidence Slowly Rising." https://www.unwto.org/news/tourist-numbers-down-83-but-confidence-slowly-rising.

Weaver, D.B. 1998. *Ecotourism in the Less Developed World*. Oxfordshire, UK: CAB International.

Wilkinson, P.F. 1989. "Strategies for Tourism in Island Microstates." *Annals of Tourism Research* 16:153–77.
Wilkinson, P.F. 1997. *Tourism Policy and Planning: Case Studies from the Commonwealth Caribbean.* New York: Cognizant Communication Corporation.
Wood, D.P.J. 1967. "The Smaller Territories: Some Political Considerations." In *Problems of Smaller Territories*, edited by B. Benedict, 23–34. London: Athlone Press.
World Health Organization (WHO) Media Centre. 2013. "New World Report Shows More than 1 Billion People with Disabilities Face Substantial Barriers in their Daily Lives." https://www.who.int/news/item/29-10-2013-new-world-report-shows-more-than-1-billion-people-with-disabilities-face-substantial-barriers-in-their-daily-lives.
World Travel and Tourism Council (WTTC). 2021. "Economic Impact Reports." https://wttc.org/Research/Economic-Impact.

2.
Niche Tourism Development

Acolla Lewis-Cameron

Introduction

The governments and leaders of the Caribbean have finally and almost unanimously realized that tourism is anything from "an important" to "the most important" to "the only" means of economic survival for their states (Pattullo 1996). It was during this period of time in the 1990s that Mather and Todd (1993) noted that the Caribbean is the most tourism-dependent region in the world. Twenty years later, tourism remains the lifeblood of the majority of the English-speaking and non-English-speaking islands. Given the context presented earlier, it is expected that tourism will continue to be core to the economic survival of the islands for some time to come. The conundrum for Caribbean destinations over the years has been a reliance on the mass tourism development model which has been economically beneficial but, in many cases, environmentally detrimental. As these destinations look towards 2030 and beyond and consider their future competitiveness and sustainability, the mass tourism model that has dominated Caribbean development comes under scrutiny.

The social, economic and environmental ills of mass tourism have plagued Caribbean tourism over the last three decades. As tourism-dependent islands look to the future, they should consider alternative approaches to tourism development in order to counteract the ills of mass tourism and contribute to improving the Caribbean's competitive position in the global tourism space. It is against this background that this chapter seeks to critically examine the concept of niche tourism development as an alternative to the mass tourism development model. This chapter which discusses in detail the various niche tourism development strategies adopted by respective destinations as well as potential niche products that can be adopted.

The Concept of Diversification

Niche tourism development is premised on the concept of diversification. According to Berry (1971), diversification allows firms, countries and institutions to expand their product range by adding and seeking out items which they did not previously have and investing in them. It involves the movement of a country's economy away from a reliance on specialization of production, in accordance with the theory of comparative advantage, and towards investment into new areas of production. The outcome of diversification is that a growing range of economic outputs are produced. This expansion in production suggests that a failure or an economic slump affecting one product will not be disastrous since it will only impact one economic area. Diversification is therefore an important consideration for countries so that they do not have all their eggs in one basket.

In support of the movement towards economic diversification, Rodrik (2005, 10) noted that countries that are moving from lower to higher levels of income have production patterns which become "much more diversified". Diversification therefore allows countries to be flexible and bold with their policies (Hendrix 2017; Auty 2017) since more diversified economies carry a higher margin for error than resource dependent economies (Hosein 2010). According to Carneiro et al. (2014, 6), "a resource-rich economy that diversifies its economic structure, its products, and its partners – and that becomes less reliant on its most abundant endowment – is also less sensitive to macroeconomic shocks transmitted through large fluctuations in commodity prices. And with resource extraction highly capital-intensive, diversification creates additional sources of employment for the labour force".

Based on the above, alongside the development of new products, diversification creates new and sustainable revenue streams which increases export variety and economic performance. Further, there is the opportunity to develop specialized labour for a wide array of jobs. The tourism industry has been a prime target for diversification efforts for many countries due to its overall growth potential: opportunities for forward and backward linkages and the multiplier effects. Several oil-dependent countries in particular have experienced success by diversifying into tourism, notably, Qatar (Morakabati, Beavis and Fletcher 2014), Bahrain, Kuwait, Oman, Saudi Arabia (Peterson 2009) and Dubai (Cherif and Hasanov 2014).

Tourism Diversification

As established earlier, in the Caribbean context, tourism remains the dominant sector driving economic development in the region with no sign of abating, given the restricted resource endowments. While countries around the world are diversifying towards tourism as an economic development tool to complement their existing products, Caribbean destinations have to consider diversification within tourism. This calls for a shift from a total reliance on mass tourism to alternative tourism product offerings. This shift comes at a time when the negative effects of mass tourism are being highlighted and the "new tourist" is being characterized. The concept of alternative tourism or niche tourism caters to the uniqueness of the individual tourist while mitigating the negative environmental and socio-cultural effects of mass tourism within a destination.

By way of a definition, Robinson, Heitmann and Dieke (2011, 9) referred to alternative tourism as "catering to the needs of specific markets by focusing on more diverse tourism products". According to Weaver (1995), alternative tourism is "a generic term encompassing a range of tourism strategies (e.g. appropriate, eco, soft, responsible, people-to-people, controlled, small-scale, cottage and green tourism), all of which purport to offer a more benign alternative to conventional mass tourism in certain types of destinations". Novelli (2005) further described alternative tourism as niche tourism which involves breaking down tourism into large homogenous market sectors and further dividing these sectors into smaller groups through further segmentation. At the core of alternative or niche tourism is a response to the ills of mass tourism and the changing dynamics in the market.

In terms of the former, concerns for the delivery of sustainable tourism using the mass tourism model of development are a key driver of alternative tourism. Some characteristics of mass tourism are underpinned by unsustainable practices, for example, the high levels of foreign exchange leakage owing to a large import bill, poor linkages within the economies and the construction of large-scale tourist facilities in environmentally sensitive areas. According to Macleod (2003), alternative tourism is a reaction to the exploitation of developing countries in which the notion of a "just" tourism arises, further mutual understanding and preventing environmental or cultural degradation and exploitation. Benur and Bramwell (2015, 214) also agreed that "alternative products" can potentially be more socially and environmentally sustainable for destinations. The rationale provided is that these products "encourage appreciation of a destination's special character, involve businesses that are locally owned, and are small-scale in terms of tourist numbers and infrastructure requirements". While small scale, local ownership and lower volume present an attractive contrast to the high volume, high impact and foreign dominance of mass tourism, there is a noteworthy concern that alternative tourism can spread the negative influences of mass tourism over a wider area. From an economic standpoint, there is also the harsh reality that in some cases, alternative tourism is too small scale to offer a realistic economic option.

The latter driver of alternative tourism, the changing dynamics in the market, can be viewed from two perspectives. On the one hand, the global competitive landscape for tourism continues to evolve and destinations are under intense pressure to ensure that they remain relevant, at the cutting edge and responsive to the market in order to survive let alone be competitive. At the time of writing, destinations the world over are trying to cope with the fallout of the COVID-19 pandemic, which has the potential to redefine the operating environment for global tourism. The United Nations World Tourism Organization designated 2020 the worst year in tourism history, citing a 74 per cent decline in international arrivals and an estimated loss of US$1.3 trillion in export revenues, a loss that is eleven times greater than the fallout of the 2008–9 global economic crisis (UNWTO 2021). This crisis has exacerbated hyper-competition among tourism businesses and destinations as they seek to gain a competitive advantage in an increasingly challenging environment.

According to Lew (2008) and Macleod (2003), it is this hyper-competition, which was evident pre-COVID-19, which has led to product development and new niches as a method of market differentiation. This differentiation allows for economies of scope, as opposed to the economies of scale afforded by mass tourism. As Manente (2008) and Ritchie and Crouch (2003) argued, in order to be competitive, destinations should propose as many products as tourism demand segmentation requires, which will allow the destination to sell itself to different typologies of clients, thereby generating profits and employment and leading the way for economic development. This sentiment is also shared by Benur and Bramwell (2015), who intimated that destinations require a suitable number and mix of products to maintain a competitive advantage.

Underlying this drive towards market differentiation lies the other aspect of the changing dynamics in the market: the emergence of a more experienced, discerning and sophisticated traveller. Poon (1993, 14) referred to these travellers as the "new tourists" who she defines as "consumers who are flexible, independent and experienced travellers, whose values and lifestyles are different from those of the mass tourists". These tourists are characterized as being more flexible and more independent-minded and having changed values and changed lifestyles. They are products of changing population demographics. As Benur and Bramwell (2015, 216) stated, "these 'new tourists' are interested in the opportunities that destination products offer them to help create their own experiences, sensations, lifestyles, identities and social status, albeit within the context of the product offering and wider society". As such, alternative tourism provides destinations with the opportunity to carefully craft experiences that match the expectations of the market based on the available resources.

The ongoing COVID-19 pandemic has further impacted the dynamics of the market. A recent report by Booking.com indicated a growing demand for sustainable travel and revealed that 61 per cent of travellers want to travel more sustainably in the future due to the pandemic (2021). Findings indicated that 69 per cent of travellers are committed to reducing the carbon footprint of their trip or paying to offset this when possible and look forward to actively participating in energy, water and waste-reduction activities at the destination. There is also an increasing demand for more environmentally friendly modes of transport. Notably, 72 per cent think travel businesses should offer more sustainable choices, with 41 per cent of travellers indicating that they do not know how to find sustainable travel options. Other research is pointing to the rise of the conscious traveller, someone who is far more discerning about the journeys they go on, who is willing and able to be away from home for longer, who is more appreciative of local people and who is less reckless in their spending. These individuals want more unorthodox experiences that involve engagement with local communities in a safe and respectful manner; they are driven by a need to volunteer and give back to a worthy cause, and they truly desire "off the beaten path"' experiences that enhance their health and wellness and which provide a greater connection to people, the environment and life. Adjusting the tourism product to new preferences is vital for Caribbean destinations to fully participate in the global recovery of the tourism sector during and after the pandemic. This shift results in the access to new markets, additional streams of income, the creation of new job opportunities and increased entrepreneurial activity.

Tourism Product Portfolio

For Caribbean islands with a restricted resource base, it is not a question of alternatives to mass tourism but rather complementary tourism products that will form part of a broader tourism portfolio that is developed in a sustainable manner. According to Lewis-Cameron and Ramgulam (2018, 128), "the development of a product-mix allows the destination to produce in a way that maximizes the total contribution to profit/throughput subject to constraints imposed by resource limitations, market demand, and sales forecast". This product development must be well planned, well implemented and appropriately supported to be a success. Pine and Gilmore (1999) aptly describe product development as the assembling and careful engineering of tourism experiences to meet the demands of the market. Many destinations in the region are actively engaged in diversifying their product portfolio, notably: ecotourism in Dominica, yachting in the Grenadines, medical tourism in Cuba and festival tourism in St Lucia and Jamaica, to name a few. As discussed in later chapters, there is tremendous potential for assembling diverse product experiences throughout the Caribbean.

Destinations may diversify their product portfolio by creating "new bundles or combinations of products in destinations" (Benur and Bramwell 2015, 217) through promoting and packaging existing tourism products or through developing new tourism products, including developing new products that are closely related to existing products. New products can also be developed by connecting with established alternative or niche tourism products. Benur and Bramwell (2015) referred to the pairing of mass tourism products such as beach resorts, which provide a significant number of tourists, with niche tourism products, including cultural tourism.

Diversifying the tourism product by integrating the tourism product portfolio can be useful to a destination, as seen above. However, Benur and Bramwell (2015, 219) noted that this integration cannot be done simply as an extension to the current tourism package offerings but must instead reflect the "strong compatibilities and complementarities" among the product offerings to offer a clear image to the tourist. Additional products must offer value to the tourist and are more likely to be effective when they "offer distinctive cultural meanings". Their framework of tourism product development options provides a useful classification of the diverse options available to destinations as they consider their product portfolio.

In figure 2.1, the authors described tourism product intensification as the scale of the particular tourism operation, whether large or small, and whether it caters to the niche or mass tourism markets. Tourism product diversification refers to the number and variety of tourism products, particularly primary tourism products, offered by the destination. The five tourism product typologies provide a good picture of the strategic options for consideration as Caribbean islands build their product portfolio. In practice, the complexities of island destination development may not allow destination managers to neatly fit product development into these categories. However, the framework is useful because it allows destination managers to not simply view mass tourism and niche tourism as polar opposites but to appreciate the extent of the relationships and inter-relatedness between product intensification and diversification.

Benur and Bramwell (2015) defined concentrated niche tourism as the offering of a limited number of primary tourism products and attracting a limited number of tourists. This may occur at the early stages of the destination's life cycle or later in the development of the destination. Notably, niche tourism products such as volcano

Figure 2.1: Framework of Tourism Product Development Options

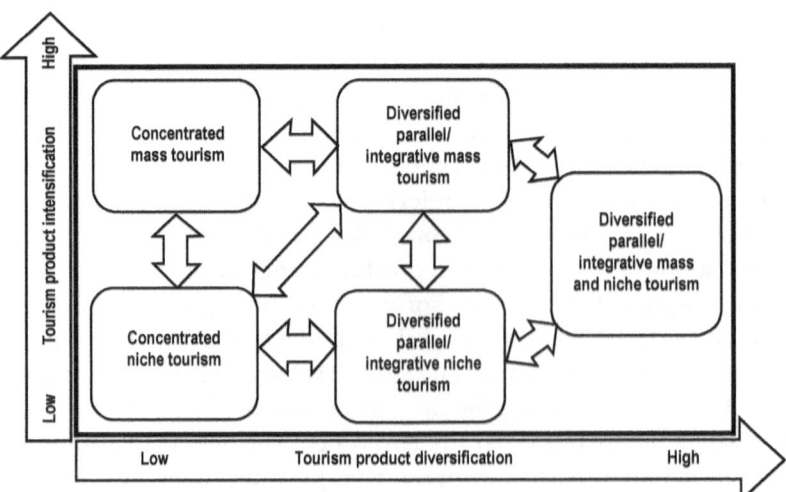

Source: Benur and Bramwell (2015, 220)

tourism in Iceland may eventually attract large numbers of tourists. On the other hand, the authors described concentrated mass tourism as focused on the development of a few primary tourism products which attract large numbers of tourists. Most islands in the Caribbean and the Mediterranean have followed this development pattern. Diversified parallel/integrative niche tourism describes a destination where the primary tourism products are based on small scale, niche markets. These products may develop separately and may not necessarily incentivize producers to cooperate. Alternatively, they may also develop in an integrated way, with tourists being interested in several of them and producers cooperating in product development.

Similarly, diversified parallel/integrative mass tourism is done in destinations whose products are intensely developed, mass tourism products. These may develop for separate markets in parallel, with limited cooperation among providers. Alternatively, several products may be consumed by significant numbers of tourists during their trip, encouraging cooperation among product providers. Finally, and perhaps the preferred option for more mature island destinations, diversified parallel/integrative mass and niche tourism is the combination of both forms in a pattern that is similar to the two described above, that is, separate or parallel development based on tourists' product use and providers' cooperation or lack thereof.

For vulnerable Caribbean islands operating in a highly competitive global space, the choice of approach is heavily dependent on the destination's context. There are a number of factors to be considered in selecting an appropriate approach, which will be explored in the concluding chapter of this book. Each approach comes with benefits and disadvantages depending on the context. While there is strong support for niche product development among a wide cross section of researchers (Dwyer et al. 2009; Croes 2003; Toften and Hammervoll 2011; Novelli, Schmitz and Spencer 2006), some researchers are against niche product development (Schilling and Hill 1998). These sceptics argue that developing new niche products is expensive, and it takes time to train staff and bring products to market. However, these new niche products are entering an already competitive marketplace where other niche products already exist. Without the right strategy, new niche products are likely to fail.

Apart from the wary warnings, the literature recognizes that the main advantage of new niche product development is value creation, allowing destinations to be more competitive in their offering.

Sun Lust to Sun Plus

Caribbean island destinations have a longstanding relationship with tourism from as far back as the 1950s. This relationship has earned these islands the title of the "most tourism-dependent region in the world". The mass tourism model of high-rise hotels and air-conditioned tour buses has dominated the Caribbean tourism product, where the focus has been the exploitation of the standard 3S (sun, sea, sand) product. The heavy reliance on mass tourism has brought with it some gains, as evidenced by the varying infrastructural development, employment opportunities and foreign exchange generation. However, many islands struggle to effectively exploit the developmental benefits of tourism and also be competitive in the global tourism market.

The COVID-19 pandemic has exacerbated this struggle as island destinations now have to re-examine the traditional mass tourism model and consider how to manage this tourism relationship so that the quality of life of locals remains at the core. There is growing recognition of the important role that sustainable, authentic, high quality and distinctive visitor experiences play in the future success of island destinations. They must shift from a production-oriented approach to tourism to meaningful tourist engagement. The following chapters will critically examine how tourism product diversification in select Caribbean destinations is embracing many potential types of innovative assembly processes.

References

Auty, R.M. 2017. "Natural Resources and Small Island Economies: Mauritius and Trinidad and Tobago." *Journal of Development Studies* 3 (2): 264–77.

Benur, A., and B. Bramwell. 2015. "Tourism Product Development and Product Diversification in Destinations." *Tourism Management* 50:213–24.

Berry, C. 1971. "Corporate Growth and Diversification." *Journal of Law and Economics* 14 (2): 371–83.

Booking.com. 2021. "Booking.com's 2021 Sustainable Travel Report Affirms Potential Watershed Moment for Industry and Consumers." https://globalnews.booking.com/bookingcoms-2021-sustainable-travel-report-affirms-potential-watershed-moment-for-industry-and-consumers/.

Carneiro, F.G., R. Longmore, R.M. Cazorla, and P. Jaupart. 2014. "A Future without Oil? Diversifying Options for Trinidad and

Tobago." *The World Bank Report on Poverty Reduction and Economic Management Network*. May 2014, No. 142.

Cherif, Reda, and Fuad Hasanov. 2014. "Soaring of the Gulf Falcons: Diversification in the GCC Oil Exporters in Seven Propositions." No. 14–177. International Monetary Fund, 2014.

Sr, M.V., and R.R. Croes. 2003. "Growth, Development and Tourism in a Small Economy: Evidence from Aruba." *International Journal of Tourism Research* 5 (5): 315–30.

Dwyer, L., D. Edwards, N. Mistilis, C. Roman, and N. Scott. 2009. "Destination and Enterprise Management for a Tourism Future." *Tourism Management* 30 (1): 63–74.

Hendrix, Cullen S. 2017. "Kicking a Crude Habit: Diversifying Away from Oil and Gas in the Twenty-First Century." *International Review of Applied Economics* (2017): 1–21.

Hosein, Roger. 2010. "Booming Mineral Resources and the Imperative of Economic Diversification." *The West Indian Journal of Engineering* 32 (1/2): 76–84.

Lew, A.A. 2008. "Long Tail Tourism: New Geographies for Marketing Niche Tourism Products." *Journal of Travel and Tourism Marketing*, 25 (3/4): 409–19.

Lewis-Cameron, A., and N. Ramgulam. 2018. "Niche Focused Tourism Development in Small Island Developing States: The Case of Trinidad." In *Development, Political and Economic Difficulties in the Caribbean*, edited by A. Bissessar, 75–89. London: Palgrave McMill.

Manente, Mara. 2008. "Destination Management and Economic Background: Defining and Monitoring Local Tourist Destinations." *International Conference on Measuring Tourism Economic Contribution at Sub-National Levels*, 29–31.

Mather, S., and G. Todd. 1993. *Tourism in the Caribbean*. (Special Report No. 455). London: Economist Intelligence Unit.

Macleod, D.V.L., ed. 2003. *Niche Tourism in Question – Interdisciplinary Perspectives on Problems and Possibilities*. Glasgow: University of Glasgow.

Morakabati, Yeganeh, John Beavis, and John Fletcher. 2014. "Planning for a Qatar without Oil: Tourism and Economic Diversification, a Battle of Perceptions." *Tourism Planning and Development* 11 (4): 415–34.

Novelli, M., ed. 2005. *Niche Tourism: Contemporary Issues, Trends and Cases*. Oxford: Butterworth-Heinemann.

Novelli, M., B. Schmitz, and T. Spencer. 2006. "Networks, Clusters and Innovation in Tourism: A UK experience." *Tourism Management* 27 (6): 1141–52.

Pattullo, P. 1996. *Last Resorts: The Cost of Tourism in the Caribbean*. London: Cassell.

Peterson, John E. 2009. "Life after Oil: Economic Alternatives for the Arab Gulf States." *Mediterranean Quarterly* 20 (3): 1–18.

Pine, B., and J. Gilmore. 1999. *The Experience Economy: Work is Theatre and Every Business a Stage*. Boston: Harvard Business Press.

Poon, A. 1993. *Tourism, Technology and Competitive Strategies*. Oxford: Cab International.

Ritchie, J.R. Brent, and Geoffrey Ian Crouch. 2003. *The Competitive Destination: A Sustainable Tourism Perspective*. Wallingford: CABI.

Robinson, P., S. Heitmann, and P. Dieke, eds. 2011. *Research Themes for Tourism*. Wallingford: CAB International.

Rodrik, D. 2005. "Policies for Economic Diversification." *CEPAL Review. Economic Commission for Latin America and the Caribbean*, 7–23.

Schilling, M.A., and C.W. Hill. 1998. "Managing the New Product Development Process: Strategic Imperatives." *The Academy of Management Executive* 12 (3): 67–81.

Toften, K., and T. Hammervoll. 2011. "International Market Selection and Growth Strategies for Niche Firms." *International Journal of Entrepreneurship and Innovation Management* 13 (3–4): 282–95.

United Nations World Tourism Organization (UNWTO). 2021. "Worst Year in Tourism History With 1 Billion Fewer International Arrivals." https://www.unwto.org/news/2020-worst-year-in-tourism-history-with-1-billion-fewer-international-arrivals#:~:text=Global%20tourism%20suffered%20its%20worst,World%20Tourism%20Organization%20(UNWTO).&text=The%20crisis%20has%20put%20between,small%20and%20medium%2Dsized%20enterprises.

Weaver, D.B. 1995. "Alternative Tourism in Montserrat." *Tourism Management* 16 (8): 593–604.

3.
The Development of a Framework for Educational Tourism

Elizabeth Ince-Peters

Introduction

Caribbean countries are highly dependent on tourism, which contributed 14.1 per cent to the Caribbean's gross domestic product (GDP) in 2019 (WTTC 2021) but represents a much higher percentage contribution to GDP in individual islands, for example, 29.6 per cent (Barbados), 68.1 per cent (St Lucia) and 44.4 per cent (the Bahamas) in 2019 (WTTC 2021). Due to the global pandemic, these figures were significantly reduced in 2020 (6.4 per cent – Caribbean region, 7.9 per cent – Barbados, 28.7 per cent – St Lucia, 20.0 per cent – the Bahamas).

Though dependent on tourism, the region "on the whole ... has suffered from stagnation [within the tourism sector], partly on account of insufficiently varied attractions" (CEPAL 2006). In fact, between 2005 and 2011, the region "substantially lagged behind its counterparts in Central America and South America" (Bourne 2013, 1), with CARICOM destinations performing worse in tourism growth than non-CARICOM destinations between 2005 and 2012. Overall, CARICOM destinations have been losing market share in the Americas, while Central and South America have been gaining market share, even among Caribbean travellers (ibid.).

The region focuses mainly on the development of tourism products which are linked to its "natural assets (sea and beach)" and has, therefore, focused on sun, sea and sand and cruise tourism but has not truly developed other potential tourism products (Zappino 2005, 3). This opens the door to a discussion on alternative and special interest tourism.

Characteristics of Alternative and Special Interest Tourism

Alternative and special interest tourism targets niches in the market. These must "produce sufficient business" while being "small" in the eyes of competitors (Robinson and Novelli 2005, 5). This form of tourism attracts tourists who are higher spenders and offers a greater feeling of intimacy despite potentially being experienced by many (Robinson and Novelli 2005).

One way to diversify the tourism sector in Caribbean countries is educational tourism (ET). As an alternative form of tourism, ET has the major benefit of having "minimal negative impacts on [the] cultural and natural environment" (Pawar and Nagaraj 2013, 2) while allowing the tourist to "experience the cultual roots" of a foreign country (Quezada 2004). Though the niche may not necessarily be small-scale, ET's characteristics match those of alternative or special interest tourism, particularly due to the desire of the "new" tourist to move "beyond sheer relaxation towards the opportunity to study and learn" (Mowforth and Munt 2008, 131).

Study abroad benefits the home country, as it can anticipate the addition of the graduate to the pool of skilled labour upon their return (WTTC 2012). The connections made by students in the host country are also a means towards "global social cohesion and the development of trade" (ibid., 12) for the home country. It is also "a major tourism opportunity" for the host country (Tarrant et al. 2014). To drive study abroad, institutions must "promote study abroad within their academic curricula" (ibid., 404). Ritchie, Carr and Cooper (2003) also highlight the importance of stakeholders, including the government at the local, regional and national levels, as well as organizations from the education and tourism sectors, in the development and promotion of ET. Overall, the development of ET requires macro-level action as well as institutional level action. To further understand ET in the Caribbean region, St George's University (SGU) in Grenada will be assessed.

Literature Review
The Need for Alternative Tourism

Alternative tourism products are highly varied. They have the potential to mitigate or significantly reduce the problems associated with mass tourism (Ursache 2015), serve to disperse the benefits of tourism away from solely the destination's honey pot areas and "into the hinterland" (Sharpley 2002a, 234) and cater to the increasing sophistication of tourists and their demand for specialized products. They also allow for greater intimacy with the tourist and the building of "long-lasting relationships" (Ursache 2015). This last characteristic is supported by the tendency of youth travellers to return later in life to countries visited while they were young. This also gives an indication of the long-term earnings that may result from attracting young tourists through offering alternative tourism products.

ET encompasses travelling with the aim of "formal learning through attending classes or participating in further, higher or work based education" (Pawar and Nagaraj 2013, 2), including teaching in a foreign country. When viewed from the perspective of the primary aim of travel, ET has its roots in the Grand Tour, which spanned the seventeenth to nineteenth centuries and facilitated the education of young, male, British aristocrats in the culture of other major European destinations (Ritchie, Carr and Cooper 2003), usually over a period of three years (Theobald 2005). Since then, ET has evolved to include persons of varying income levels and, in more recent times, presents itself in the form of studying abroad (Ritchie, Carr and Cooper 2003). Study abroad programmes have increasingly become a "mainstream component of the higher education environment" (Pabel and Prideaux 2012), offering benefits to students including "better chances in the employment market" as study abroad prepares them to operate in a global work environment (Niser 2010, 49).

For the purposes of this study, ET will be defined as per the definition of Pawar and Nagaraj (2013) above, focusing particularly on students at higher education institutions and encompassing both study abroad and travelling to another country for the completion of an entire degree.

Push and Pull Motivating Factors within ET

ET can be considered in terms of time or in terms of the achievement of learning objectives and is facilitated by push and pull factors (Pabel and Prideaux 2012). The push factors (Llewellyn Smith and McCabe 2008) are students' desire to:
- travel,
- seek excitement,
- meet new people,
- learn or improve a new language, and
- experience a different teaching style and culture.

Pull factors on the side of the destination encompass host country, host city and host university elements, including:
- safety,
- natural offerings of the country,
- affordability,
- available facilities of the city and campus,
- prior establishment of an exchange programme,
- the ability to transfer course credits, and
- attractiveness of the university.

In their study, the authors discovered that "internal 'socio-psychological'" push factors, particularly the desire to travel, are more important drivers than pull factors, and host country pull factors were "more important" than those of the host university (Llewellyn-Smith and McCabe 2008, 598).

Benefits of ET

> If managed in a sustainable way, ET has shown its earning potential over the years as higher education institutions gain the most from the activities of the youth travel segment, followed by youth travel accommodation (Student Marketing 2016). Considering both study abroad and students' completion of an entire degree abroad, international students in the United States generated US$44.7 billion in 2018 (Reuters 2020). International students in the United Kingdom generated £28.8 billion in 2021 (Hepi 2021). International students in Australia generated AU$40.3 billion in 2019. (University World News 2021)

The number of international students in the United States was 1,095,299 in 2018/2019 (Statista 2020) and "few will disagree that one of America's greatest exports is its system of higher education" (Brustein 2010, 261). However, the impression of increasing xenophobia alongside stricter immigration policies enacted by the United States since the 9/11 terrorist attacks has led to a rise in competition from East and Southeast Asian universities for international students (Brustein 2010). This shows the potential for stable ET if government policies support ET, but also shows the dynamism of ET, where unfavourable policies can leave room for new destinations to enter the market. There has been a rise of new study abroad destinations with a wide array of cultural and historic experiences that they offer to international students. This introduces the possible socio-cultural benefits, particularly to the host country, of ET.

Universities can focus on improving their "teaching and research capabilities" (Pabel and Prideaux 2012, 25), as well as bundling education with other attractions or conveniences within the surrounding locale. Overall, the development and promotion of the culture can bolster ET, and this form of alternative tourism has minimal impact on the environment and the culture (Pawar and Nagaraj 2013).

Challenges in the Development of ET

In developing ET, challenges may be encountered in packaging it (Ritchie, Carr and Cooper 2003). Educational institutions, the public sector and the destination's attractions must work with the private sector to service the educational tourists' needs and wants. This means the merging of "four cultures" (CTC 2001, 44, cited in Ritchie, Carr and Cooper 2003, 110) involving a focus on tourism and commercialism in the private sector, as opposed to working within a budget within the higher education institution. Additionally, the type of international student attracted may introduce challenges. For example, language students, who usually come during the summer for a language programme, introduce the issue of seasonality into ET (Ritchie, Carr and Cooper 2003). This results in the challenge of spreading the benefits of ET throughout the year. Language schools also face the challenge of protecting the students from crime while simultaneously allowing them to be immersed in the "culture and nightlife" (ibid., 168). Lack of support for the development of ET also creates issues. In the case of Nigeria, major challenges to the development of ET stem from the lack of investment in the education system, the state of the economy, incidence of cult-related violence, the low standard of education and the misconduct of university staff, among other factors (Adekalu and Oludeyi 2013).

Key Stakeholders in ET

Stakeholder involvement is essential and can be achieved through taking a collaborative approach to tourism planning and development. Waligo, Clarke and Hawkins (2013) categorized stakeholders in tourism development into "six broad categories: tourists, industry, local community, government, special interest groups and educational institutions" (343).

Stakeholder Group 1: The Tourist

Since "young travellers aged 15 to 29 comprised 23% of international arrivals before the COVID-19 pandemic" (WYSE Travel Confederation 2021), the current and potential impact of this sector cannot be ignored. This sector has been attracting attention as there is "growing lust and spending power" (Richards and Wilson 2005, 39). Firstly, young people are time rich and, therefore, stay longer in the destination, spending money while there. Secondly, young people are often backed by their time poor but money rich parents and may seek employment during their travels to earn extra money (UNWTO and WYSE Travel Confederation 2011).

Their desire to travel is less likely to be dampened by terrorism, socio-political unrest, economic crisis or threat of disease and natural disaster. They are keen to seek out new destinations, are tech savvy and give back to the places they visit (UNWTO and WYSE Travel Confederation 2011). Youth and student travellers are also forging the path towards responsible tourism and are leaders in innovation (ibid.). In this vein, youth travellers seek out local suppliers above international ones, allowing for a reduction in leakages.

Young people who travel for study also invite friends and relatives (UNWTO and WYSE Travel Confederation 2011), add a "buzz" element to the destination and have a "thirst for more travel", which points to the snowball effect of starting to travel at an early age (Richards and Wilson 2005). Doyle et al. (2010) also noted that word of mouth, particularly from friends who had previously studied abroad, was the most prominent means by which undergraduate students learned about study abroad.

Stakeholder Group 2: The Industry

Once within the destination, students have an estimated "20 weeks of free time...[and] have a high propensity for travel because they have few external commitments" (Ritchie 2003 quoted in Llewellyn-Smith and McCabe 2008, 594). This implies that the country gains not only from payments made toward accommodation, food and entertainment but also leisure travel, opening the door to collaboration with other stakeholders, particularly the Destination Management/Marketing Organization (DMO), in the destination.

Stakeholder Group 3: The Local Community

Though not widely assessed in the literature, the community has an impact on ET. Analysis of college towns and university cities has shown that "many college faculty and staff, along with towns-people, do not want to live near college students because of their lifestyles" (Gumprecht 2003, 60), while students prefer to live "relatively free from adult interference".

Conflict can arise when students move into residential neighbourhoods because enrolment in educational institutions is expanded without the requisite expansion of student accommodation. Further conflict can arise as a result of the actions of students, particularly under the influence of alcohol. The expansion of campuses into the town without paying equal land taxes can also create issues. These cause tensions between the educational institutions and surrounding communities as the economic benefits to the institutions are at odds with the apparent disregard of the interests of permanent residents (ibid.).

Stakeholder Group 4: The Government

Political will is the driving force for the advance of ET as it propels initiatives, creates stability and raises investor confidence in the future of ET in the destination (Townsend 2015). The government also determines how easy it is for students to enter through visa requirements and administration, taxation policies, industry standards and working holidays (UNWTO and WYSE Travel Confederation 2011).

Stakeholder Group 5: Special Interest Groups – producer, non-producer, single interest

Interest groups refer to recognized bodies which represent "the shared views or interests of a group" (McCarthy and Zald 1977, cited in Needham and Rollins 2005, 3). They play a role in both policymaking and the forming of institutional arrangements in tourism (Hall and Jenkins 1995; Tosun 2000). Within ET, special interest groups can include student groups within and outside of institutions.

Stakeholder Group 6: Educational Institutions

To successfully establish and grow study abroad programmes, institutions must build commitment to study abroad programmes, establish the requisite infrastructure, provide the necessary resources and ensure "clarity and accountability" (NAFSA 2008, 3). Establishing study abroad in a university requires more than a statement by the institution that it facilitates the service. It requires dedication and strategic implementation, a point that is supported in Doyle et al. (2010).

Methodology

For this study, data were collected using a mixed methods approach. A case study approach was taken using in-depth, semi-structured interviews with persons of influence in three of the six stakeholder groups outlined above:

- The educational institution:
  - Interview Participant (IP) 1 – Assistant Director of Communications, Office of University Communications and Publications, St George's University, Grenada;
  - IP 2 – Associate Dean of Enrolment Planning, Office of Enrolment Planning, St George's University, Grenada;
- The government:
  - IP 3 – The Grenada Airport Authority under the Ministry of Tourism, Civil Aviation and Culture;
- The industry:
  - IPs 4, 5 and 6 – Grenada Tourism Authority.

Also, a questionnaire was selected for the fourth stakeholder group (the tourist). A simple random sampling technique towards the pre-determined sample size was used whereby paper questionnaires were handed out to students at random on the SGU True Blue campus over the period 22–25 May 2016. Where students did not have the time to complete the paper questionnaire, they were given the option of completing it online. Sixty-eight paper questionnaires and seven online questionnaires, via email, were distributed, giving a total of seventy-five respondents, a 78.9 per cent success rate.

Local community and special interest groups were not included in the interview process because defining the extent of these groups created an obstruction. Additionally, the Grenada Chamber of Industry and Commerce was unavailable to be interviewed as a representative of the producer groups. Rather, stakeholder groups interviewed were asked questions about these two remaining groups and their involvement.

Findings and Discussion

ET as a Means of Diversifying Tourism

The Grenadian case study demonstrates the partnership among SGU, the Grenadian government, the tourism industry, producer groups and the local community towards producing an ET product. This is evidence of tourism diversification as the country has diversified its tourism product to include both ET and the 3S offering it had before. IP 2 noted, "The creation was built on the vision of recognizing the value in educational tourism, something that ... is probably very strange in our Caribbean thought process because Caribbean internationally is not viewed as a destination for education. Sun, sea, sand, rum ... along with music. We're seen as destinations for that".

However, through SGU, Grenada "from inception has positioned itself as an exporter of medical education". Sharpley (2002b) highlighted factors that determine the effect of tourism on economic growth and diversification, and these are seen in the Grenadian case study, as SGU had contributed "upwards of 20% of the island's GDP", as referenced by IP 2 in 2016, and contributed more than 22 per cent in 2018 (Straker 2019). It is the largest private employer of Grenadian workers, with a staff of over eight hundred in 2016 and, though an American institution, over 947 Grenadian students were enrolled in 2020 (SGU 2020). This demonstrates the ability of tourism to redistribute wealth between developed and developing countries.

SGU also links to other sectors in the economy, particularly through its relationship with the health sector and its stimulation of the construction sector as accommodation must be provided for students. The presence of ET also supports the traditional 3S (sun, sea and sand) tourism industry in Grenada, as relatives visiting SGU students make use of the tourism products offered by the island. SGU partners with the Grenada Tourism Authority (GTA) to promote 3S and eco-tourism products to students. This shows that Grenada has diversified its tourism offering rather than simply shifting the island's tourism focus from one tourism product to another.

From the interview with IP 2, the SGU identified a niche in a specific target market, the United States, expanding thereafter to other nations. Grenada has subsequently benefitted from the advantages of niche tourism as seasonality has been reduced. ET is, "a staple because we [SGU] move 3,800 students plus an additional probably 500 or thereabouts faculty, another 200 family members into the university for the start of classes a couple of times per year".

It is noted also that students have "a minimum stay of two years" on the island. Hence, for Grenada, the challenges of seasonality highlighted by Ritchie, Carr and Cooper (2003) do not appear to be a concern. Furthermore, the "long-lasting relationships" referred to by Ursache (2015) are evident in the SGU alumni who return to Grenada to give back to the country, particularly through partnership with the Ministry of Health. The willingness of 71 per cent of respondents to return after their studies are completed shows that current students are also forming that long-lasting relationship. Respondents demonstrated that culture was an important factor in their minds by mentioning culture (six respondents) and cultural activities (ten respondents) when asked to share their recommendations about Grenada. The destination can, therefore, focus on the promotion of its culture through backward linkages between ET and cultural tourism (Sharpley 2002b). This will promote diversification of the tourism product to include arts and culture.

ET has also demonstrated aspects of sustainable development through its consistent economic contribution, its strides towards solar energy use, its support of marine biological research and forestry support, and its outreach into communities within Grenada, Carriacou and Petite Martinique. This shows the economic, environmental and social impact of ET in Grenada over the last four decades. A staple of the economy, ET also helped Grenada's economy to recover after Hurricane Ivan in 2004 and the global financial crisis of 2007 and 2008.

Though Grenada's tourism product has been successfully diversified by ET, research shows that SGU can go further. For example, it can collaborate with the GTA to create packaged offers for students beyond the offers it currently makes during the orientation period. It can also collaborate with the Ministry of Tourism and Civil Aviation to facilitate students' easy access to Grenada.

Requirements for the Sustainable Development and Management of ET

Support for the Initiative

The political will supporting the development of SGU is evident in the 1976 Act of Parliament allowing SGU into Grenada; the visas that are issued for international students; the inclusion of SGU-related travel on the International Air Transport Association database; and the inclusion of SGU within the Grenadian budget. Political will facilitated foreign investment into SGU from the start and continued governmental support can be seen in the promotion of the Citizenship by Investment programme linked to SGU housing.

This government support has allowed students from 140 countries to enter over the course of SGU's establishment, with ninety-six countries being represented within SGU in 2016. This willingness to open up to foreigners has allowed Grenada to fully access its target market, that is, students seeking a Western medical education. This is reflected in the statement of one French student of SGU in his questionnaire response where he stated that the United States is "not foreign friendly", a statement that supports Brustein's comment on the barriers raised by increasing xenophobia in the United States (2010).

Special interest groups also play a role in supporting ET. Producer groups in Grenada offer special deals and discounts to SGU students and others visiting SGU, though collaboration with SGU and other stakeholders is minimal.

Interaction between international and local students is promoted through events organized by the various special interest groups within SGU, for example, the Indian Cultural Students' Association. This relates to Brustein's recommendation to encourage interaction through organized events, facilitating the assimilation of the international student into the new environment (2010). Similar to the findings in Llewellyn-Smith and McCabe's study (2008), a higher number of organized social activities, groups and teams at SGU was related to high levels of satisfaction.

For ET to be successful, the educational institution must also support the tourist, and this can be seen in the Grenada case. SGU representatives spoke about support measures like those highlighted in the Llewellyn-Smith and McCabe study (2008), including guaranteeing SGU accommodation for first-time students. Also, SGU has established a buddy system for new students that is aligned with the work of Doyle et al. (2010). The importance placed on the dedication of specific departments and campus areas, print and study rooms, to serving the students' needs within the case highlights the value of this measure to ET. Overall, the educational institution's focus on supporting the educational tourist and making them feel comfortable plays a significant role in the enablement of ET.

The local community's involvement through investment and providing accommodation is similar to the type of participation seen in the college towns assessed by Gumprecht (2003). However, unlike the Gumprecht study, complaints received from the community in Grenada appear to be minimal, that is, those related to students being a little rowdy after examinations are completed. Furthermore, IP 2 spoke to the benefits received by the community due to SGU students living in or frequenting their areas, for example, increased security patrols. Overall, though there may have been scepticism from the local community when SGU was introduced, it has been replaced by a "sense of pride" in relation to SGU among Grenadians. The Grenadian people are also seen as a "strategic strength", as they are friendly and are willing "to accept and accommodate visitors". This support is important for ET as the comfort and enjoyment of the students play a major role in word-of-mouth marketing.

Responding to the Demand

The educational institution has certainly established itself as an institution which promotes ET, though the term may not have been used in its initial development. IP 2 made a particular note of the niche filled by SGU, a medical university which could offer a Western medical education in an English-speaking destination close to the United States. IP 2 stated that foundationally, it positioned itself as an "exporter of education", "as the Chancellor would have conceptualized this idea in the early 70s, it was a recognition that there was a demand for training in medicine. And the number of seats in US medical schools were far short than the demand".

This shows that the major point leveraged by SGU in the Grenada case is the response to the youth segment's demand for a Western medical education. This point was supported by the students' responses, which demonstrated that a major push factor for them was not being accepted to a medical school in the United States or Canada. Hence, the destination seeking to diversify into ET must ensure that the ET product being offered meets the demands of the target market.

SGU is also in alignment with the recommendation of Pabel and Prideaux (2012), as the use of the Department of Educational Services to improve teaching skills and engaging in research in partnership with foreign universities and directly related to Grenada shows expansion of "teaching and research capbilities". Additionally, the expansion of the university over the years so that it now encompasses four schools shows the growth to suit the demand for tertiary-level courses.

The push factors of Llewellyn-Smith and McCabe (2008) were also relevant to case study respondents with the exception of travelling to learn a new language. Certainly, the search for excitement and adventure, experiencing a new culture and increasing knowledge through attending medical school were significant motivations for the youth travellers to Grenada, which related to the work of the

UNWTO and WYSE Travel Confederation (2011) and Richards and Wilson (2005). Pull factors selected for the questionnaire from the work of Llewellyn-Smith and McCabe (2008) were relevant, though the affordability of studying at SGU and tourism offerings, that is, host country offerings, festivals and events, were not frequently selected as pull factors.

It is noteworthy that the Destination Management/Marketing Organization (DMO) was aware of the itineraries of the students, evidenced in IP 4 and 6 listing activities that linked to the self-identified itineraries of the student respondents, with the exception of hashing, which was mentioned by the GTA but not the students. The knowledge of the students' itineraries links to the study done by Ryan and Huimin (2007), which spoke to the importance of this knowledge. Having knowledge of the itineraries of the students, the GTA has crafted tours such as the "discovery train tours" which allow students to "club hop or bar hop". Hence, the DMO is knowledgeable about the demands of the target market and has begun to craft products to meet the demand. The DMO also revealed plans to introduce a "bowling alley and entertainment hub", which speaks to the evolution of the product offerings to suit the youth segment's demand for "nightlife". As a DMO seeks to support ET, it should study the target market's desires and seek to provide tourism products to suit. Furthermore, it should make its presence known among the tourists, a factor which could have been improved in the Grenada case as 38.7 per cent of respondents did not know about the GTA or its role.

Noted also in the case study is the proportion of students, 70.7 per cent, who have been visited by friends and relatives during their stay in Grenada. Family Weekends support this. In addition, welcoming significant others through the Significant Others Programme allows SGU and Grenada to gain more from the tourism aspect. An area where there is unmet demand is the SGU policy on earning money while studying. The students of SGU, particularly those in the School of Medicine, were not allowed to work to earn money during their study, and their dissatisfaction, 40 per cent of respondents, with this restriction indicates their desire to earn. This supports the point made by UNWTO and WYSE Travel Confederation (2011) concerning the incidence of youth travellers working during their trips. Making it possible for students to earn money while studying can allow the destination to gain more from ET.

Safety of the Destination

The issues highlighted by Adekalu and Oludeyi (2013) do not pose a threat to Grenada, which offers high-quality education through SGU, which is accredited, safe and politically stable. It is noted that there were political disturbances in Grenada from 1979 to 1983 due to the Marxist coup. This affected SGU "students, faculty, families and others, there were nearly 1,000 Americans on the island" (St George's University 2016). However, when events escalated in 1983, "within days, the students were flown to safety and classes were temporarily suspended" (St George's University 2016). This shows SGU's effective response to the threat.

Noting the resilience of SGU through the Grenadian political uprising in 1983, Hurricane Ivan of 2004 and the Global Financial Crisis of 2007 and 2008, the fact presented by UNWTO and WYSE Travel Confederation (2011) concerning the reduced volatility of youth travel patterns is proven in the small island developing state's case. ET in Grenada remained active and has not only recuperated but grown in the years following the socio-political unrest, natural disaster and economic crisis.

Collaboration Among Stakeholders

Though there is collaboration between the government and SGU, improved collaboration between stakeholders through formalizing institutional arrangements can further develop ET in Grenada. The DMO and the educational institution collaborate to a fair extent to promote tourism within the destination. The study of Llewellyn and McCabe (2008) is also confirmed in the Grenada case, as students and regular tourists engaged in the same tourist activities, particularly visits to the beach. This gives an indication that Grenada has more room to capitalize on the GTA and SGU partnership to promote tourism products.

As seen in the research of Gumprecht (2003), the tax concessions given to the university may raise concerns in the local community. However, though SGU receives tax credits, it was noted by IP 2 that these are re-invested into the local community through scholarships offered to Grenadians to attend SGU. Additionally, stakeholders spoke to the investment of the local community into accommodation for SGU students in areas close to the campus. This shows the two-way collaboration between the educational institution and the local community.

Collaboration with students is also possible. The fact that 42.7 per cent of current students learned of SGU from friends or relatives shows that word of mouth is an effective promoter, one which is also used by the SGU Office of Enrolment. In this vein, SGU has included features highlighted by Doyle et. al (2010) in its ET offering by facilitating current students to speak with prospective students, harnessing word-of-mouth marketing.

Recommendations

The stakeholders referred to above play different roles in the development and management of ET in the case study and have different intensities of relationship with one another. This can be summarized in the framework for the development of ET shown in figure 3.1. This highlights the necessary relationships a destination seeking to pursue ET should develop and their intensities.

Figure 3.1 shows that development of ET is premised on a foundation of strong governmental support, as has been demonstrated in the Grenada case. This governmental support should extend beyond the political will to launch into ET and into putting the mechanisms in place to facilitate it over time. Making it easy for students to enter and exit, including providing sufficient transportation, user-friendly visa procedures and efficient airport structures, is necessary. Within the framework, there is a two-way relationship between the government and the educational institution: the institution also gives back to the government. This is seen in the translation of tax credits into scholarships for Grenadian students and the conducting of clinics by students and alumni in the communities of Grenada. The importance of the two-way relationship is indicated by the thick two-way arrow.

A similarly thick dual arrow connects the tourists and the educational institution. In both this case and the literature, ET depends particularly upon the word-of-mouth marketing of the youth travel sector. The tourists depend on the educational institution for quality education and a high-quality experience at the at the university. This extends to the experience in the destination on a whole, which is reflected in the encasement of all elements in the "Conditions in the Destination". Hence, the safety of the destination is an important factor. In turn, the educational institution depends on youth travellers to spread a favourable report of their experience.

As the educational institution seeks to offer an overall good experience to the students, it partners with the tourist industry, the local community and special interest groups. The Grenadian case

Figure 3.1: The Framework for the Development and Management of ET

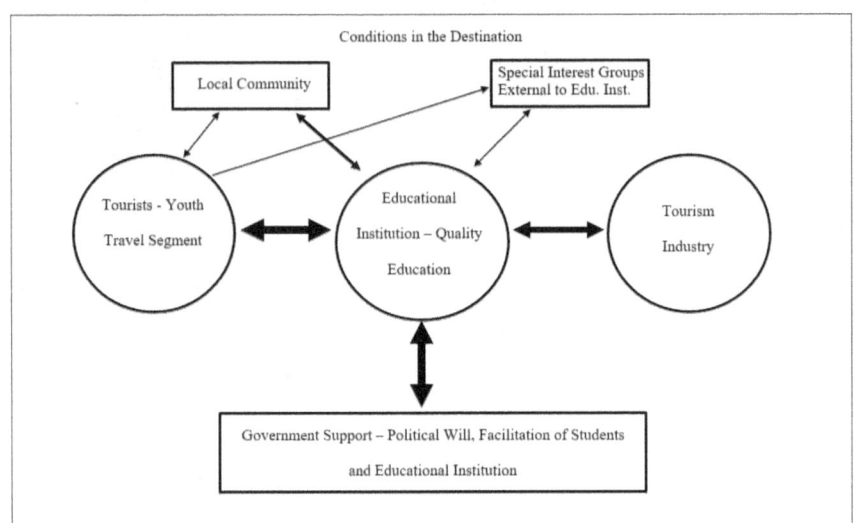

shows that the strongest connection of the three is between the educational institution and the tourist industry as they partner to provide students and their visiting friends and relatives with packaged deals, allowing the benefits of ET to extend to the destination as a whole.

The second strongest connection is with the local community, which the institution depends on for support, especially for accommodation. The student tourists also interact with the local community since they live in the area and give back to the community through outreach activities. The third relationship is between the educational institution and special interest groups, particularly producer groups. This is evident not only in the institution's partnership with supermarkets but also in the businesses' unilateral decision to offer special deals to students without seeking partnership with the university, hence the weaker arrow connection. The connection also involves collaboration towards furthering research and development in Grenada also involving students, though this seems to be unidirectional, which is signified by the one-way, thin arrow between tourists and special interest groups.

For a destination seeking to diversify into ET, it is important to recognize these stakeholders and establish relationships with them. However, as with the Grenada case, there can be varying levels of collaboration in the facilitation of ET. Within the framework, the intensity of the relationships has been represented by the thickness of the arrows connecting the stakeholders. This gives an indication of the importance of certain stakeholder relationships but does not give specific measurements or frequencies.

Conclusion

As a niche tourism product, there is the potential for ET to develop in small island developing states sustainably and with its benefits accruing to the economy, environment and society. The resilience and success of ET in the case study of Grenada, which was vastly improved by the underlying governmental support, show the potential for this niche to thrive in small island developing states. In Grenada, there is room for expansion of and more diversity within the tourism product through closer partnership among key stakeholders. This can be achieved through formalized institutional arrangements that improve the ET product offering.

Collaboration between and among key stakeholders is represented in a framework which highlights the necessary relationships and their intensities of the same within the destination based on the case study. The framework created in this study opens the door for further research into the measurable extent of contribution each stakeholder has to give towards the development of ET. Of interest would be an analysis of the econometric weights which could be assigned to the different stakeholder groups' contributions to the development of ET. Further research can also delve into the particular areas that each stakeholder should manage or have oversight of so that each stakeholder can effectively do their part.

References

Adekalu, Samuel Olutokunbo, and Olukunle Saheed Oludeyi. 2013. "Edutourism: The Nigeria Educational Challenges and International Students' Choice of Study in Nigerian Universities." *International Journal of Academic Research in Progressive Education and Development* 2 (4): 53–64.

Association of International Educators (NAFSA). 2008. "Strengthening Study Abroad: Recommendations for Effective Institutional Management for Presidents, Senior Administrators, and Study Abroad Professionals." *NAFSA's Task Force on Institutional Management of Study Abroad Report.* https://www.nafsa.org/_/File/_/final_imsa_taskforce.pdf.

Bourne, Compton. 2013. "Some Trends in Caribbean Tourism." *Caribbean Centre for Money and Finance Newsletter* 6 (2).

Brustein, William. 2010. "It Takes an Entire Institution – A Blueprint for the Global University." In *The Handbook of Practice and Research in Study Abroad: Higher Education and the Quest for Global Citizenship*, edited by Ross Lewin, 249–65. Taylor and Francis e-Library.

Doyle, Stephanie, Philip Gendall, Luanna H. Meyer, Janet Hoek, Carolyn Tait, Lynanne McKenzie, and Avatar Loorparg. 2010. "An Investigation of Factors Associated with Student Participation in Study Abroad." *Journal of Studies in International Education* 14 (5): 471–90.

Gumprecht, Blake. 2003. "The American College Town." *The Geographical Review* 93 (1): 51–80.

Hall, Colin Michael, and John M. Jenkins. 1995. *Tourism and Public Policy*. New York: Routledge.

Hepi. 2021. "International Students Are WORTH £28.8 Billion to the UK." *FE News*. https://www.fenews.co.uk/press-releases/75590-international-students-are-worth-28-8-billion-to-the-uk.

Llewellyn-Smith, Catherine, and Vivienne S. McCabe. 2008. "What is the Attraction for Exchange Students: The Host Destination or Host University? Empirical Evidence from a Study of an Australian University." *International Journal of Tourism Research* 10 (6): 593–607.

Mowforth, Martin, and Ian Munt. 2008. *Tourism and Sustainability: Development, Globalisation and New Tourism in the Third World.* Taylor and Francis e-Library.

Needham, Mark D., and Rick B. Rollins. 2005. "Interest Group Standards for Recreation and Tourism Impacts at Ski Areas in the Summer." *Tourism Management* 26:1–13.

Niser, John C. 2010. "Study Abroad Education in New England Higher Education: A Pilot Survey." *International Journal of Educational Management* 24 (1): 48–55.

Pabel, Anja, and Bruce Prideaux. 2012. "Education Tourism – Linking Pleasure Travel with Tertiary Education in the Youth Market." *Journal of Hospitality and Tourism Education* 24 (4): 22–31.

Pawar, J., and H. Nagaraj. 2013. "Educational Tourism – A Strategy for Sustainable Development." *Indian Streams Research Journal* 3 (1).

Quezada, Reyes. 2004. "Beyond Educational Tourism: Lessons Learned While Student Teaching Abroad." *International Education Journal* 5 (4): 458–65.

Reuters. 2020. "Explainer: What 1.1 Million Foreign Students Contribute to the U.S. Economy." https://www.reuters.com/article/us-usa-immigration-students-economy-expl-idUSKBN2492VS.

Richards, Greg, and Julie Wilson. 2005. "Youth Tourism – Finally Coming of Age?" In *Niche Tourism – Contemporary Issues, Trends and Cases*, edited by Marina Novelli, 39–46. Oxford: Elsevier Butterworth-Heinemann.

Ritchie, Brent W., Neil Carr, and Christopher P. Cooper. 2003. *Managing Educational Tourism.* Bristol: Channel View Publications.

Robinson, Mike, and Marina Novelli. 2005. "Niche Tourism: An Introduction" In *Niche Tourism – Contemporary Issues, Trends and Cases*, edited by Marina Novelli, 1–11. Oxford: Elsevier Butterworth-Heinemann.

Ryan, Chris, and Gu Huimin. 2007. "Spatial Planning, Mobilities and Culture – Chinese and New Zealand Student Preferences for Californian Travel." *International Journal of Tourism Research* 9 (3): 189–203.

Sharpley, Richard. 2002a. "Rural Tourism and the Challenge of Tourism Diversification – The Case of Cyprus." *Tourism Management* 23 (3): 233–44.

———. 2002b. "The Challenges of Economic Diversification through Tourism: The Case of Abu Dhabi." *International Journal of Tourism Research* 4:221–35.

Statista. 2020. "International Students in the U.S. 2003/2004 to 2021/2022. https://www.sgu.edu/academic-programs/school-of-mdicine/.

St George's University. 2016. "School of Medicine." Accessed 16 June 2016. http://www.sgu.edu/school-of-medicine/.

———. 2020. "Enrollment and Demographics." Accessed 31 August 2021. https://www.sgu.edu/about-sgu/enrollment-and-demographics/.

Straker, Linda. 2018. "2018 To Mark 6th Year of Economic Growth." NOW Grenada. https://www.nowgrenada.com/2018/10/2018-to-mark-the-6th-year-of-economic-growth/.

Student Marketing. 2016. "Market Overview and Trends." Accessed 26 January 2016. http://www.student-market.com/youth-travel

Tarrant, M. A., K. Lyons, L. Stoner, G. T. Kyle, S. Wearing, and N. Poudyal. 2014. "Global Citizenry, Educational Travel and Sustainable Tourism: Evidence from Australia and New Zealand." *Journal of Sustainable Tourism* 22 (3): 403–20.

Theobald, William F. 2005. The Meaning, Scope, and Measurement of Travel and Tourism." In *Global Tourism*, edited by William F. Theobald, 5–24. Massachusetts: Elsevier.

Tosun, Cevat. 2000. "Limits to Community Participation in the Tourism Development Process in Developing Countries." *Tourism Management* 21 (6): 613–63.

Townsend, Mark. 2015. "A Race for Economic Diversification." *Global Finance* 29.1:19–20, 22–23.

United Nations Economic Commission for Latin America and the Caribbean (CEPAL). 2006. "Challenges to Caribbean Tourism." *ECLAC Subregional Headquarters for the Caribbean (Studies and Research)* Issue 14.

United Nations World Tourism Organization (UNWTO) and WYSE Travel Confederation. 2011. "The Power of Youth Travel." *UNWTO and WYSE Travel Confed_lw.pdf*. https://www.wysetc.org/wp-content/uploads/2014/12/wysetc-unwto-report-english_the-power-of-youth.pdf.

University World News. 2021. "University Income from Foreign Student

Fees Collapses." https://www.universityworldnews.com/post.php?story=20210428132839972.

Ursache, Mara. 2015. "Niche Tourism Markets – Means of Enhancing Sustainable Economic Development in EU's Eastern Periphery." CES Working Papers 7 (2A): 648–61.

Waligo, Victoria, Jackie Clarke, and Rebecca Hawkins. 2013. "Implementing Sustainable Tourism: A Multi-Stakeholder Involvement Management Framework." *Tourism Management* (36): 342–53.

World Travel and Tourism Council (WTTC). 2012. "The Comparative Economic Impact of Travel & Tourism." *World Travel and Tourism Council.* https://s3.amazonaws.com/tourism-economics/craft/Case-Studies-Docs/The_Comparative_Economic_Impact_of_Travel_Tourism.pdf.

———. 2021. "Travel & TOURISM Economic IMPACT." World Travel and Tourism Council. Accessed 12 August 2021. https://wttc.org/Portals/0/Documents/Reports/2021/Global%20Economic%20Impact%20and%20Trends%202021.pdf.

WYSE Travel Confederation. "Projecting the Recovery Timeline for Youth Travel." 12 March 2021. https://www.wysetc.org/2021/03/projecting-the-recovery-timeline-for-youth-travel/.

Zappino, Vincenzo. 2005. "Caribbean Tourism and Development: An Overview." European Centre for Development Policy Management Discussion Paper No. 65.

4.
Accessible Tourism: A Case Study of Two of Grenada's Main Tourist Attractions

Jovari Hagley

Introduction

As the travel and tourism industry continues to grow, the travelling population has increased. The World Tourism and Travel Council (WTTC n.d.a) reported that the travel and tourism sector accounted for 10.3 per cent of global GDP and supported the livelihoods of 330 million people in 2019, outpacing the growth of the global economy for nine consecutive years. However, there is still a segment of society that is unable to equally enjoy tourism services. The World Bank (2022) highlighted that over a billion people (approximately 15 per cent of the world's population) are people with disabilities. Consequently, organizations, including the United Nations World Tourism Organization (WTO), have appealed to stakeholders to guarantee that their facilities, attractions and services are accessible to everyone. Moreover, the World Health Organization Director-General, Dr Margaret Chan, outlined that: "almost every one of us will be permanently or temporarily disabled at some point in life. We must do more to break the barriers which segregate people with disabilities" (WHO Media Centre 2013).

Approximately 150 countries are signatories to the United Nations (UN) Convention on the Rights of Persons with Disabilities. An additional hundred countries ratified the resolutions of the convention to remove hindrances to people with disabilities participating in society (WHO Media Centre 2013). Accessible tourism has become a buzz term for tourism stakeholders, although there is no universally accepted definition. The term "accessible tourism" is also referred to as tourism for all, inclusive tourism, universal tourism and barrier-free tourism. For this study, the definition endorsed by the WTO will be adopted: "[Accessible tourism] is a form of tourism that involves a collaborative process among stakeholders that enables people with access requirements, including mobility, vision, hearing and cognitive dimensions of access, to function independently and with equity and dignity through the delivery of universally designed tourism products, services and environments" (Darcy and Dickson 2009, 34).

Accessible tourism attempts to meet the needs of people otherwise marginalized within the sector, such as senior citizens, pregnant women and people with special needs. As accessible tourism demand increases, tourism stakeholders should view it more as an obligation and opportunity rather than a risky option. There are several benefits to be derived from fulfilling the needs of people with disabilities and special needs. As a result, several countries have now mandated that their tourist destinations promote universal accessibility.

Tourism is important to small island developing states such as Grenada. According to the World Tourism and Travel Council (WTTC 2021, 10) in 2019, tourism accounted for 40.7 per cent of Grenada's total GDP. According to Grenada's Strategic Plan of 2011–2014, which is still in use, Grenada appeals to leisure travellers in areas such as dive, cruise, soft adventure and community tourism (GBT 2011). Moreover, Grenada's brand "Pure Grenada: The Spice of the Caribbean" focuses on geo-tourism, dive tourism and ecotourism (Government of Grenada 2021). Importantly, the strategic plan also noted that tourism stakeholders were unhappy with the poor conditions of the natural tourism product in Grenada (GBT 2011).

As a signatory to the UN Convention on the Rights of Persons with Disabilities, Grenada is obligated to ensure universal access to its tourist destinations. Therefore, accessible tourism should be an important part of Grenada's tourism policies. The purpose of this chapter is to determine the extent to which Grenada should develop two of its main tourist attractions to achieve universal accessibility for all visitors.

Literature Review

Tourism Sector

The tourism industry has directly and indirectly contributed significantly to several countries' GDPs. The World Tourism and Travel Council stated that: "prior to the pandemic, Travel & Tourism (including its direct, indirect and induced impacts) accounted for 1 in 4 of all new jobs created across the world, 10.6 per cent of all jobs (334 million), and 10.4 per cent of global GDP (US$9.2 trillion).

Meanwhile, international visitor spending amounted to US$1.7 trillion in 2019 (6.8 per cent of total exports, 27.4% of global services exports)" (WTTC 2021).

Several Caribbean countries rely on tourism for their continued growth and development. Pacheco and Lewis-Cameron (2010, 149) wrote that "the tourism sector is a major and sometimes only provider of foreign exchange for many of the [small island developing states]". Pacheco and Lewis-Cameron (2010, 149) postulated that "the Caribbean's tourism industry is based upon a fragile natural environment". The preceding claim has been evidenced in Grenada and Haiti, as both islands' natural environments were damaged by natural disasters, Hurricane Ivan in 2004 and the 2010 Haiti earthquake, respectively.

Hugh Riley (2017, np) stated that despite the region not reaching its forecasted thirty million arrivals in 2016: "Caribbean tourism continues to break new ground, surpassing 29 million arrivals for the first time in our history, and once again we have grown faster than the global average".

This demonstrates that the tourism industry is one of the fastest growing industries in the Caribbean.

Accessible Tourism

The concept of accessible tourism has long existed. Bordeianu (2015, 42) wrote that the accessible tourism concept was first crafted in 1989, at the International Year of Disabled Persons forum. As authors such as Bordeianu (2015) and Darcy (2009) have stated, accessible tourism does not have a single definition and many authors have tried to subjectively define the term, even referring to accessible tourism using different names, including tourism for all, inclusive tourism, universal tourism and barrier-free tourism.According to Darcy and Dickson (2009, 34) accessible tourism is "a form of tourism that involves a collaborative process among stakeholders that enables people with access requirements, including mobility, vision, hearing and cognitive dimensions of access, to function independently and with equity and dignity through the delivery of universally designed tourism products, services and environments".

This definition is endorsed by the WTO and used as the main definition of accessible tourism in much of the literature. Irrespective of varying definitions, the concept of accessible tourism has three underlying principles: equality; respect for all people, including people with disabilities; and independence. Accessible tourism encompasses all categories of people with special needs. It creates a barrier-free environment such that no sub-category of people with disabilities is put in a position where their disability becomes an inability. Therefore, stakeholders should ensure that all categories of people with disabilities can equally enjoy the tourism experience.

An Understanding of Disabilities

The International Classification of Functioning, Disability and Health defines disability as "an umbrella term for impairments, activity limitations, and participation restrictions. Disability is the interaction between individuals with a health condition (e.g. cerebral palsy, down syndrome and depression) and personal and environmental factors (e.g. negative attitudes, inaccessible transportation and public buildings, and limited social supports)" (WHO Media Centre 2013).

These factors are important for tourism stakeholders to consider in designing a tourist attraction that satisfies universal accessibility. As Darcy (2009, 816–826) noted, disability is a multidimensional construct, and each one has its own needs and requirements. The term "person with a disability" as it relates to the tourism industry refers to "any person whose full and effective participation in society on an equal basis with others in travel, accommodation and other tourism services is hindered by the barriers in the environment they are in and by attitudinal barriers" WTO (2013, 4).

Tourism stakeholders need to consider all forms of disabilities in developing their attractions. Ban Ki-Moon (2016) pointed out that "even with modern technologies, those with visual, hearing, mobility or cognitive impairments are being left behind in many tourism destinations".

According to the WTO, the term "people with disabilities": "include[s] all persons who, owing to the environment being encountered, suffer a limitation in their relational ability and have special needs during travel, in accommodations, and other tourism services, particularly individuals with physical, sensory and intellectual disabilities or other medical conditions requiring special care, such as elderly persons and others in need of temporary assistance" (WTO 2005).

These people should be catered to in addressing the accessibility of tourist sites, and stakeholders must work assiduously to accommodate every person with a disability as far as is possible.

Benefits of Accessible Tourism

The benefits of making tourism accessible include, but are not limited to:

- **Customer Satisfaction** – The improved quality of services and facilities offered through accessible tourism allows for otherwise marginalized people to feel included and partake in the tourism experience, thus improving their satisfaction with the tourism product as it caters to them and their needs. A practical example of this is the thriving Prado Museum's Collection in Spain, which exhibits three-dimensional copies of works of art, to accommodate people with visual impairments.
- **Enhanced Publicity** – As destinations develop universal design spaces, the reputation of those destinations will improve, thereby leading to increased recognition among people with disabilities and international organizations.
- **Investment Opportunities** – Noting the economic and reputational benefits to be derived from catering for people with disabilities in the tourism product, investors can be attracted by stakeholders to develop universal spaces.
- **Increased Visitors** – The European Network for Accessible Tourism (n.d.) reported that accessible tourism in Europe is estimated at 130 million people with annual spending of 68 million euros from the disabled community. People with disabilities often do not vacation alone but travel with their spouse, a friend or a caregiver for assistance. Through facilitating accessible tourism, a destination's competitiveness can be increased, thereby leading to more visitors with disabilities and their companions journeying to the destination and becoming loyal guests.
- **Meeting the Needs of Service** – Through moving towards accessible tourism, which will necessitate education regarding people with disabilities, catering for people with disabilities will eventually become the norm, thereby leading to the service needs of people with disabilities being met universally.

Rights of People with Disabilities

Several legislative instruments have addressed the rights of people with disabilities. The legislative objective was to remove barriers facing persons with special needs and to create universal access to all tourist sites for them. However, there is a lack of evidence to prove that such legislative instruments have improved the lives of those they agreed to protect (Huang-Chicago 2015).

The WTO and Fundación ACS (2015, 5) reported that the General Assembly accepted the Declaration on the Rights of Disabled Persons in December 1975. Years later, the UN declared 1981 the "International Year of Disabled Persons". The primary purpose of the declaration was to create a social life for people with disabilities and have them participate in the development of society (UN 1981). Other objectives were to increase public awareness, to accept and understand people with disabilities, and to allow them to create a voice for themselves and others (UN 1981). One of the outcomes of this programme is that people with disabilities became eligible for the same rights and equal opportunities as other individuals (UN 1983, np). Another outcome was that legislation to protect people with disabilities from discrimination was enacted (UN 1983). The programme set a clear mandate for the tourism stakeholders in section 134 of the World Programme of Action. It reads:

> the Member States should ensure that persons with disabilities have the same opportunities for recreational activities as other citizens. This involves the possibility of using restaurants, cinemas, theatres, libraries, as well as holiday resorts, sports arenas, hotels, beaches and other places for recreation. Member States should act to remove all obstacles to this effect. Tourist authorities, travel agencies, hotels, voluntary organisations and others involved in organising recreational activities or travel opportunities should offer their services to all and not discriminate against persons with disabilities. This involves, for instance, incorporating information on accessibility into their regular information to the public. (United Nations 1983)

The UN declared 1982–1992 as the "United Nations Decade of Disabled Persons". This period brought light to the definitions of people with disabilities and the relationship between people living with disabilities and their environment. Thereafter, the Standard Rules on the Equalization of Opportunities for Persons with Disabilities was sanctioned by the UN in 1993. The purpose of the rules according to section 15 was:

> to ensure that girls, boys, women and men with disabilities, as members of their societies, may exercise the same rights and obligations as others. In all societies of the world, there are still obstacles preventing persons with disabilities from exercising their

rights and freedoms and making it difficult for them to participate fully in the activities of their societies. It is the responsibility of States to take appropriate action to remove such obstacles. (UN 1993)

In 2007, the International Convention on the Rights of Persons with Disabilities was hosted. According to article 1, its purpose was "to promote, protect and ensure the full and equal enjoyment of all human rights and fundamental freedoms by all persons with disabilities, and to promote respect for their inherent dignity" (UN 2007, 4).

From a WTO context, in 1980, the Manila Declaration was approved by the WTO. Section 4 of the declaration noted that:

> the right to access holidays and freedom of travel and tourism, a natural consequence of the right to work, is recognized as an aspect of the fulfilment of the human being by the Universal Declaration of Human Rights as well as by the legislation of many States. It entails for society, the duty of providing for its citizens the best practical, effective and non-discriminatory access to this type of activity. (WTO 1980)

Thereafter, the WTO Assembly General approved Resolution A/RES/284(IX) in 1991. The resolution outlined a list of guidelines for member states to follow in order to regulate tourism services and establish new tourism facilities (WTO 1991). Resolution A/RES/406(XIII), accepted in 1999 by the General Assembly of the WTO, adopted the Global Code of Ethics for Tourism (WTO 1999). According to the WTO (1999), the code established ten principles that set the framework for tourism stakeholders to develop global tourism in more responsible and sustainable ways. Articles 2 and 7 of the principles allude to the rights of people with disabilities. Article 2 of the code states that "tourism activities should respect the equality of men and women; they should promote human rights and, more particularly, the individual rights of the most vulnerable groups, notably children, the elderly, the handicapped, ethnic minorities and indigenous peoples".

More recently, in 2005, the WTO renamed "Creating Tourism Opportunities for Handicapped People" to "Accessible Tourism for All". The term "handicapped" was seen as being insensitive and having disrespectful undertones. "Accessible Tourism for All" is a more inclusive term and incorporates not just people with health conditions but personal and environmental conditions. The document established a definition of the term "people with disabilities" and guidelines such as tourist information and publicity, preparation of staff, common requirements and requirements concerning specific facilities (WTO 2005). In 2016, the WTO celebrated World Tourism Day under the theme "Tourism for All – promoting universal accessibility", highlighting the importance of universal accessibility and its advantages for destinations (WTO 2016, 4).

Each legislative instrument discussed demonstrates the need for all people to have equal opportunities and enjoy tourism accommodation, services and activities. It is important, therefore, to create an environment that does not discriminate against people with disabilities. It is critical for governments to uphold the conventions on the rights of people with disabilities and to ensure that their destinations facilitate universal access for all. Thus, governments should take the bold step to develop their local legislation and policies to cater for people with disabilities. The residual effect will be that tourism stakeholders will pay more attention to the development of universal design and view it as obligatory rather than optional.

Creating Universal Design

Government and tourism stakeholders must lead the way in ensuring all tourism services, facilities and attractions are universally designed. Article 2 of the International Convention on the Rights of Persons with Disabilities in 2007 defines universal design as "the design of products, environments, programmes and services to be usable by all people, to the greatest extent possible, without the need for adaptation or specialized design. Universal design shall not exclude assistive devices for particular groups of persons with disabilities where this is needed" (UN 2007, 4).

Universal design creates barrier-free environments while incorporating planning that identifies the relationship between aging, disability and people's abilities over their lifetime (Darcy, Cameron, and Pegg 2010, 519). In Spain, the Tourism Authority has taken great initiatives to ensure the country's tourism products and services (including the airport and transportation services) are universally designed, which has led to increased benefits for the destination.

In 1997, the Center for Universal Design at the North Carolina State University developed seven principles for universal design. These are:

- Equitable Use
- Flexibility in Use
- Simple and Intuitive Use
- Perceptible Information

- Tolerance for Error
- Low Physical Effort
- Size and Space for Approach and Use" (National Disability Authority 2012).

The principles above can be used by stakeholders with a vested interest in tourism to guide the design of their environments, products and communications. Additionally, the principles can be used to guide future development, existing designs and to educate stakeholders. Rains (2004) wrote that if the tourism industry conforms to the principles listed above, it can be used as a pillar to achieve greater social sustainability.

To date, the International Organization for Standardization has set no international standard for accessible tourism, specifically regarding the development of a universal design for tourism attractions. An internationally accepted standard will assist in guiding all destinations, including small island developing states, in the best practices for accessible tourism. Due to the lack of international standards, more developed countries have established their own standards through entities such as the Spanish Association for Standardization in Spain and the Hérault General Council (2016, 64) in France, which developed the Open Sea for All programme aimed at making all beaches on the Mediterranean coast universally accessible and providing specialized workers to help people with special requirements.

Caribbean islands have also taken the initiative to develop some of the destinations' product offerings to ensure universal accessibility. However, as there is no regional entity to establish and enforce accessible tourism standards, there is still much to be done to ensure universal access in the Caribbean.

Case Study – Grenada

The Tourism Industry – Grenada

Past and present governments have named the tourism industry as one of the pillars of growth and transformation for Grenada's economy. According to the Government of Grenada prospectus (2009, 26), the tourism industry began to play, the tourism industry began to play a leading economic role around the 1990s. Pacheco and Lewis-Cameron (2010, 158) noted that with the decline of the agricultural sector, the Grenadian government developed a greater dependence on tourism. According to the National Portal of the

Government of Grenada, Grenada's brand "Pure Grenada: The Spice of the Caribbean" focuses on geo-tourism, dive tourism and ecotourism (Government of Grenada 2021). The report suggested that based on the Tourism Area Life Cycle, Grenada is positioned between the development and consolidation stages (Ministry of Finance and Planning 2006, 54).

In 2018, "all visitor categories reflected an increase including stay-over, at 31,815 visitors, an increase of 13 per cent; cruise, at 82,797 visitors, up by 37 per cent; and yachting, at 4,042 visitors, up by 43 per cent" (Niland n.d.). Niland (n.d.) also mentioned that room stock was projected to increase by 32 per cent in the next two years (2019 and 2020). All future growth projections were significantly affected by the COVID-19 pandemic, which resulted in an overall decline of the sector.

Disabilities in Grenada

The Population and Housing Census in 2011 reported that 14 per cent of the population had some form of infirmity or disability (The Commonwealth 2016). Forty-two per cent of those individuals were born with a disability, while 58 per cent were living with a disability due to illness, accident or some other cause (Crawford and St Bernard 2009, 89). Statistics show that in 2014 about 85.3 million Americans (27.2 per cent of the population) had a disability (Taylor 2018). The United States is Grenada's top tourism market. Thus, if Grenada develops its tourism product to cater for people with disabilities, it can tap into the 27.2 per cent of the US population living with disabilities.

Accessible Tourism in Grenada

Currently, Grenada has no local legislation specific to the rights of people with disabilities. However, Grenada is a member of the UN and has ratified the UN Convention on the Rights of Persons with Disabilities. Thus, the Grenada Tourism Authority uses the guidelines of the UN as it relates to the rights of people with disabilities. The result has been that many tourism practitioners in Grenada view the development of universal design facilities, services and attractions as voluntary as opposed to mandatory. Moreover, most tourism stakeholders in Grenada conceive of disability as only referring to people who use a wheelchair; thus, they design their facilities, services, and products to cater for people who use a wheelchair and ignore other forms of disability.

For this chapter, two of Grenada's main tourist attractions, the Grand Anse Beach and Grand E'tang National Park and Forest Reserve, were assessed to determine their accessibility to all visitors. The attractions were chosen based on their popularity.

The Grand Anse Beach is located on the southwest coastline of Grenada, in the parish of St George. The beach has approximately three kilometres of white sand (GTA 2021), attracting both locals and foreigners (including stay-over and cruise passengers). Located along the beach are a park, vendors' mall, several accommodations (Spice Island Beach Resort, Coyaba Beach Resort, Radisson Grenada) and restaurants (Umbrella's Restaurant). The beach also has a lifeguard station and one paid public washroom. The Grand E'tang National Park and Forest Reserve is in the parish of St Andrew. It is well known for its volcanic lake and forest reserve, its wide variety of vegetation and wildlife (including the famous Mona monkey, hummingbirds, ferns and pine and mahogany trees). The national park has a wide range of hiking trails. There is also a craft vendors' booth and a visitors' welcome centre.

Methodology

A mixed method approach was used. Data were collected from both primary and secondary sources to gain maximum insight. Primary data were gathered through 112 questionnaires administered to residents and visitors, using convenience sampling. Additionally, interviews were conducted with the product and development manager at the Grenada Tourism Authority (GTA) and a representative from the disabled community. These people were selected using purposive sampling because of their expertise in the field of research and their willingness to participate in the survey. The questionnaire contained twenty-four close-ended questions. In comparison, the interviews consisted of eleven open-ended questions.

Limitations experienced while conducting the research included early withdrawal by the Grenada National Council of the Disabled, difficulty in scheduling interviews and the refusal of respondents to answer questions. The data collected were analysed using Statistical Package for the Social Sciences software. The interviews were analysed using the coding process.

Findings and Discussion
Level of Accessibility for People with Disabilities at Main Attractions
Grand Anse Beach

Respondents were asked if the facilities provided at the attraction ensured a barrier-free environment. Of the forty-five respondents, thirty-two said that Grand Anse Beach does not provide ramps. The member of the disabled community stated that "at Grand Anse beach a mat for wheelchair access from the sand to the water is needed". This implies that the beach does not provide facilities that ensure a completely barrier-free environment in Grenada. Developed nations such as Spain and France have already implemented measures at their beaches that cater to the disabled community. Additionally, international sustainable certification regimes such as Blue Flag require beaches to have a barrier-free environment to be certified. Therefore, Grenada needs to make its beaches more accessible to the disabled community.

Respondents were also asked about signage, interpreters and washroom facilities at the Grand Anse beach. Thirty-nine respondents stated that Grand Anse Beach does not provide interpreters. Such results demonstrate the importance of staff development, through training and education, in achieving a barrier-free environment. Properly trained staff will be better able to fulfil the needs of people with disabilities. For example, through training in interpretation, lifeguards will be able to adequately communicate to blind tourists the areas of the beach safe for swimming. If training is facilitated and staff are developed, Grenada will become recognized for its development of a barrier-free tourism product and the tourism market will be expanded to include people with disabilities. An increase in arrivals will positively impact the overall tourism market and the local economy.

Grand E'tang National Park and Forest Reserve

All twelve respondents indicated that Grand E'tang National Park and Forest Reserve does not provide ramps and interpreters to ensure a barrier-free environment. Additionally, ten of the twelve respondents noted that this site does not provide railings and washroom facilities. As stated earlier, implementing such infrastructure and services will aid in the development of an accessible tourism product.

Approximately 50 per cent of the Greek population of people with disabilities, including mobility restrictions, indicated that they would travel more if access were improved (Voulgaropoulos, Strati and Fyka 2012, 56). From the survey conducted, of the fifteen respondents, only one person stated that they would be willing to visit an attraction alone. This reiterates the profit-earning potential of adopting practices compatible with accessible tourism and the need for ensuring that all members of society can fully enjoy the tourism product. However, as Darcy et al. (2011, 309) explained, "tourism providers need to have some basic knowledge, skills and competencies to meet the expectations of tourists with disabilities".

Table 4.1: Amenities Provided at the Sites for People with Disabilities

Sites	Amenities															Total
	Ramps			Railings			Signage			Interpreters			Washroom Facilities			
	Yes	No	N/A	Yes	No	N/A	Yes	No	N/A	Yes	No	N/A	Yes	No	N/A	
Grand Anse Beach	14	32	0	12	34	0	10	36	0	1	45	0	11	35	0	46
Grand E'tang National Park and Forest Reserve	0	12	0	10	2	0	4	8	0	0	12	0	2	10	0	12
N/A	0	0	7	0	0	7	0	0	7	0	0	7	0	0	7	7
Total	14	44	7	22	36	7	14	44	7	1	57	7	13	45	7	58

Challenges That May Hinder Key Stakeholders in Grenada from Catering to People with Disabilities

According to Puhretmair and Buhalis (2008), "tourism and travel experiences are still highly restricted by physical accessibility barriers, such as transportation constraints, inaccessible accommodation and tourism sites as well as information barriers such as a general lack of information, inadequate or incomplete information or poorly designed websites" (969). Based on the interviews, the major obstacles to key stakeholders in Grenada catering to people with disabilities include the lack of government funding, little to no collaboration among stakeholders, inadequate enforcement of laws concerning people with disabilities and insufficient education among stakeholders concerning people with disabilities.

Lack of Government Funding

Fourteen per cent of Grenada's population is living with some form of disability (The Commonwealth 2016). Tourism was not listed among the ten largest budget allocations in Grenada's 2018 budget (Mitchell 2018, 12). The entire health care section of the budget presentation did not address people with disabilities (Mitchell 2018, 14–15). This demonstrates that little or no financial provisions were made for people with disabilities or accessible tourism. Without enough funding, it is impossible to make significant changes to tourist sites. In order for accessible tourism to be developed, materials must be bought and workers must be paid. As a result, the government of Grenada has leased numerous tourism sites across Grenada (including the Annandale Waterfall) to firms with the sensitivity and capacity to develop the sites so that they are disability-friendly (Mitchell 2016, 37–38). This demonstrates that the government has found it difficult to finance tourism sites and is moving toward privatization of the sites (Mitchell 2016, 37–38).

A lack of funding is a challenge because it restricts or delays the development of facilities, which can harm visitorship. Of the forty-five respondents surveyed regarding Grand Anse Beach, sixteen disagreed and three strongly disagreed that the site was well equipped to cater to people with disabilities. If the site is unable to cater to the needs of people with disabilities, they and people who accompany them are unlikely to visit.

Collaboration among Stakeholders

The Product and Development Manager noted that "the GTA is not the sole owners or managers of any tourism attractions found in Grenada". This creates a challenge since the GTA must depend on other organizations or individuals when making decisions. It becomes difficult to find common ground if the stakeholders have different goals and objectives for tourism sites. An article from the *Daily Mail* stated that "some of the things holiday companies need to consider for the disabled travellers are accessible hotel rooms, equipment hires such as shower chairs, airport assistance and adapted transfers" (Gordon 2011).

Based on that statement, each stakeholder has an equally important role in developing sites towards accessible tourism. Even if the government enhances the airport and tourist sites, it is still up to hoteliers to provide accessible rooms and up to tour operators to make their tours accessible to people with disabilities. Both interviewees pointed out that there are standards for tourism stakeholders to follow as outlined by the Grenada Bureau of Standards. However, there remains a disconnect among stakeholders around abiding by those standards.

Lack of Enforcement of the Laws

Grenada has signed the International Convention on the Rights of Persons with Disabilities. Additionally, as highlighted by the interviewees, there are standards for tourism stakeholders to follow as outlined by the Grenada Bureau of Standards. However, presently in Grenada, there are few legislative frameworks to enforce the rights of people with disabilities, generally or concerning tourism specifically. Grenada is not the only country that has faced challenges when it comes to enforcing the goals of the treaty. Hoffman, Sritharan and Tejpar (2016, 1) found that "while the Convention is clearly an important step forward, there remains a divide, even in Canada, between the Convention's goals and the experiences of Canadians with disabilities".

The lack of legislative framework and enforcement of laws regarding people with disabilities thus allows stakeholders to ignore the rights of people with disabilities without fear of sanction, thus leading to the standards set by the Grenada Bureau of Standards and the UN not being upheld.

Lack of Education among Stakeholders

According to the Economic and Social Commission for Asia and the Pacific (2003, 86), "training and education are one of the major challenges facing the tourism industry in relation to meeting the needs of persons with disabilities". Of the seventy-three respondents, twenty-two knew nothing about accessible tourism. Additionally, when asked about their familiarity with the Convention on the Rights of Persons with Disabilities, 48 per cent of respondents stated that they were not at all familiar. This proves that awareness is lacking among the public. To boost the accessible tourism niche, general knowledge among the public and training for staff members is critical. If stakeholders are unaware of accessible tourism and conventions which promote it, it is unlikely that they will feel a sense of urgency to develop facilities towards achieving accessible tourism.

As stated by Butler and Jones (2001, 305), "there is a great deal of money to be made by meeting the demands of specific groups". However, accessible tourism will not be as profitable a niche if there is a lack of education among stakeholders, the major effect of which was highlighted in the paragraph above. With a lack of education and a consequent lack of development towards achieving accessible tourism, people with disabilities and those who accompany them will likely avoid sites that do not cater to their needs. This is validated by the data which show that out of seventy-three respondents, thirty-five agreed and twenty-three strongly agreed that tourists choose a site based on accessibility and their needs. It is therefore evident that the lack of training and education regarding accessible tourism can negatively impact the tourism industry, particularly since the global disabled community is projected to increase and travel more in the future (Butler and Jones 2001, 305).

Benefits of Accessible Tourism

Tourism provides many benefits to the global economy. Specific to this study, of the seventy-three respondents, thirty-seven strongly agreed and eight agreed that tourism is beneficial to the Grenadian society. The product and development manager noted that "tourism does not only raise tax revenues, but it also creates jobs". The tourism industry can be even more beneficial if accessible tourism is fully implemented. Both interviewees referred to the financial benefits to be derived from accessible tourism. Portugal has seen its market share increase as accessible tourism has increased in the territory. As outlined earlier, destinations that develop universally designed spaces enhance their competitiveness in the global arena and boost destination loyalty among visitors. Additionally, the representative from the disabled community noted that the development of accessible tourism "will not only benefit the disabled but all of society". All of society will benefit from the increase in foreign exchange, jobs and the expansion of the sector. Additionally, accessible tourism will allow everyone to exercise their right to participate in tourism, thereby fulfilling the goals of sustainable tourism, which should be practised by all destinations.

Creating Universal Design

As stated in the literature review, "'universal design' shall not exclude assistive devices for particular groups of people with disabilities where this is needed" (UN 2007, 4). When asked whether there was "proper" access to the two tourist sites, 51 per cent of respondents agreed and 37 per cent strongly agreed. However, when respondents were asked about the accessibility of these sites for people with disabilities, seventeen disagreed and ten strongly disagreed that these sites cater to people with disabilities. This suggests that respondents viewed "proper" access to sites from the perspective of non-disabled people, as opposed to the "universal design" perspective.

The general public's understanding of universal design needs to be increased. As mentioned earlier, there must be the theory of universal design to fully support and accommodate guests (Wattanayrangkul 2016). A site should never be deemed as "proper" unless all necessary infrastructure is in place. Services for tourists with disabilities are equally important. Therefore, universal design should become a critical part of Grenada's policies and plans in all sectors of society, but particularly the tourism sector.

For Grenada to develop a tourism product that adheres to universal design, it will take a collaboration of the public and private sectors and civil society. Entities such as the Ministry of Tourism must develop infrastructure such as airports, public transportation and tourism sites to reflect universal design. The GTA must also promote awareness of universal design within the private sector. With this knowledge, the private sector will be able to tailor products such as tours and accommodation to suit all tourists. The civil society should also share in building awareness in order to bring about the mindset change that is required. These combined efforts will lead to more and more visitors from the disabled community, which will lead to Grenada becoming a benchmark for best practices in accessible tourism.

Rights for People with Disabilities

The literature review highlighted that the rights of people with disabilities is not a new concept. Both interviewees stated that there are laws and policies in place to protect people with disabilities. These laws are in place because governments recognize that "all persons are equal before and under the law and are entitled without any discrimination to the equal protection and equal benefit of the law" United Nations (2007, 6). Policies are important to ensure that all stakeholders follow set guidelines in creating universal designs.

Policies will also be important for training staff to be equipped with the knowledge and skills necessary to cater to tourists with disabilities.

People with disabilities face discrimination and barriers that restrict them from participating in society on an equal basis with others every day (OHCHR n.d.). According to the representative from the disabled community, Grenada sees disability as mainly immobility. As a result, most of the attractions cater to people using wheelchairs but do not take into consideration other forms of disabilities. This denies the rights of those individuals who have disabilities other than immobility. Including everyone in the travel and tourism industry will aid in satisfying their human rights and stimulate the further growth of the industry.

Recommendations

The researcher has developed a conceptual framework based on the research conducted. This framework showcases several aspects necessary to create a barrier-free environment that will ensure an all-inclusive approach to tourism sites and attractions (see figure 4.1). Training and education among staff, collaboration among stakeholders, government funding, development of sites and stricter enforcement of laws are pillars of the framework.

Figure 4.1: Conceptual Framework for Barrier-Free Tourism Sites and Attractions

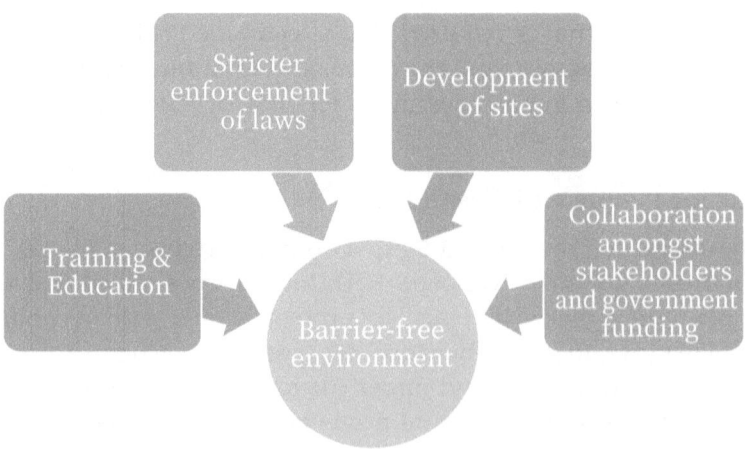

Education and Training

Based on the results presented, 48 per cent of respondents knew nothing about the Convention on the Rights of Persons with Disabilities. Moreover, out of the seventy-three respondents, only twelve were familiar with the term "accessible tourism". This, therefore, highlights the need for more public knowledge and awareness about people with disabilities and by extension accessible tourism. One way the GTA can eradicate this problem is through promotion, for example, via stakeholder conferences, social media, radio, TV and print. This awareness can educate stakeholders on their roles and the importance of having a barrier-free environment.

Additionally, when asked about staff helpfulness at the sites, twelve out of thirteen respondents stated that the staff at the tourist sites were not helpful. This low result underscores the need for staff training at each of the sites so that employees are better able to attend to people with access needs. The European Network for Accessible Tourism provides online training to tourism professionals on accessibility; as of 2013, the programme has successfully trained 259 participants (WTO 2016) – this programme can therefore be explored by the GTA. Staff training can help to decrease some access problems in access or address unforeseen difficulties, which can help to minimize the barriers that people with disabilities face.

Collaboration among Stakeholders and Government Funding

For Grenada to develop accessible tourism as a niche market, all stakeholders, including the government, private sector, community and non-profit organizations, are needed. Grenada is a member of the UN and a signatory to the Convention on the Rights of Persons with Disabilities. Therefore, the Grenadian government should abide by its international treaty obligations under the UN convention. Additionally, the government should lead the way in developing all state-owned attractions towards a barrier-free environment as an example for private stakeholders, who will, in turn, feel a sense of urgency to follow suit.

Only four respondents strongly agreed that stakeholders are presently committed to catering to people with disabilities. The government can help to change this by providing incentives such as tax breaks or grants for private sector bodies to improve their facilities and services towards a barrier-free environment, as seen in the example of Turismo de Portugal. As a result, Grenada will not only be catering to the local disabled community but also to tourists with disabilities.

The government can also source much-needed funding from agencies such as the European Union under its enhancement tourism accessibility programmes or the UN Voluntary Fund on Disability. The government can work with other stakeholders to write an effective proposal to access funding.

Development of Sites

Based on the research, several developments are needed at all the sites for Grenada to take advantage of the accessible tourism market. As outlined in the interview, most of the sites failed to cater for people with needs outside of mobility, such as visual and hearing impairments. Therefore, the sites must be designed to cater for all people, for example, through proper signage using audio and print to guide visitors in an unfamiliar environment. The sites should be universally designed to ensure a barrier-free environment.

Additionally, during the interview, both interviewees agreed that Grenada should develop a rating scheme for its attractions. This can be conducted and monitored within the GTA under the Product and Development Department. The rating scheme can act as an indicator of the accessibility of each attraction. Additionally, the GTA can develop a subpage on its website highlighting various attractions and their levels of accessibility, generating awareness.

Stricter Enforcement of Laws

From the primary data collected, it was noted that Grenada is a member of the UN and a signatory to the Convention on the Rights of Persons with Disabilities. Thus, the government must ratify the convention into local law so that laws regarding people with disabilities can be developed and enforced. The government can then enact stricter penalties as fines for stakeholders who are non-compliant with the convention. Moreover, the GTA can also ensure that they only endorse tourism activities and businesses that ensure a barrier-free environment, demonstrating to tourism stakeholders the seriousness with which accessible tourism should be treated.

Suggestions for Further Work

Research focusing on the disabled community's views on the accessibility of tourism sites and attractions via a simple random approach is suggested. This will allow for a greater understanding of the needs of people with disabilities since results will be based on their own perspective. The research can focus on tourist sites and attractions in Grenada such as Concord Waterfall and La Sagesse Beach. Similar research can be conducted in other Caribbean islands. A formal assessment of the accessibility of the accommodation sector in Grenada can also be conducted. Ultimately, a report can be generated detailing the viability of accessible tourism as a niche market for Grenada, as well as the benefits to be derived from it.

Conclusion

Accessible tourism is an increasingly important tourism sub-sector. Its existence presents a great economic opportunity for Grenada while simultaneously ensuring that the destination meets its UN obligations. However, for accessible tourism to elevate from being an aspirational ideal for Grenada to an achieved goal, there must be formal research regarding the current status of, and potential for, accessible tourism in Grenada, such that appropriate planning and strategies can be put in place to achieve extensively accessible tourism. Additionally, training and educating staff in the tourism sector in the importance of accessibility and the needs of people with disabilities is vital. Further, there must be collaboration between the government and the private sector to fund the development necessary for accessible tourism to become a reality in Grenada. Additionally, the government must develop laws that protect people with disabilities and promote accessible tourism. Once these and other necessary steps are taken, accessible tourism can become a viable niche market for Grenada.

References

Ki-moon, Ban. 2016. "Tourism for All – Promoting Universal Accessibility." Message delivered at the World Tourism Day Celebration 2016, Thailand, September 2016. World Tourism Day 2016: Promoting Universal Accessibility | UNWTO.

Bordeianu, Otilia Maria. 2015. "Accessible Tourism – A Challenge for Romanian Tourism." *Journal of Tourism – Studies and Research in Tourism* 20:42–49.

Butler, Richard, and Peter Jo. 2001. "Conclusions – Problems, Challenges Solutions." In *Tourism and Hospitality in the 21st Century*, edited by A. Lockwood and S. Medlik, 296–310. Oxford: Elsevier Butterworth-Heinemann.

Crawford, Wendy, and Godfrey St Bernard. 2009. *Caricom Capacity Development Programme, 2000 Round of Population and Housing Census Data, Analysis Sub-Project, National Census Report, Grenada.* Guyana: Caribbean Community (CARICOM) Secretariat.

Darcy, S, I. Ambrose, S. Schweinsbery, and D. Buhalis. 2011. "Conclusion: Universal Approaches to Accessible Tourism." In *Accessible Tourism: Concepts and Issues,* edited by Dimitrios Buhalis and Simon Darcy, 300–311. UK: Channel View Publications.

Darcy, Simon. 2009. "Inherent Complexity: Disability, Accessible Tourism and Accommodation Information Preferences." *Tourism Management* 31 (6): 816–26. https://doi.org/10.1016/j.tourman.2009.08.010.

Darcy, Simon, Bruce Cameron, and Shane Pegg. 2010. "Accessible Tourism and Sustainability: A Discussion and Case Study." *Journal of Sustainable Tourism* 18 (4): 515–37. https://doi.org/10.1080/09669581003690668.

———, and Tracey J. Dickson. 2009. "A Whole-of-Life Approach to Tourism: The Case for Accessible Tourism Experiences." *Journal of Hospitality and Tourism Management* 16:32–44. https://doi.org/10.1375/jhtm.16.1.32.

European Network for Accessible Tourism. n.d. "Working Together to Make Tourism in Europe Accessible for All." Accessed 8 February 2017. http://www.accessibletourism.org/resources/enat-a3_2010_en_for_web.pdf.

Economic and Social Commission for Asia and the Pacific. 2003. *Barrier-Free Tourism for People with Disabilities in the Asian and Pacific Region.* New York: United Nations.

Gordon, Sarah. 2011. "Travel Industry 'Not Doing Enough for Disabled Travellers.'" *Daily Mail,* 13 January 2011. http://www.dailymail.co.uk/travel/article-1346753/Disabled-travel-Holiday-industry-doing-disabled-travellers.html.

Government of Grenada. 2021. "Tourism." Web Portal. Accessed 28 September 2021.

Grenada Tourism Authority (GTA). 2021. "Grand Anse Beach." Accessed 21 July 2021. grenadagrenadines.com/explore/attractions/beaches/grand-anse-beach/#.WK-z3vkrLIU.

Grenada Board of Tourism (GBT). 2011. *Strategic Plan 2011–2014.* Burns Point, Grenada: GBT.

Hérault General Council. 2016. "Case Study: La mer ouverte à tous, Hérault General Council (France)." In *Manual on Accessible Tourism for All: Principles, Tools and Best Practices – Module V: Best Practices in Accessible Tourism,* edited by World Tourism Organisation, 64–66. Madrid: UNWTO.

Hoffman, Steven J., Lathika Sritharan, and Ali Tejpar. 2016. "Is the UN Convention on the Rights of Persons with Disabilities Impacting Mental Health Laws and Policies in High-Income Countries? A Case Study of Implementation in Canada." *BMC International Health and Human Rights* 16 (28): 1–18. https://doi.org/10.1186/s12914-016-0103-1.

Huang-Chicago, Wen. 2015. "Are Human Rights Treaties Actually Working?" https://www.futurity.org/human-rights-937172/.

Ministry of Finance and Planning. 2006. *Grenada Export Strategy*. St George's: Government of Grenada.

Mitchell, Keith. 2016. "Budget Statement 2016." Speech delivered at the House of Representatives 2015, Grenada, November 2015. Accessed 17 November 2017. http://www.gov.gd/egov/docs/budget_speech/Budget-2016.pdf.

———. 2018. "Budget Statement 2018." Speech delivered at the Grenada Trade Centre 2017, Grenada, November 2017. Accessed 28 September 2021. http://www.grenadagov.info/egov/docs/budget_speech/budget-2018.pdf.

National Disability Authority. 2012. "The 7 Principles." Accessed 15 February 2017. http://universaldesign.ie/What-is-Universal-Design/The-7-Principles/.

Niland, Dana. n.d. "Grenada Tourism Continues Boom into 2018." *Caribbean Journal*. Accessed 28 September 2021. https://www.caribjournal.com/2018/03/03/grenada-tourism-continues-boom-2018/.

Office of the High Commissioner for Human Rights (OHCHR). n.d. "Human Rights of Persons with Disabilities." Accessed 17 November 2017. http://www.ohchr.org/EN/Issues/Disability/Pages/DisabilityIndex.aspx.

Pacheco, Barney G., and Acolla Lewis-Cameron. 2010. "Weathering the Storm – Crisis Marketing for Small Island Tourist Destinations." In *Marketing Island Destinations: Concepts and Cases*, edited by Acolla Lewis-Cameron and Sherma Roberts, 149–71. New York: Routledge.

Puhretmair, Franz, and Dimitrios Buhalis. 2008. "Accessible Tourism: Introduction to the Special Thematic Session." In *Computers Helping People with Special Needs:11th International Conference, ICCHP 2008, Linz, Austria, July 9–11, 2008 Proceedings*, edited by Klaus Miesenberger, Joachim Klaus, Wolfgang Zagler, and Arthur Karshmer, 969–72. Heidelberg: Springer.

Rains, Scott. 2004. "Universal Design and the International Travel and Hospitality Industry." Paper presented at the Designing for the 21st Century III, Rio de Janeiro, Brazil, 7–12 December 2004. http://www.designfor21st.org/proceedings/proceedings/precon_rains.html.

Riley, Hugh. 2017. "Caribbean Tourism Industry Performance Report 2016." Speech delivered at the Caribbean Tourism Industry Performance Report news conference outlining the Caribbean's performance in 2016 and the outlook for 2017, Barbados, February 2017. http://www.onecaribbean.org/events-calendar/cto-2017-calendar/state-industry-2017/.

Taylor, Danielle. 2018. "Americans with Disabilities: 2014." https://www.census.gov/content/dam/Census/library/publications/2018/demo/p70-152.pdf.

The Commonwealth. 2016. "Grenada Referendum and the Protection of Persons with Disabilities." https://thecommonwealth.org/media/news/grenada-referendum-and-protection-persons-disabilities.

The World Bank. 2022. "Disability Inclusion." Last modified 14 April 2022. https://www.worldbank.org/en/topic/disability.

United Nations (UN). 1981. "The International Year of Disabled Persons 1981." https://www.un.org/development/desa/disabilities/the-international-year-of-disabled-persons-1981.html.

———. 1983. *United Nations Decade of Disabled Persons 1983–1992: World Programme of Action Concerning Disabled Persons*. New York: United Nations.

———. 1993. "Standard Rules on the Equalization of Opportunities for Persons with Disabilities." http://www.un.org/esa/socdev/enable/dissre00.htm.

———. 2007. "Convention on the Rights of Persons with Disabilities and Optional Protocol." http://www.un.org/disabilities/documents/convention/convoptprot-e.pdf.

Wattanayrangkul, Kobharn. 2016. "Tourism for All – Promoting Universal Accessibility." Message delivered at the World Tourism Day Celebration 2016, Thailand, September 2016. http://wtd.unwto.org/content/official-messages-world-tourism-day-0.

World Health Organization (WHO) Media Centre. 2013. "New World Report Shows More than 1 Billion People with Disabilities Face Substantial Barriers in their Daily Lives." https://www.who.int/news/item/29-10-2013-new-world-report-shows-more-than-1-billion-people-with-disabilities-face-substantial-barriers-in-their-daily-lives.

World Tourism Organization (WTO). 1980. *Manila Declaration On World Tourism*. Madrid: UNWTO.

———.1991. *Resolution A/RES/284(IX)*. Madrid: UNWTO.

———. 1999. *Global Code of Ethics for Tourism: For Responsible Tourism*. Madrid: UNWTO.

———. 2005. *Resolution A/RES/492(XVI), Accessible Tourism for All*. Madrid: UNWTO.

———. 2013. *Recommendations on Accessible Tourism for all*. Madrid: UNWTO.

———. 2016. *Highlights of the 1st UNWTO Conference on Accessible Tourism in Europe*. Madrid: UNWTO.

———, and Fundación ACS. 2015. *Manual on Accessible Tourism for All – Public-Private Partnerships and Good Practices*. Madrid: UNWTO.

World Tourism and Travel Council (WTTC). n.d.a. "Security and Travel Facilitation." Accessed July 18, 2021. https://wttc.org/Initiatives/Security-Travel-Facilitation#:~:text=WTTC%20Members%20have%20identified%20security%20and%20travel%20facilitation,of%20the%20global%20economy%20for%20nine%20consecutive%rch 2021.

———. 2021. "Economic Impact Reports." https://wttc.org/research/economic-impact.

Voulgaropoulos, Nikos, Eleni Strati, and Georgia Fyka. 2012. "Accessible Tourism in Greece: Beaches Bathing for All." In *Best Practice in Accessible Tourism: Inclusion, Disability, Ageing Population and Tourism*, edited by Dimitrios Buhalis, Simon Darcy, and Ivor Ambrose, 55–62. Bristol: Channel View Publications.

5.
Stop Making Noise, Make Image – Unleashing the Possibilities of Music Tourism in Trinidad through Participation

Leandra Simon-Richards

Introduction

This chapter looks at a potential music tourism niche in Trinidad, a Caribbean destination with a post-colonial governance structure and economically dominant energy sector (Ministry of Energy and Energy Industries n.d.). Trinidad has a society with high levels of dependency on distributive and redistributive governmental inputs, from oil and gas into development and an associated dependency philosophy among many in the population (Augustine 2017). With central government-led tourism niches in "Events, Sport, and Conferences", and a large and seasonal festival tourism product through their "Trinidad Carnival", there is still a vast amount of untapped potential, particularly in music, which can be explored for the purpose of year-round tourism development (Tourism Trinidad Limited 2020).

According to Guilbault (2014, 308):

> In the context of tourism, music enables diverse and contrasting types of encounters and affects social relations locally, regionally, and internationally. It reveals how music acts in many contrasting capacities: how it intervenes as a cultural broker, generates income, and also produces pleasure; how it features local and cosmopolitan knowledge; how in some cases it serves as a spiritual medium; and how it turns political and private interests into economic possibilities as well as, inadvertently, social liabilities.

The power and impact of music on the emotional and cultural experiences of tourists has long been recognized as it has always been intertwined with various tourism experiences in a supportive role.

Music as a tourism driver requires the harnessing of this power towards the delivery of a unique and memorable tourism experience.

This can be facilitated within a destination by an adequate pool of resources and talent with a wide variety of capabilities, including music, entrepreneurship and administration, working collaboratively to create and extract social and economic value through tourism interactions.

Despite the pervasive role of music in the lives and identity of the local population of Trinidad, a comprehensive music tourism offering has not yet made its way into public policy, and despite the Creative Music City designation of its capital city, Port of Spain (UNESCO 2019), its tourism destination development organization – Tourism Trinidad – does not yet consider music to be a market-ready option on its own strength (Tourism Trinidad Limited 2020). Given the country's long-standing musical footprint, globally and regionally, as well as the scarcity of research into music tourism among Caribbean music ethnologists (Guilbault 2014, 308), there is a question of whether there is a lack of interest and a lack of capacity within the destination which hinders the development of a successful music tourism niche.

In addressing the phenomena that Caribbean music ethnologists have "largely failed" to address the relationship between music and tourism until recently, Guilbault (2014) refers to Crick's (1989) view that "what distinguishes entertainment for tourism in the circum-Caribbean" is "its postcolonial history and the vexed relationships it has entailed with the so-called 'First World'" (Guilbault 2014, 308). Pattullo (1996) noted that "cultural attitudes, racism, patterns of control and ownership have all contributed to the perceptions of many black Caribbeans that they remain bunched at the bottom end of the tourist industry with few opportunities for career advancement" (65).

Together with the seasonality of Carnival and its sustainment by heavy government subventions (Paul 2020), small local markets and a population overflowing with unfulfilled musical capabilities, this apparent lack of interest in tourism by researchers in music fields may possibly reflect or explain in some small way the attitudes and perceptions held by the wider music fraternity. This chapter seeks to bring about an appreciation of:
- the significance of music and the definition and nature of music tourism from various perspectives,
- the way in which participation in music activities and processes both contributes to and is influenced by tourism and the rationale for a participatory approach to music tourism development,

- the characteristics of the Participatory Tourism Development Framework as a construct of intrinsic and extrinsic elements of interest and power, respectively, and
- the concept of Participatory Tourism Development (PTD) as a strategic approach for increasing tourism benefits to local communities.

Literature Review
Understanding Music Tourism

Researchers of ProColumbia and Sound Diplomacy (2018) describe music tourism as encompassing "any activity undertaken by a tourist where the primary motivation to travel is music related" (13). They explain that boosting tourism begins with identifying music-related assets and thereafter unpacking the music history, heritage, experiences and stories that can "uncover new means to share stories, develop travel packages and expand one's tourism offer (ProColumbia and Sound Diplomacy 2018, 10).

Similarly, Watson (2018) draws on Bolderman and Reijnders's (2016) statement that one of the main motives for travel is seen in the role music plays in creating a "story of self" (Bolderman and Reijnder 2016, quoted in Watson 2018, 73). Watson (2018) also states that there is a strong attachment between styles of music and particular places, whereby these places are often connected with certain musical scenes and "sounds" (73).

Music tourism, as such, can be built on places with musical heritage or it may be built on contemporary music scenes and live music performances or a combination thereof (Watson 2018, 74–81). Whatever typology is used, it is usually clear that psychological identification is key to the development of music tourism. At a personal level, people develop an intimate relationship with music, and it forms an important part of individual identity. Music therefore has an emotive power, evoking personal memories and allowing people to recall particular periods of their lives. As Connell and Gibson (2003) noted, music tourism taps into this, providing people with opportunities to relive their emotional attachments to music (Connell and Gibson 2003, quoted in Watson 2018, 73).

Prior (2015) examined "the texture of material practices in the everyday lives of musicians and associated cultural workers" and explains the importance of "situated interactions" that are required to "contribute to the flourishing of local music cultures" (82). When one asks what practices operate at a local level, the picture that unfolds is one of "people actively engaging in intensely human practices in which they took trouble and pains, in which they experienced disputes and sociability" (Finnegan 2007, xv). To understand why music matters to people is, in other words, to be oriented to the encounters, moments and events through which particular music-based attachments are given shape and meaning (Cohen 2007; DeNora 2000) (Prior 2015, 82).

A similar approach is seen in the case of Cuba. Takashi Aoki notes and explains the manner in which music tourism influenced the government and society through observing Cuba's musical and cultural setting and analysing "the manner in which culture can be utilised by and for Cubans through tourist activities" (Aoki 2002, 78). Along with history, heritage and experiences, these spaces would contribute to the "recognised structure" to tell the story, which would generate jobs and demand for accommodation, food and amenities, which allow value extraction towards participant benefits. Prior agrees that "If 'musicking' is essentially about doing music in location with others, then one way to identify these practices is to examine processes of collaborative interaction in vivo – in other words, to examine creative endeavours as collective accomplishments of flesh and blood actors, situated and contextualized in specific locations" (Martin 2006, quoted in Prior 2015, 86).

Prior's approach of examining collaborative interactions considers four corresponding activities that he saw as the basis of the flourishing music culture in Reykjavik (see figure 5.1).

Figure 5.1: Interactive Music Activities

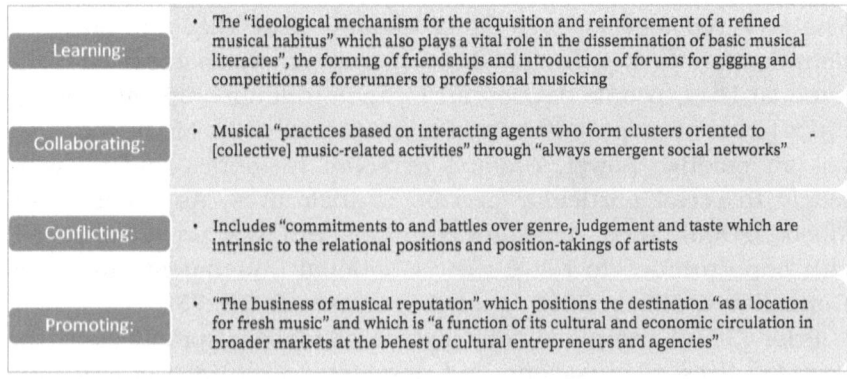

Source: Prior (2015, 88–89)

Participation in these activities necessitates varying degrees of cognitive and affective investment (Prior 2015, 83) and is also influenced and shaped by the dynamics of political, social and economic circumstances within the spaces and places where people engage in music processes, that is, the socio-spatial configuration.

Participatory Tourism Development (PTD)

It is within the socio-spatial configuration of music spaces that the level and quality of participation by stakeholders in the processes that facilitate music tourism development may be analysed. PTD, according to Tosun (2006), is tourism development that seeks "to sustain tourism as an agent for sociocultural and economic development" (493). Tosun states, "It is believed that participatory development approach would facilitate implementation of principles of sustainable tourism development by creating better opportunities for local people to gain larger and more balanced benefits from tourism development taking place in their localities (Tosun 2000), resulting in more positive attitudes to tourism development and conservation of local resources (Inskeep, 1994), and by increasing the limits of local tolerance to tourism" (Tosun 2006, 493).

It should not be assumed, however, that residents are willing and able to participate equally. Thetsane's (2019) research indicated that in the general local community there is an "unclear description" of the community's roles and "how their views are incorporated in the whole tourism planning and development process" (124). To this end, Tosun provides a useful synopsis of the forms (typologies) of participation towards the development of a model to better understand how to involve local communities effectively in tourism (Tosun 2006, 503). Table 5.1 summarizes the attributes of Tosun's community participation in tourism typologies.

A comparison of Tosun's and Thetsane's studies of the expected nature of participation by local communities shows that although respondents generally wanted to take part in the tourism development process, the level at which they preferred to participate varied (Tosun 2006; Thetsane 2019).

Behavioural theory has shown that human beings have bounded, instead of perfect, rationality and, therefore, it is unlikely that "human exchange relationships are always characterised by rational economic optimisation, but instead by human expectations" and limitations (Mermoud et al. 2019, 2). This has been explored in the tourism literature through theoretical frameworks such as social exchange theory (regarding residents' perceived costs and benefits of tourism development) and Weber's theory of formal and substantive rationality (Boley et al. 2014, 33–50).

Table 5.1: Community Participation in Tourism

Typology	Main Attributes
Coercive	• Enables power holders to educate or cure host communities to turn away potential and actual threats to [the] future of tourism development • Heavily skewed towards the fostering and development of tourism • Primarily concerned with meeting the needs and desires of decision makers, tourism's operators and tourists
Induced	• Allows the host community to hear and be heard • They have a voice in the tourism development process, but they do not have power to ensure that their views will be taken into account by other powerful interest groups such as government bodies, multinational companies, international tour operators, etc.
Spontaneous	• Provides full managerial responsibility and authority to host communities

Source: Tosun (2006, 494–95)

Considering Ajzen's (2016) theory of planned behaviour, it can be argued that given favourable and accommodating behavioural and normative beliefs and "a sufficient degree of actual power" or control over participation (empowerment)", people are expected to be willing and able to participate "when the opportunity arises" (1). Boley et al. (2014) emphasized "the importance of developing tourism in a manner that increases residents' pride and self-esteem in their community" and suggested "that if members of the tourism industry wish to cultivate favourable attitudes towards tourism, they need to consider how residents perceive themselves to be empowered or disempowered through tourism" (47). They suggest that fostering psychological empowerment among residents requires "marketing strategies that highlight the special features of the region from a local's perspective". This is supported in the special interest tourism literature where the psychological construct of "interest" is linked to the value gained from the experiences of tourists, allowing the development of several scales to measure the influence of the multidimensional construct of "involvement" on tourist and consumer behaviour.

In the context of tourism, according to Trauer (2006, 191), involvement "has been interpreted as a process of psychological identification resulting in varying degrees of behavioural, cognitive, and affective investment in an activity, product or situation" (Trauer, 2006 cited in Agarwal, Busby and Huang 2018, 9). This process of psychological identification captures the relationship between customers and producers, which involves a joint effort in the creation of value and describes the movement from passive to active consumers as per the co-creation and service-dominant logic theorizations (Agarwal, Huang and Busby 2018, 7). There might also be merit in describing local producers' efforts in terms of passive and active value creation, which may be seen to influence stakeholder behaviour at a destination, specifically participative behaviours that contribute to tourism development.

The participatory approach to identifying stakeholders is the "identification of those who have legitimate and important views but need to have their capabilities raised to enable them to put these views forward and to negotiate in collaborative decision-making arrangements" (Carroll 1993, 238). Such stakeholders may:

> lack technical knowledge about tourism planning or skills in presenting their views in meetings, and these might be developed through education and training. Warner (1997: 418) adopts a normative position that "stakeholder targeting" is needed to create an equitable basis for collaborative negotiations, and that "a 'consensus' model of participation should direct early effort towards those stakeholders who are most polarized from a capability to negotiate collaboratively". (Warner 1997, 418 as cited in Araujo and Bramwell 1999, 359)

Stakeholder interest in music may therefore translate into participation in music tourism only in the presence of an appropriate structure which increases the capability of music stakeholders to negotiate collaboratively in the tourism arena. A participatory approach to music tourism development may facilitate the creation of such a collaborative structure.

Methodology

The case study sought to determine to what extent the local music community in Trinidad is willing and able to participate in the development of music tourism. A dominant/ or less dominant (deductive/ or inductive) multi-strategy approach was used, where qualitative strategy was dominant and quantitative strategy was less dominant (Wilson 2014, 17).

Exploratory research was used to develop better insights into the music community, while qualitative and quantitative descriptive research were used to describe the interest group. Primary data was collected using a survey, interviews and participatory observations. A total of thirty-nine completed survey responses were received. Interviews with several private and public sector stakeholders were conducted. Nine one-on-one interviews and one focus group interview with six participants were completed. Participatory observation took place in a six-week music industry technical camp by Dian Jen Music School, a music symposium hosted by Music TT in 2018, three (gospel) artist network meetups and one high-level stakeholder engagement organized by Tourism TT on 14 January 2020.

Secondary data was used to collect the archival data on Trinidad's music stories from the works of music ethnologists, history books, articles and documentaries relating to local music stakeholders, music heritage and contemporary music scenes.

The target population for the primary research consisted of stakeholders with a "legitimate interest" in music (as per the participatory approach to stakeholder targeting) or tourism organizations, groups and individuals who could potentially engage in or support the use of music-related activities as a tourism driver. The chosen sampling technique was non-probability sampling, using a combination of convenience and purposive sampling, which allowed researchers to use their judgement to select people who would best answer the research questions and meet the objectives of the study.

Data analysis was quantitative and qualitative. Descriptive analysis was used to report central tendency and variability with respect to:

- how respondents thought the music community should participate in music tourism development (spontaneous, induced, coercive),
- whether there was a positive or negative attitude towards music tourism development from the music community,
- whether there was a high (or low) level of psychological, social and political empowerment within the community towards engaging in the behavioural, cognitive and affective investment in music tourism-related activities, and
- respondent opinion on adequacy and availability of local music-related spaces, assets and resources.

With respect to qualitative analysis, the study used discourse analysis whereby "formal written records" such as news reports and industry-related online articles, policy documents, academic texts, documentaries, transcripts of interviews, survey responses and the group discussion were analysed.

The major limitation of the study was the challenge of obtaining the cooperation of the cultural gatekeepers and the inconsistent level of willingness of the relevant personnel in the various ministries and other organizations to assist. Another major difficulty was the drastic change in the overall environment being studied with the COVID-19 pandemic beginning after the field research had been conducted. However, this was not found to have a deleterious effect on the overall research value.

Discussion

Trinidad, in the language of Gibson and Connell (2005), has been viewed as the "authentic birthplace" or "place of creation" of Steelpan and Calypso music with subsequent fusions and variations from other diverse cultures, which resulted in the creation of Soca, Rapso, Chutney and Parang. These would meet the criteria to be considered the "unique sounds" of destination Trinidad (Gibson and Connell 2005, 44). One part of its musical history is a struggle with achieving equity and inclusion. This comprises a story of colonial and post-colonial disparity in the allocation of resources, cycles of political and social discontent, conflict, and creative rebellion. It includes chance occurrences and experimentation within the various musical movements and their cycles of rejection, placation and acceptance – or recognition of opportunities of economic exploitation – of each new musical movement by wider society and particularly by those who held political and economic power, influence and access to resources.

Another aspect of Trinidad's musical history is a fight for cultural preservation against the passage of time and changing tastes and values between and within generations. This history, as well as the present resistance to change from stalwarts of earlier musical movements and their battle to preserve their art in its original forms and in its original spaces, can be used to understand the socio-spatial configuration of Trinidad's creative networks.

Participation in Music Tourism in Trinidad

Interest (Music Tourism Participation Push Factors)

The collective results of the research into the willingness of Trinidad's music community to participate in music tourism indicated an overall interest in music tourism on both cognitive and affective levels by music stakeholders. This supports the finding that there is a positive or favourable attitude towards music tourism development and that there is willingness to participate. The Kendall's tau b and Spearman's rho tests of non-parametric correlations confirmed the assumptions of correlations between interest and willingness to participate (Correlations of .428 and .570 were significant at the 0.00 level [2-tailed]). The summated result is seen in table 5.2.

The positive attitude may be a good indicator of psychological identification with music and thus interest and support for music tourism. This means that if given the opportunity, resources, access and knowledge, the stakeholder may be willing to actively participate.

Active interest is indicated when the interest reflects a fluid and dynamic identification with the destination image (shared stories, heritage and experiences) as it relates to stakeholder's pride and self-esteem and thus characterized by substantial psycho-social investment in stories of national identity, music identity, and music activities and processes within local spaces of creativity. Conversely, passive interest may be characterized by low risk or no personal or affective investment in creative music activities and processes.

The research indicated that there is an opportunity for the development of music tourism in resident populations such as in Trinidad, which have historically shown a lack of interest in tourism unless there is direct economic benefit in the form of employment outside of the Carnival season. It also indicated that this favourable attitude is tempered by lower identification with national identity.

The high level of affective and cognitive interest in music tourism shifts the movement from passive towards active participation, and onward to the final goal of authentic value-creation. This can be see as the "psychological identfication" which researchers such as Trauer (2006) referred to as having influence on consumer and tourist behaviour in terms of increasing both the likelihood of involvement and the positive attitude towards a behaviour (such as support for music tourism, as per Boley et al. [2014]), and which is a good indicator of behavioural intention according to Ajzen (2016). This psychological identification with music on the stakeholder side

Table 5.2: Willingness to Participate in Music Tourism

Behavioural Construct	Minimum	Maximum	Mean	Std. Deviation
Interest in Music Tourism	2.92	5.00	4.4477	.47839
Participation in Music Tourism	3.71	5.00	4.3114	.34039

*Statistically significant correlation between interest and participation

can be seen to influence their behaviour, increasing the likelihood of support in the form of participation in music interactions if given the opportunity to so do for their benefit, which will contribute to tourism development.

As with special interest tourists, special interest stakeholders must have the interest and value-based motivations to pursue opportunities for interaction and engagement within the special interest tourism system based on psychological identification with that specific activity, product or situation (in this case, musicking), and can therefore be targeted as willing tourism stakeholders based on that specific interest.

The joint effort in the creation of value and the movement from passive to active consumers described in the special interest tourism literature may be extended to describe the movement from passive to active stakeholders which identify specifically with various and diverse musical movements (Agarwal, Busby and Huang 2018, 7). There were several musical movements of active participation in Trinidad, each with its own unique identity as seen in table 5.3, which, for simplicity, may be categorized into participants within indigenous and non-indigenous music scenes. These movements have varying levels of access to spaces of various capacities and music-related resources. Dedicated or repurposed music spaces ranged from micro-spaces (which facilitate less than one hundred) to mega-spaces (which facilitate over five thousand).

Table 5.3: Examples of Music Movements in Trinidad

Indigenous: Festival Music Scene	Non-Indigenous: Traditional and Contemporary Music Scenes
• Calypso – the pulse of Afro-Trinidadian culture • Soca – the pulse of carnival • Indian and African Drumming – the pulse of spirituality/victory/ancestry. • Pan-Trinidad's Heartbeat – A living vibration – the pulse of Trinidad • Indo-Trinidadian music – the pulse of Indian culture • Parang – the pulse of Spanish/Latino culture	**Traditional Music Scene** • Classical music – the pulse of European elitism **Contemporary Music Scene** • Hip-Hop/Jazz/R&B – the pulse of black American pop-culture • Reggae – the pulse of Jamaican "Bingi" (Rastafari) culture • Rock – the pulse of white American/European pop-culture • Dancehall – the pulse of Jamaican/Caribbean youth

The findings add credence to the consensus model of stakeholder participation (Araujo and Bramwell 1999). It supported the view that an approach to stakeholder identification that targets stakeholders with legitimate interests can contribute to sustainable tourism development if the facilitators and inhibitors of participation are calibrated in a way that enables authentic participation. These pull factors include political empowerment and a facilitative socio-spatial configuration.

Power (Music Tourism Participation Pull Factors)

In the Trinidad case, psychological, social and political variables that ask about perceptions of empowerment related to the country's music were designed to determine whether there was a high (or low) level of perceived control over extracting benefits from music activities and processes in local spaces. The summated result of the study is shown in table 5.4.

Psychological and social empowerment are significant as they have been shown to have a "direct and significant relationship with resident perceptions of the negative and positive impacts of tourism" (Boley et al. 2014, 45–48). Additionally, only psychological empowerment had a direct relationship with support for tourism. The research may support the proposal that psychological and (to some extent) social empowerment, as per the resident empowerment through tourism scale, may be considered as parallel to the construct of interest in the participation framework in as much as they better reflect intrinsic motivational factors and personal identity, as opposed to the extrinsic perceived control factors.

Table 5.4: Ability to Participate in Music Tourism Development (Empowerment)

Behavioural Construct	Minimum	Maximum	Mean	Std. Deviation
Psychological empowerment	1.60	5.00	4.1590	.81973
Social empowerment	1.00	5.00	3.8034	.86423
Political empowerment	1.00	5.00	2.4615	1.09204

Statistically significant correlation between psychological and social empowerment (.735, sig .000) and between social and political (.409, sig .010)

The case study supported the view that political empowerment is an important antecedent to Tosun's (2006) spontaneous typology which is characterized by active interest and shared benefits. It was seen that due to low perceived control, in terms of political empowerment, there are members of the community who, though willing and invested, do not perceive themselves to be positioned to share the benefits of the value they create from music processes and activities, which indicates active interest and benefit deprivation, that is, a frustrated participation typology.

As per Ajzen (2016), high perceived control through low levels of inhibitors and high levels of facilitators to interactive music activities allows for greater chances of spontaneous participation in the development of music tourism, as per Tosun's (2006) typology. As such, the ability to participate moves along a continuum from low to high power or control. The findings support the following statements suggested by Prior's (2015) multidimensional approach:

A socio-spatial configuration which increases music stakeholders' ability to benefit from music tourism development likely:
- facilitates integrative music education and learning,
- facilitates collaborative interactions between or within stakeholder clusters and agents,
- inhibits (or effectively manages) excessive conflict, and
- facilitates the promotion of local music through local and international networks.

Conversely, a configuration which inhibits integrative learning, inhibits collaboration, facilitates excessive conflict (or fails to adequately manage conflict) and inhibits promotion decreases their ability to share the benefits of participation.

The Participatory Music Tourism Development Framework

Building on Tosun's (2006) typologies of community participation in the area of tourism (induced, coercive and spontaneous), the PTD framework looks at interest and power as indicators of willingness and ability to participate in music tourism. As such, an additional typology (frustrated participation) has been included, where stakeholders have high levels of interest in terms of motivation, participative rationality, change seeking behaviour and sensitivity to music tourism impacts, as seen in Tosun's (2006) spontaneous participation category. However, they may not have any real power or opportunity to engage in planning, decision-making, implementation or sharing of benefits.

The inclusion of this category was influenced by the grievance theory literature, which best represented the discourse provided by stakeholders over the lack of access to the right support, resources and opportunities, resulting in a feeling of frustration. Frustration, according to the grievance models, is caused by the "disparity between what people expect to have and what they actually get, as well as the means available to getting what they want", that is, "actors' perception of discrepancy between their value expectations and their capabilities" (Gurr 1970, 23–24).

After an exploration of the socio-spatial configuration was undertaken, along with the constructs of interest and empowerment, a proposed theoretical special interest framework for participation was conceptualized. This framework attempts to categorize and understand stakeholder participation in terms of the "movement from passive to active [interest] stakeholders" and the movement from benefit deprivation to benefit sharing (Agarwal, Busby and Huang 2018, 7). The resulting model, or framework, for participatory music tourism development is seen at figure 5.2.

Figure 5.2: Participatory Framework for Music Tourism Development

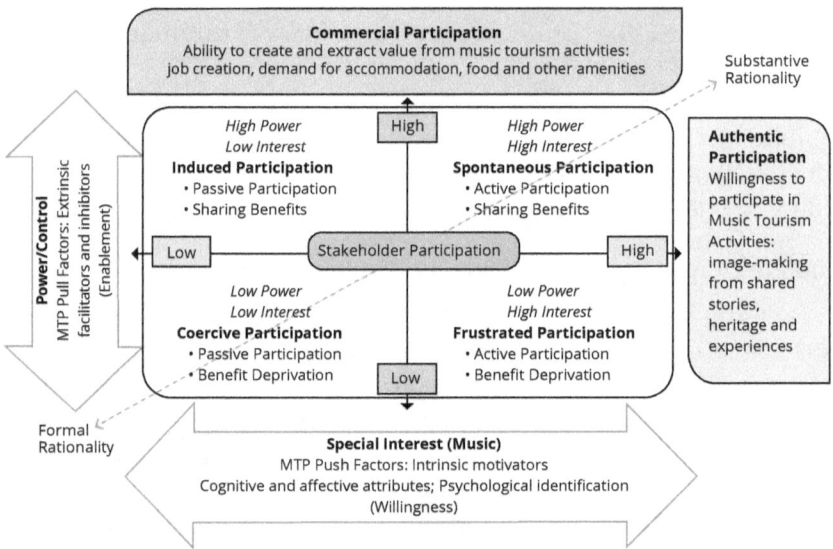

Tables 5.5 and 5.6 provide a descriptive summary of the four typologies for the purposes of the PTD framework.

Table 5.5: Participation Typologies as a Construct of Behavioural Intention – Interest

		PARTICIPATION TYPOLOGY			
		Coercive	**Induced**	**Frustrated**	**Spontaneous**
BEHAVIOURAL CONSTRUCT INDICATOR: INTEREST	Motivation	Usually extrinsic	Usually extrinsic	Intrinsic	Intrinsic
		(Financial incentives/ compensation, career advancement, social status, etc.)		(Desire to express oneself, relationships, competence, enjoyment, self-efficacy, etc.)	
	Participative Rationality	Formal	Formal	Authentic	Authentic/ substantive
	Change/ Action-seeking Behaviour	Passive	Passive	Active	Active
	Impact Sensitivity	Low susceptibility to negative impacts in area of interest	Low susceptibility	Highly susceptible to impacts in area of interest	High susceptibility
	Interest Group Membership	Disorganized: No organized interest group	Organized: May be part of other interest groups (e.g., Chambers of Commerce, etc.)	Disorganized or in an organization limited/ affected by excessive conflict	Organized in relevant and functional interest groups

Table 5.6: Participation Typologies as a Construct of Behavioural Intention – Empowerment

		PARTICIPATION TYPOLOGY			
		Coercive	**Induced**	**Frustrated**	**Spontaneous**
BEHAVIOURAL CONSTRUCT INDICATOR: POWER/CONTROL	**Planning Input**	No input/ tokenistic	Pseudo-participation	Informal planning	Self-planning
	Decision-Making Input	Manipulative/ tokenistic	Indirect/limited to proposed choices	Opportunity-dependent	Direct, self-initiated
	Implementation Capabilities	incapable of implementation	Capable	Incapable	Capable
	Value Creation and Extraction Process Flows	Top-down	Top-down	Bottom-up	Bottom-up

Strategic Participation

Following the participation assessment of local stakeholders, various strategies for stakeholder targeting and engagement may be prioritized and developed with an emphasis on specific stakeholders, depending on the quadrant which best describes their interest and power dynamic. A destination may have some combination of specific strategies for various stakeholders related to the typologies, such as empowerment, collaboration, education and support, based on the vision and associated strategic objectives of the destination, as seen in table 5.7.

Table 5.7: PTD Strategy Selection

Induced	Collaborate
Coercive	Educate
Spontaneous	Support
Frustrated	Empower

Music Tourism Participation Push Strategies – Moving from Passive to Active Interest

Strategies which engage existing active interest, or push stakeholders towards active interest, may be more likely to contribute to authentic music value creation through the creation of myths, stories and an overall authentic socio-spatial configuration that

Figure 5.3: Music Tourism Participation Push Strategies towards Active Interest

Collaborate
- Results-driven (rewards-based, compete for profits and income)
- Connect rewards to authentic creativity/sites of creation
- Exposure to musical experiences that connect to community and culture and show opportunity for investment towards situated value creation
- Open linkages/connections/communication with active (interest) stakeholders

Educate
- Knowledge-driven (learning/skills-based, improve music-related capacity and capabilities)
- Information and awareness on the musical stories and myths of the destination and potential impacts of music tourism value creation
- Information on organizing for music tourism-related activities (membership, activism)
- Encourage staycations to local sites of creativity (local consumption/localized first-customer approach)

moves towards diversity and preservation of cultural identity. This supports a flourishing music tourism community. Strategies which do not promote existing interest, or which do not push stakeholders towards active interest, are likely to result in activities which reflect indifference with the local musicscape unless immediate commercial benefit, with or without a flourishing socio-spatial configuration, is made available. Figure 5.3 highlights possible strategic approaches to increase active interest.

Music Tourism Participation Pull Strategies – Reducing Benefit Deprivation towards Sharing Benefits

Strategies which increase shared benefits for stakeholders are more likely to result in the effective commercialization of music-related activity that may encourage positive attitudes and support for tourism and yield sustainable results for music tourism development. Strategies where the gap or discrepancy between stakeholders' value expectation and capabilities is not intentionally bridged and which, therefore, ultimately fail to address benefit deprivation are unlikely to result in effective commercialization, which is linked to sustainability.

If relative deprivation is an actor's perceived discrepancy between their value expectations and their value capabilities then, alternatively, relative satisfaction may be seen as an actor's perceived consistency or synchronicity between their value expectations and their value capabilities. Strategies which move towards equity and inclusion in the sharing of benefits are thus more likely to contribute to music tourism, which allows for satisfactory value extraction through the development of structures for the commercialization of myths, stories and experiences and an overall socio-spatial configuration that allows value expectations and capabilities to connect sustainably.

Strategies that allow benefit deprivation to continue unaddressed are likely to result in activities that lack authenticity even as they have a large impact on the tourist area, and to encourage exclusivity and disparity between beneficiaries and non-beneficiaries, thereby increasing stakeholder frustration. Figure 5.4 highlights possible strategic approaches which may increase benefit-sharing or decrease benefit-deprivation to achieve relative satisfaction, thereby reducing stakeholder frustration.

Figure 5.4: Music Tourism Participation Pull Strategies – Towards Sharing Benefits

Support
- Preventative control measures (encourage stakeholder initiative)
- Provide support system for stakeholder-initiated problem-solving
- Provide administrative support as required
- Assist organized/engaged communities with legislation, policy and regulatory issues
- Assist with continued commercialization/promotion of existing products as well as research and development
- Recognize and support expansion of authentic local value creation

Empower
- Facilitative control measures (reduce barriers to participation)
- Raise tourism capabilities or balance capabilties and value expectations
- Bridge gaps in ability to participate with respect to organization of stakeholders and policy structures
- Improve or increase access to spaces and tourism resources and share knowledge to aid or facilitate commercialization in local spaces

Conclusion and Recommendations

Participation

Participatory music tourism entails inviting residents and tourists alike to places where music is created in order to consume diverse types of music in place-based social interactions. To do this, they need to travel to the "birthplaces", "places of creation" and "sacred locations" of the music to experience it. In a time of widespread global changes in tourism and travel – as seen in the unprecedented COVID-19 pandemic, lockdown of tourism-dependent countries, border closures and general uncertainty – the value of localized inter-regional, domestic tourism development which provides world-class entertainment options for local tourists within localized music spaces is a possible method of meeting the social and economic value-extraction needs of local producers and consumers and developing or maintaining tourism readiness.

Increasing Collaboration: Strength in Diversity

Destination Trinidad has had a substantial share of musical ambassadors who have penetrated the international music market in the Caribbean region, Europe and the United States of America. The sounds of Calypso and the Trinidadian national instrument, the steelpan – which is the only original non-electronic instrument created in the twentieth century – are known and recognized throughout the world as the most prominent sounds of the Caribbean. The story of Trinidad's music, and by extension the spaces related to the music, is deeply connected to and affected by the diverse origins of the population, especially the political and social relations of various social groups related to ethnicity, race, class and religion.

What is lacking, however, is the collaborative networks that can capture and convert these achievements into the type of reputational capital that is required to form dense creative tourism networks throughout the country. Given that "people's personal motivations are difficult to change using policy", a reasonable approach to capturing these achievements is to acknowledge the motivations and interest that already exist as a foundation that can be built upon for participatory behaviour (Involve Foundation 2018).

Managing Conflict: Reducing Frustration

Consensus among private sector interviewees was that there were several causes of frustration:

- There were insufficient structure and weak institutional arrangements in the laws and regulations that guide various agents and agencies, protect their interests and allow them to benefit from their creative and financial investments.
- There was a lack of development, access and control of (non-religious or clique-controlled) community spaces that would allow them to build their local creative networks.
- There was a lack of dedicated institutions where integrative learning of "all things music", – including technical and creative skills as well as the business of music: promotion, production and marketing – is available to people at every level of society who have an interest in drawing value from music. These institutions should expose people to the possibilities of the industry.
- Regardless of any natural talent that may or may not exist, whether a person is exposed to music in any meaningful way can strongly depend on where they live, the financial means of their family and other chance interactions and circumstances that emphasize socio-economic vulnerabilities and reinforce capitalistic inequalities.
- There is a lack of investment into music outside of Carnival and other festivals, especially at the community or regional level. While the live music district was a source of pride for the public servants involved, private sector stakeholders expressed disappointment that it focused only on the capital city while other regions had little to nothing in place for their creatives. This continues to widen the developmental gap between urban

cities and rural areas. No real attempt seems to be made towards bringing programmes and development to outlying regions to alleviate poverty and inequity.

Affirmative and deliberate action should be taken towards detecting, managing and reducing conflict and disconnectedness in the creative policy or decision-making environment. There should be a greater emphasis on pursuing initiatives that focus on bringing balance to competitive musical environments, creating win–win programmes and initiatives that build and nurture social networks, and shaping inclusive opportunities that encourage participation and facilitate enablement and willingness.

Priority should be placed on limiting market distortion by encouraging a more equitable distribution of government resources while ensuring that there are catchment spaces in place for creatives to benefit from a trickledown of taxpayer's investment in "culture and heritage" beyond seasonal festivals.

Promotion and Identity: Reconceptualizing Trinidad's Music and Tourism

Music ethnologists, industry analysts, policymakers and even musicians, artists and producers have focused on increasing the added value of music production and export in Trinidad. Many practical improvements to the processes of music production and supply have been suggested over the years. Trinidad's musical value has traditionally been relegated to a supporting position within the wider context of festival or events tourism based on perceptions of its low economic potential and the elevation of economic development over the socio-cultural dimension.

Soca has thus emerged as the only truly internationally marketed music format, commercialized heavily as the key supplement to festival stage performances and party-culture, which remain its main mediums. This approach has contributed to the present ad hoc local music environment where the flourishing of urban and (particularly) rural music communities is stymied.

A tourism approach that focuses on preserving musical stories and developing various musical identities into authentic experiences in a flourishing structure for storytelling would create the balance and inclusivity needed for development grounded in diversity, equity and inclusion. Natural preservation of culture is a likely consequence of nurturing creativity and perfecting the timely retelling of stories in ways and spaces that make it relevant to the audience. This is opposed to forced preservation, which is done in an environment of suppressed creativity and reactionary policy or an environment that is not nurturing to diverse creatives and offers minimal opportunity to facilitate the ideas or initiatives of interested stakeholders. Successful promotion would become the natural culmination of such a flourishing culture.

Music TT's music industry conferences and the live music district display the results of a holistic understanding of the music environment and how people can be empowered to function effectively or participate spontaneously in that environment. It also demonstrates the way that these dynamics eventually progressed into the place-based activities that are essential for music tourism development. People who are empowered with positions in organizations that give them access to funding and stable incomes are removed from a "conflict/competition" environment and into an achievement/goal-focused environment. This combined with explicit knowledge has created a foundation for the basics of healthy musicking despite budgetary limitations. However, this model also demonstrated the limitations of top-down development and prolonged dependence on public money allocated at the discretion of public officials.

Destinations considering music tourism as an alternative must understand that any potential for sustained tourism value to be harnessed from music through sites or scenes beyond economic measures can scarcely be realized in the face of a suppressed, uninvolved or disempowered local music community. Though specific indicators of a flourishing music culture may vary according to the destination, broadly speaking, a flourishing music tourism structure cannot be sustained artificially and must originate from the interest and capabilities of stakeholders who are willing to consistently participate in value creation and extraction through music-related interactions. If this is established via a reliable assessment framework, stakeholders who seek to extract value from their creative input should be strategically supported and empowered accordingly.

It should also be noted that developing a flourishing music tourism structure for storytelling requires:
- deliberate, targeted, research-driven and strategic identification and assessment of local stakeholders and investment in the development of inclusive spaces of musical creativity that aim to allow diverse creative communities to flourish or benefit across regions all year round,
- an integrative approach that uses various music interactions to create and relay the existing and potential stories about the

destination's art, history, literature, religion, politics, language, food, film, sports, events, festivals and other prevailing offerings,
- policies and institutional arrangements across sectors that focus on reducing inequity and the exclusion of creatives by providing them with informed and proactive representation, access to spaces, resources and planners, and the power to organize themselves and initiate and participate in decisions at various levels of government, and
- a collaborative environment that seeks to organize stakeholders and manage conflict towards the creation and expansion of shared benefits for win–win outcomes.

Music tourism can enable a more meaningful set of experiences to be created as it widens the focus of niche tourism from a narrow set of highly specialized, seasonal and disjointed products to one that appeals to a more mainstream audience in a permanent, year-round setting. PTD is a viable strategic approach to developing music tourism in destinations with existing or potential music-related resources in a sustainable manner. It seeks to consider the local stakeholder and their views on the opportunities that may result from tourism activity in their environment. This consideration should be a precursor to co-creating memorable and authentic experiences within the destination for the mutual benefit of tourists and the local population.

References

Agarwal, Sheela, Graham Busby, and Rong Huang. 2018. "Special Interest Tourism: An Introduction." In *Special Interest Tourism: Concepts, Contexts and Cases*, edited by Sheela Agarwal, Graham Busby, and Rong Huang, 1–17. Oxfordshire: CABI International.
———, Rong Huang, and Graham Busby. 2018. *Special Interest Tourism: Concepts, Contexts and Cases*. Oxfordshire: CABI.
Ajzen, Icek. 2016. "Constructing a Theory of Planned Behavior Questionnaire." https://www.researchgate.net/publication/235913732_Constructing_a_Theory_of_Planned_Behavior_Questionnaire.
Aoki, Takashi. 2002. "The Role of Cultural Tourism for Sustainable Development: The Case of Music in Cuba." *Thesis*, Dalhousie University.
Augustine, Marlene. 2017. "Dependency Syndrome Must End." *Trinidad and Tobago Newsday*, 8 August 2017. http://newsday.co.tt/2017/08/08/dependency-syndrome-must-end/.

Boley, B. Bynum, and Nancy G. McGehee. 2014. "Measuring Empowerment: Developing and Validating the Resident Empowerment through Tourism Scale (RETS)." *Tourism Management* 45:85–94.

———, Richards R. Perdue, and Patrick Long. 2014. "Empowerment and Resident Attitudes towards Tourism: Strengthening the Theoretical Foundation through a Weberian Lens." *Annals of Tourism Research* 49:33–50. https://doi.org/10.1016/j.annals.2014.08.005.

Carroll, G.R. 1993. A Sociological View on Why Firms Differ. *Strategic Management Journal*, 14 (4): 237–49.

Gibson, Chris, and John Connell. 2005. *Music and Tourism : On the Road Again*. Clevedon: Channel Viel Publications.

Guilbault, Joycelyn. 2014. "Afterword." In *Sun, Sea and Sound: Music and Tourism in the Circum-Caribbean*, edited by Timothy Rommen and Daniel T. Neely, 308. New York: Oxford University Press.

Gurr, Ted Robert. 1970. *Why Men Rebel*. New York: Princeton University Press.

Involve Foundation. 2018. "How and Why do People Participate?" *Involve.org.uk*. Accessed 1 September 2020.

Madeiros de Araujo, L., and Bill Bramwell. 1999. "Stakeholder Assessment and Collaborative Tourism Planning: The Case of Brazil's Costa Dourada Project." *Journal of Sustainable Tourism* 7 (3–4): 356–78. https://doi.org/10.1080/09669589908667344.

Mermoud, Alain, Marcus Matthias Keupp, Kévin Huguenin, Maximilian Palmié, and Dimitri Percia David. 2019. "To Share or Not to Share: A Behavioural Perspective on Human Participation in Security Information Sharing." *Journal of Cybersecurity* 5 (1): 1–13. https://doi.org/10.1093/cybsec/tyz006.

Ministry of Energy and Energy Industries. n.d. *Oil and Gas Industry*. Accessed April 29, 2020. https://www.energy.gov.tt/our-business/oil-and-gas-industry/.

Pattullo, Polly. 1996. *Last Resorts: The Cost of Tourism in the Caribbean*. Kingston: Ian Randle Publishers.

Paul, Anna-Lisa. 2020. "NCC Gets $25m More for 2020 Carnival, Still Paying 2019 Debts." *Trinidad and Tobago Guardian*, Febuary 1, 2020. https://www.guardian.co.tt/news/ncc-gets-25-m-more-for-2020-carnival-still-paying-2019-debts-6.2.1044611.e073206725.

Prior, Nick. 2015. "'It's a Social Thing, Not a Nature Thing': Popular Music Practices in Reykjavík, Iceland." *Cultural Sociology* 9 (1): 81–98.

ProColombia and Sound Diplomacy. 2018. *Music is the New Gastronomy: White Paper on Music and Tourism – Your Guide to Connecting Music and Tourism, and Making the Most Out of It*. White Paper. Colombia: ProColombia. https://www.sounddiplomacy.com/music-is-the-new-gastronomy.

Thetsane, Regina M. 2019. "Local Community Participation in Tourism: The Case of Katse Villages in Lesotho." *Athens Journal of Tourism* 6 (2): 123–40. https://doi.org/10.30958/ajt.6-2-4.

Tosun, Cevat. 2006. "Expected Nature of Community Participation in

Tourism Development." *Tourism Management* 27 (3): 493–504. https://doi.org/10.1016/j.tourman.2004.12.004.

Tourism Trinidad Limited. 2020. "Strategic Action Plan." *Stakeholder Engagement Meeting-Business Chambers and Associations*. Port of Spain: TTL, 14 January.

Trauer, Birgit. 2006. "Conceptualizing Special Interest Tourism – Frameworks for Analysis." *Tourism Management* 27 (2): 183–200. https://doi.org/10.1016/j.tourman.2004.10.004.

UNESCO. 2019. "Port of Spain Designated as UNESCO Creative City of Music." *UNESCO Cluster Office for the Caribbean*. 18 November 2019. https://www.unesco.org/en/articles/port-spain-designated-unesco-creative-city-music.

Watson, Allan. 2018. "Music Tourism." In *Special Interest Tourism: Concepts, Contexts and Cases*, edited by Sheela Agarwal, Graham Busby, and Rong Huang, 73–84. Oxforshire: CABI International.

Wilson, Jonathan. 2014. *Essentials of Business Research: A Guide to Doing your Research Project*. London: SAGE Publications.

6.
Festival Tourism in the Caribbean: A Comparative Analysis of the Barbados and St Lucia Jazz Festivals

Leslie-Ann Jordan

Introduction

The purpose of this research is to examine the challenges, evolution, management and impacts of the two oldest jazz festivals in the English-speaking Caribbean: the St Lucia Jazz Festival and the Barbados Jazz Festival. More specifically, this chapter will discuss some of the similarities and differences in these festivals in terms of their strategies for marketing and promotion, economic impact and financial management, and community engagement. Based on a comparative analysis of the festivals, it will recommend some sustainable strategies and best practices for managing jazz festivals in small island developing states (SIDS).

In order to increase tourist arrivals in the low season, many Caribbean islands have created music and other festivals. In fact, a study done in 2008 identified festival and music tourism as one of the main niche markets for the Caribbean (Acorn 2008). They defined festival and music tourism as "travel for the main purpose of attending cultural and/or music festivals" (Acorn 2008, 38). Religious pilgrimages and sporting events were excluded from the definition. Festival tourism in the Caribbean makes a significant contribution to the wider economy in that it increases government tax receipts, generates employment and sectoral linkages, attracts business sponsorship and cross promotions, and has a spill over effect on ancillary sectors like the media and advertising industries, auto rentals, hotels and restaurants (Rivera, Semrad and Croes 2016; Nurse 2003).

Literature Review
Festival Tourism – Helping to Establish a Sense of Place

According to Acorn (2008, 38), "an estimated ten million people travel internationally each year for the main purpose of watching or participating in a music or cultural festival". Interest in cultural events in other countries is on the increase, and experiencing festivals is perceived by tourists as one of the most authentic ways of immersing themselves in local culture. Consequently, there is considerable interest in the "global festival calendar". Overall, growth in this segment is expected to remain very strong, attaining growth rates in excess of 10 per cent per annum (Acorn 2008, 38). Historically, there have always been reasons for people to come together to celebrate, to demonstrate, to worship, to honour, to remember, to socialize and to relive (Kuuder, Adongo, and Abanga 2012). The desire to participate in festivals and events is not new or specific to any particular culture, religion or community group (Douglas, Douglas, and Derrett 2001, 356). Festivals fall within the parameters of event tourism and according to Hall (1992) and Getz (2008), events are seen as an important motivator of tourism, as well as an effective enhancer of destination image.

In more recent times, destinations are not only selected based on natural beauty but are marketed in relation to events, as well as "people and contemporary themes" (Herbert 1995, cited in MacLeod 2006). In this regard, festivals can play an important role in the tourist's choice of destination as well as in the formation of the unique sense of place related to the destination. According to Amsden, Stedman and Kruger (2011, 33), the idea of place "is ultimately constructed around what a particular place means and how people evaluate it based on those meanings". In this way, the sense of place within a destination is an important facet as it ensures that destinations do not become meaninglessly exchangeable or "highly standardised" (MacLeod 2006). In such cases, destinations may become "non-places" (Augé 1995, cited in MacLeod 2006) which display a high level of commodification. Hosting festivals and events, like jazz festivals, helps to prevent destinations from becoming exchangeable. A study by Lee, Kyle and Scott (2012, 754) revealed that "satisfied visitors at a festival develop a moderate level of emotional attachment to the festival host destination and ultimately become loyal to that destination". In this way, a visitor will be encouraged to also visit a destination outside of the festival or event time. Curtis (2010) also notes that music festivals in particular, which already have the ability to build "a sense of community or belonging", can help the destination to establish a long-term relationship with visitors.

Festival and Music Tourism in the Caribbean

Festival tourism is now growing throughout the region as a result of the success of a few festivals, such as Reggae Sunsplash (Jamaica), Trinidad and Tobago Carnival, St Lucia Jazz Festival, the Barbados Crop Over and the St Kitts Music Festival (Nurse 2003). The festival context in the Caribbean is such that there is now an increasing number of jazz festivals in the region (see table 6.1). According to Nurse (2003), countries like Barbados and St Lucia have developed what can be described as a festival tourism strategy that forms an integral part of their cultural policy and strategy. Cultural policy relates to "the way the state interacts with, supports, represses or regulates different cultural forms", which can be "highly selective" (Bell and Oakley 2015, 16). Policies related to culture, therefore, can be used to foster the development of events and festivals which

Table 6.1: List of Jazz Festivals in Caribbean Region

Country	Name of Festival	Time	Started
Anguilla	Tranquillity Jazz Fest	November	2002
Aruba	Caribbean Sea Jazz Festival	September	2007
Barbados	Barbados Jazz Festival	January	1993
Cayman Islands	Cayman Jazz Fest	December	2004
Cuba	Havana International Jazz Festival	December	1984
Curaçao	Curaçao North Sea Jazz Festival	September	2010
Dominican Republic	Dominican Republic Jazz Festival	November	1997
Jamaica	Jamaica Jazz and Blues Festival	January	1996
	Jamaica Ocho Rios International Jazz Festival	June	1991
Puerto Rico	Puerto Rico Heineken Jazz Fest	May	1991
St Lucia	Saint Lucia Jazz	May	1992
Trinidad and Tobago	Tobago Jazz Experience	April	2005

facilitate the "perpetuating and transplanting" of culture (Nurse 2004, 223 in Quinn 2013, 7). Hence, cultural policymakers in the region have long been cognisant of the value of festivals, which have the capability to achieve not only social but economic goals, "including nurturing identity and difference, fostering social inclusion, and developing the creative and economic infrastructure of towns, cities, and nations" (Stevenson, Rowe and McKay 2010, 249). Nurse (2004) highlighted that, within the Caribbean context, "festivals contribute by 'perpetuating and transplanting Caribbean culture and values and thus influencing global culture, media and public opinion'" (cited in Quinn 2013, 7). Furthermore, Tull (2017, 292) suggested that the region has much to gain from the "establishment and implementation of a framework for the valuing of Caribbean festival arts" beyond the monetization of festivals.

Additionally, the most obvious reasons for the popularity of festivals as a tourism promotion tool are that (1) festivals increase the demand for local tourism (Smith and Jenner 1998) and (2) successful festivals can help recreate the image of a place or contribute towards the exposure of a location trying to get on the tourism map (Kotler, Haider and Rein 1993). Also, "the strategic placement of a festival in the local tourism calendar can help extend the tourism season" (Getz 2005, 152). Festivals make it possible to concentrate a big number of activities into a short period of time, developing a number of potential tourist products. Festivals are a good opportunity to improve destination image and to generate new tourism flows and to foster association between existing markets and products (Getz 2008).

It is clear that jazz festivals are now important social events as they help to increase tourist arrivals and, through international advertising, they have been instrumental in raising the profile of their destinations. Furthermore, the carnival-type festivals have stimulated entertainment sectors that generate employment for artists and cultural entrepreneurs during the season and year-round (Khan 2006).

However, despite the Caribbean region's rich cultural assets, according to Nurse (2003), the importance and potential of the creative industries in CARIFORUM countries have been underestimated and unexplored. This blind spot is due in many cases to the absence of data infrastructure to capture the economic contribution of the sector (Nurse 2003). Although festivals have emerged to be an important contributor to the tourism industry throughout the Caribbean, there is a paucity of published data on their impact in the region (Frisby and Getz 1989). Only three festivals (Trinidad and Tobago's Carnival, the St Lucia Jazz Festival and the Barbados Crop Over Festival) have done exit surveys in the past which provide quality data on visitor arrivals (Nurse 2003). What is known is limited to what has been published by individual studies such as Nurse (2003) and Nurse and Nicholls (2011). However, one of the emerging problems associated with this development is the increase in regional competition.

Challenges to Festival Management in the Caribbean

According to Frisby and Getz (1989), strategic festival management should include goal setting, marketing, strategic planning, organized fundraising ventures and appropriate structures to accurately measure attendance and economic impacts. Unfortunately, the Caribbean region faces a number of significant challenges in these areas. For example, Chaitoo (2013, 1) explains that "despite the Caribbean's great potential in the entertainment sector, important domestic challenges – emanating from both public and private sectors – have long impeded the successful growth of creative industries". With respect to the public sector, he states that challenges stem from the low level of investment that is put into the cultural industry. It is noted that developed countries "invest heavily in their cultural industries" and have carved out "sufficient policy space and set up the appropriate infrastructure to enable local creativity to flourish, allow creative persons and enterprises to develop, and ensure that their rights and obligations are respected and legally protected" (Chaitoo 2013, 23–25). However, in the Caribbean, for the most part, although there have been consultations and various government level proclamations regarding the development of the cultural sector, there has been "little support to the sector or removal of government measures that constrain the sector's development" (Chaitoo 2013, 26).

Compounding this matter is the absence of economic impact assessments, which makes applications for adequate government funding challenging and is linked to the deeper challenge of the "unsophisticated" nature of festival management in the region (Frisby and Getz, 1989, 7). There is also the threat of inconsistent funding facing festival managers, as there is an "absence of secure, long-term funding...in about half of all festival types" (Carlsen and Andersson 2011, 91). In fact, according to Burke (2013, 22), "many festivals fail due to the popular misconception that they are 'cash cows'", when in fact "most festivals (even the big ones) make small profits or barely break even and are overly dependent on solid sponsorship for success". Additionally, Bethel (2014), in her analysis of Junkanoo in the Bahamas, highlighted the issue of a lack of data to examine the return on investment of such festivals, as well as the disconnect between the festival and its potential to contribute to the tourism industry.

The lack of appropriate institutional arrangements for festival management is another key challenge in the region. As an example, Burke (2007), in conducting research on CARIFESTA (Caribbean Festival of the Arts), highlights the ad hoc planning and management of the festival due to the absence of a permanent secretariat. It was noted that "these committees generally meet once or twice annually, and as such, their responsibility for policy making and management have consistently resulted in poor festival management and decreasing levels of public interest in CARIFESTA" (Burke 2007, 178).

Another more general challenge to tourism development in the Caribbean is the issue of airlift and the lack of control, by the destinations, over the majority of air carriers. In this sense, the region is vulnerable to any adjustments to the number of direct connections or the route structure of in-transit flights (Clayton, Karagiannis and Bailey 2015). For music events and festivals, this can pose a challenge as the "flows of tourism" (Clayton, Karagiannis and Bailey 2015, 341) are not under the control of the destinations.

Methodology

This study used a qualitative case study approach using secondary data analysis (Baxter and Jack 2008; Yin 2012). Secondary data can be a valuable source of information for gaining knowledge and insight into a broad range of issues and phenomena such as festival management in the Caribbean. Review and analysis of secondary data can provide a cost-effective way of addressing issues, conducting cross-national comparisons, understanding country-specific and local conditions, determining the direction and magnitude of change and trends, and describing the current situation. Data were collected from various sources such as academic books, journals, newspaper articles, statistical reports from the St Lucia Tourist Board and from regional and international tourism organizations like the Caribbean Tourism Organization and the World Travel and Tourism Council, as well as publications in electronic media. The information was then synthesized with personal critical analysis to provide new insights for improved festival management in the Caribbean.

Findings and Discussion
Historical Overview of the Festivals

As of 2020, the St Lucia Jazz and Arts Festival celebrated its twenty-eighth anniversary, which is a rare achievement. Several other jazz festivals established in the Caribbean region over the years have failed, for example, Aruba and Curacao, and Barbados. The first St Lucia Jazz Festival was held in 1992 as an initiative to extend St Lucia's tourist season into May, a relatively slow period (Pro-Poor Tourism and Travel Foundation 2006). The festival was conceived out of a need to advance St Lucia's marketing efforts to a new dimension in order to raise the island's visibility overseas. With tourism increasingly playing a leading role in St Lucia's economic development, it became imperative to increase the awareness of St Lucia in the main tourism markets. With a limited marketing budget and significant levels of advertising being undertaken by its competitors, the objective was to develop an activity and promotional tool that would command international attention and be minimal in cost. The St Lucia Jazz Festival had two main objectives:

1. to provide a platform to showcase St Lucia to a broad cross section of potential visitors, and
2. to redress the traditional slow tourist period in May, so that visitor arrivals and occupancy levels would be on par with that of the winter period.

These objectives became broader as the St Lucia Jazz Festival developed and now additional objectives include providing an outlet for local expression and economic opportunities and developing the necessary infrastructure for event productions. Subsequently, in 2016, the festival was rebranded and renamed the St Lucia Jazz and Arts Festival. According to the St Lucia Tourist Board (2016), this redefined festival product "offers its patrons a full immersion into things culturally and creatively Saint Lucian". It goes on to explain that "at year twenty-five, Saint Lucia Jazz & Arts Festival spans a full 9 days and upwards of fifteen venues featuring some of the best live performances spliced with the celebration of Saint Lucian Arts, Culture and Cuisine. The rationale is to exploit the opportunities to be derived from the hosting of a prestigious and stellar festival, with the island's burgeoning creative industries sector" (SLTB 2016). Here, the creative sector component is defined by a literary and performing arts renaissance, a vibrant music performance and production sector, award-winning gourmet chefs, and the consistent celebration of heritage through diverse genres of dance, song, language, fashion and fine arts. The St Lucia Tourist Board has declared that "Saint Lucia, as the artistic mecca of the Eastern Caribbean Economic Union is well able to define a new and differentiated cultural component of an already unmatched touristic destination" (SLTB 2016).

In 2017, the Tourist Board announced that the St Lucia Jazz Festival would end after twenty-five years and its management was handed over to the St Lucia Tourism Authority (Dowrich-Phillips 2018). Under this new structure, the festival was rebranded as one of the events under the St Lucia Soleil Summer Festival and is now marketed as purely a jazz festival. The festival has continued to evolve. In 2019, it was put on in collaboration with the New York–based Jazz at Lincoln Center to reinvigorate the festival with a return to authentic jazz performances. In 2020, the festival was cancelled due to the COVID-19 pandemic and at the time of writing (October 2021), it has not been planned for this year.

Following close on the heels of the St Lucia Jazz Festival, in January 1993 the first Barbados Jazz Festival made its debut as a tourism product designed primarily to attract visitors and diversify the product offering to visitors (The Barbados Jazz Festival 2007). The popular Barbados Jazz Festival took place over one week in January, with the organizer, GMR International Tours, bringing in talent from around the world. Venues typically included the modern Sir Garfield Sobers Sports Complex, historic Sunbury Plantation House and the popular open air venue Farley Hill National Park. Unfortunately, the festival was abruptly cancelled in 2010.

Marketing and Promotion of the Festivals

Since its establishment in 1992, St Lucia Jazz Festival has grown in magnitude and stature, making it the most important marketing activity of the St Lucia Tourist Board. The festival has surpassed the objectives set out for it and continues to attract international and regional media attention to the island (Pro-Poor Tourism and Travel Foundation 2006). Tourist visits to St Lucia, due to awareness of the island generated by jazz, continue well beyond the May period. The festival has strong media appeal (Nurse et al. 2007) and extensive international media coverage on television and in radio and print media has resulted in added exposure, the estimated cost of which surpasses the Tourist Board's overall annual budget (Nurse et al. 2007). St Lucia Jazz has now become an internationally recognized brand. The great example of this is the "Being cool is..." advertising campaign used by soft drink giant Coca Cola. The print campaign lists St Lucia Jazz as one of the top indicators of what being cool is all about – it is no small achievement when arguably the world's number one consumer brand chooses to associate itself with your festival.

As a result of such strategic partnerships, the St Lucia Jazz Festival is considered by patrons and the press as one of the premiere jazz festivals of the Caribbean region. George Wein, who produces over thirty festivals across the world, listed the St Lucia Jazz Festival as one of the top three festivals in the world (St Lucia Hotel and Tourism Association 2016). Also, Grover Washington Jr commented that the St Lucia Jazz Festival was among the "best that he has attended" (Laurent n.d.). Over the years, word has spread about the festival, helped by coverage on the BET J television network, and it is now a well-established fixture on the jazz festival calendar, "Over the years, the Saint Lucia Jazz Festival has developed a reputation for the quality of the artistes it attracts and is considered one of the top five jazz and music festivals in the world. Similar to the St Lucia Jazz Festival, the Barbados Jazz Festival also partnered with BET J and, according to South Florida Caribbean News (2006), BET J's viewership grew enormously in the first three years of the partnership, and BET J now reaches millions more through its alliance with DirecTV. In addition to advertising heavily on BET J, VH1 Soul and other channels, including mainstream radio stations in Atlanta and New York, BET J produced and aired a full one-hour programme on the festival and on the sites and attractions of Barbados (Jazz News 2006).

In trying to gather arrival data for the Barbados case study, the researcher was severely hindered by a lack of empirical data on the jazz festival. Part of the problem with attracting visitors for the festival is the fact that there are several jazz festivals around the region. It is therefore very difficult to attract intra-regional visitors, a group that makes up a large proportion of visitors in most regional festivals (Nurse 2003).

Socio-Cultural Impacts and Community Engagement

At first, attendance at the St Lucia Jazz Festival was poor. Jazz obviously did not do as well as organizers had expected and this, combined with other factors such as limited resources and broad criticism of the event, led organizers to consider giving up. However, in 1996, in order to satisfy demand, organizers increased the range of performances by including foreign acts. This was a crucial moment in the history of the event.

The festival was now becoming more established and a full-time organizational structure was established in a partnership between the St Lucia Tourist Board and the St Lucia Chamber of Commerce. With this full-time structure came more rapid changes and the event itself evolved and improved with the addition of a stage, better sound management, food and drink concessions, a craft display, and night time shows (SLTB 2007a).

Originally, four locations were used for the festival. However, today the festival has evolved and expanded and several locations around the island are used to host performances, such as Pigeon Point National Reserve, Derek Walcott Square in central Castries ("Jazz on the Square"), the Great House, Fond D'or Estate, Vieux Fort Square, Rudy John Beach Park, Balenbouche, Soufrière Waterfront, La Place Carenage, Mindoo Phillip Park, Royal St Lucian Hotel, Rodney Bay Marina and Gaiety on Rodney Bay. This geographical spreading of the event has facilitated greater local involvement in the festival and has provided the opportunity for local jazz musicians to perform, resulting in extensive television exposure of artistes. St Lucia Jazz Festival also provides an audience ready to patronize not only musicians but all service providers. According to Meyers (2006, 71), "this opportunity is utilized by various organizations/individuals putting on exhibitions, performances, events and items for sale. This helps to encourage local participation in Jazz".

In 1999, the St Lucia Jazz Festival took on a new dimension with the addition of more side attractions, including additional jazz performances aside from main stage events. These additions have been affectionately called the "fringe activities". This created a more festive atmosphere and allowed the local St Lucian public and visitors to participate in these events free-of-charge. The recent addition of fringe activities has only enhanced this mix, shifting festival from a nucleus of small hotel and club venues to a ten-day event that permeates the entire island (Dowrich-Phillips, 2016). Virtually a separate festival in itself, the fringe activities such as Jazz in the South feature a distinct Afro-Caribbean flavour and has kept audiences growing in number and satisfaction (SLTB 2007c).

Additionally, "Monchy Mizik En Kweyol" was conceptualized in 2012 to promote local artistes and facilitate the participation of indigenous musical ensembles during the festival. The organizers endeavoured to stimulate local economic development in the community of Monchy by encouraging vendors to capitalize on the event by offering their goods and services to the public. The main objective of the event was to share in the spirit of the St Lucia Jazz and Arts Festival, promote ethno-musicality and contribute to the overall diversity of the festival through greater local community participation. The event has been branded a cultural showcase of traditional music, dance, art and food. According to the St Lucia Tourist Board (2016), from inception, members of the community have been involved in the vision for the event and were asked to participate in and contribute to the development and implementation of the show.

Over the years, the Barbados Jazz Festival also evolved and grew from an event spanning the Martin Luther King Jr weekend to a cultural experience that fed and nurtured the art form at the local level. Designed to meet all tastes in jazz, from the purist to the general music lover, the festival also supported the Barbados Jazz Academy, workshops for children led by renowned jazz masters, encouraging and promoting "young jazz", where burgeoning young jazz musicians play onstage with the greats (MyVueNews.com 2010).

Economic Impacts, Financial Management and Sponsorship

According to Nurse et al. (2007), the St Lucia Jazz and Arts Festival is the second-best performing festival in the region from an economic standpoint, after Trinidad and Tobago's Carnival. They further noted that the benefit-to-cost analysis indicated that most festivals have a healthy yield or return on investment and that the festival with the highest estimated benefit-to-cost ratio was that of the St Lucia Jazz Festival with a ratio of 9.1:1. The festival has grown from averaging nine thousand visitors in the late 1990s to averaging twelve thousand in recent years. Visitor expenditure has grown steadily throughout the period from US$14.1 million in 1998 to US$17.3 million in 2003 (Nurse et al. 2007). However, according to the Southplanet (n.d.),

> financing of the St Lucia Jazz Festival has been complicated and includes sponsorship (cash and kind), merchandising, gate receipts and contributions by the St Lucia Tourist Board. In addition, the Government of St Lucia makes a significant

contribution to Jazz through waiver of import duties and taxes. With the limited infrastructure available on the island, patronage of Jazz is limited. Hence, contributions from gate receipts are not expected to exceed thirty per cent of the Jazz's production costs.

As a result of the limitation on accommodation stock, venue seating capacity and air access, the festival cannot physically grow much larger. However, the St Lucia Tourist Board envisioned that its economic impact could increase by lengthening the festival period, increasing the number of shows or increasing ticket prices. However, festival benefits must be assessed by the overall benefits the entire island derives, not only in terms of the money circulating via spending on rooms, taxi fares, food and beverage, souvenirs, and so on, but also the promotion that the island receives. The latter is of major significance to tourism, and it is this market component that can develop and provide substantial future benefits to St Lucia. The festival is also used to increase the benefits of tourism to the local community by continuing to provide an avenue and audience for display and trade for local goods and services (SLTB 2007b).

Unfortunately, on 4 December 2010, the producers of the Barbados festival announced that it was cancelling the 18th Annual Barbados Jazz Festival due to budgetary constraints. The festival has not been held since. The Barbados Tourism Authority (BTA) had been sponsoring the festival to the tune of US$300,000 per year in addition to the First Caribbean International Bank sponsorship of US$125,000 a year (Barbados Free Press 2010). In a letter released to the media, Gilbert Rowe, one of the organizers of GMR International Tours, noted that it was with a heavy heart that his company had taken the decision due to the prevailing economic environment. According to Rowe, "our delay in making this announcement is rooted in the fact that we were exploring all possibilities which may have resulted in our being able to produce the festival for 2011 especially at this time when our nation requires all assistance possible with regards to tourism-related events" (Jamaica Observer 2010).

In an interview after, Rowe explained that they had difficulties reaching an agreement with the BTA, one of the main sponsors of the festival. According to Rowe:

> for the seventeen years of the festival, since the inception, all of the contracts between the BTA and ourselves contained three elements: 1) the funding of the festival, cash-wise; 2) the responsibility of the BTA with regards to the international marketing of the festival, as is their responsibility with every single event of international

appeal that happens in Barbados; and 3) the making available of specific rights by GMR International Tours to the BTA to facilitate the said marketing of the festival. (Thompson 2010, n.d.)

Rowe explained that he had suggested that the festival be organized by the government as in St Lucia, but he had not had a positive response by the BTA (Thompson 2010).

Recommendations

Undoubtedly, the St Lucia Jazz and Arts Festival and the Barbados Jazz Festival have been used as tourism stimulators in St Lucia and Barbados, functioning as brand builders, indirect generators of business growth, tactical levers, and vehicles for local pride and community building (Nurse and Nicholls 2011; UNWTO 2007). Based on this comparative analysis of the St Lucia Jazz and Arts Festival and the Barbados Jazz Festival, there are several best practices and recommendations for festival sustainability and successful event management that can be highlighted.

Institutional Arrangements

Based on the findings, it is recommended that a full-time organization should be dedicated to the efficient planning and development of festivals that have a national focus and impact. St Lucia's festival model of private–public sector partnership showed the importance of the collaboration and co-operation of the two sectors rather than one sector running the festival entirely, as was seen in Barbados with the private sector. Poor institutional arrangements were identified as one of the main reasons for the collapse of the Barbados festival. Nurse at al. (2007) even suggested that a regional festival association be established, noting the absence of such organizations at both the national and regional levels. Another critical success factor is the clear definition of event stakeholder roles and responsibilities to ensure efficient and effective festival management. Furthermore, Walker (2019) argued that stakeholders need to use a collaborative approach to festival management in order to progress the sustainable tourism development agenda in the region.

Financial Management and Economic Impacts

As the case studies illustrate, there are a number of factors that are critical for the economic sustainability of festivals. For example, as mentioned previously, private sector support in the form of corporate sponsorship is critical and government incentives and subsidies are also needed to support the festival. Ultimately, festivals should be self-financing and not solely dependent on government support. The creation of fringe events helps to spread the positive economic impacts of the festival by stimulating other economic sectors and providing entrepreneurial opportunities for locals. However, the long-term sustainability of these festivals depends on destinations formulating the right combination of public, private, corporate and community ownership and sponsorship. Further research should be conducted to assess the various financial management models in operation, both regionally and internationally, examining their respective strengths and weaknesses.

The sustainability of these jazz and arts festivals might be in jeopardy in the Caribbean region given that the success of these events has led to attempts to replicate them in other islands. This is resulting in increasing competition among Caribbean destinations. As this analysis shows, both festivals, before the demise of the Barbados Jazz Festival, were using similar strategies to retain their competitive advantage, such as the addition of fringe events, greater inclusion of communities, and international and regional partnerships. This would have eventually resulted in less differentiation and distinctiveness of the Caribbean jazz festival product and a homogeneity of the product, which does not bode well for sustainability. Additionally, according to Khan (2006), these festivals are also competing with traditional carnivals in the region, such as Trinidad and Tobago's Carnival and Barbados's Crop Over.

A further limitation is the reliance on the same set of international and regional artists. While the Carnival festivals in the region use mainly local and regional artistes, jazz festivals tend to depend on international artistes. While they attract tourists to the festivals, they make the events somewhat dependent on external agents and foreign currency and revenue leakage becomes a critical concern (Khan 2006). Finally, in small island developing states like St Lucia and Barbados, the economic growth and potential of the festivals are stymied given the shortage of appropriate indoor and outdoor venues for the performing arts. For example, in 2011, the St Lucia Jazz Festival was almost ruined by rain as there were no alternative indoor venues in case the weather changed. This limits the development of the product as well as media coverage.

Marketing and Promotion

From the above analysis of the St Lucia and Barbados Jazz festivals, certain key points for the effective marketing and promotion of such events can be noted. In both countries, it was noted that strategic partnerships with promoters and media in the diaspora – including television, print and radio coverage in, for example, Atlanta and New York or on BET J or VH1 Soul – were useful in the marketing of the festival. Promotion, particularly on international music channels, was complemented by sponsorships and collaborations with well-established international brands (such as Coca-Cola) so that international awareness was created, particularly in the Caribbean diaspora markets. Both festivals also included top local bands and artistes, which helped to stimulate the local and regional creative industries and strengthen and increase national pride.

Evolution of the Festival Product

The analysis of both events shows that over time, they had to change and evolve in order to meet visitors' expectations and ensure the sustainability of the event. Both festivals focused on ensuring the continued quality of the event, the combination of international acts, regional acts and local talent, as well as the provision of a wide range of musical performances. This is a significant observation as it shows the festivals catering to the changing desires of the audience, which would have included local, regional and international guests. In order to identify opportunities for growth and expansion of the festival product, event organizers must continuously monitor and evaluate the event programme, design and structure. As in the case of the St Lucia and Barbados, the festivals were restructured, rebranded and redesigned to include more components of the creative industries such as food, fashion and dance. This strategy would help to ensure the economic and socio-cultural sustainability of the events.

At the time of this publication, the COVID-19 pandemic has had a significant impact on the events industry worldwide. In the midst of stay-at-home restrictions, curfews, social distancing, health concerns and general fear and uncertainty, many events were either postponed or cancelled in 2019 and 2020. Internationally and regionally, event planners and promoters have had to pivot to virtual events and hybrid events in order to survive in this new environment. Post COVID-19, events like jazz festivals will have to be reimagined in innovative ways to remain sustainable and attract both domestic and international tourists.

Socio-Cultural Impacts and Community Engagement

Particularly in St Lucia, the expansion of the geographic spread of the festival was a key strategy in helping to manage its social carrying capacity. This worked through the creation of fringe events that were free to the public in order to secure community involvement, engagement and participation in the festival. Beyond its effect on the carrying capacity, this strategy also facilitated the increase in local pride for culture and, by extension, cultural preservation. Within Barbados, including young people in the festival through partnerships with schools and local music academies also built on this thrust.

Conclusion

Given the increased regional and international competition, Caribbean governments should continue to support festivals in order to increase the positive economic spin-offs in terms of increased tourist arrivals and multiplier effects in the local economy. Festivals can bring tourists into the destination in the low season and encourage tourists out into the community to experience the authentic culture of the destination. However, the sustainability of these festivals will be dependent on a strategic change in how their management is approached. In the first instance, there has to be greater stakeholder engagement at all levels, particularly among different sectors. Increased community engagement is also central to the longevity of festivals. Furthermore, a focus on the – "glocalizing" – (i.e. globalization and localization) of the event is needed for two reasons. First, it allows for the showcasing of indigenous talent and less reliance on repeat international acts. Second, it allows for a type of community-oriented jazz festival that increases the multiplier effect.

Another strategic change is the determination of an appropriate funding model that engages both the public and private sectors. Moreover, it is imperative that destinations monitor and measure the impacts of festivals using a triple bottom line approach, as a lack of data stymies any strategic decision making on the future development and management of festivals. The lessons learned from these case studies are valuable for other destinations engaged in the hosting of festivals. Both case studies point to the importance of and movement towards greater community involvement in the staging of festivals. This signals a need to conduct further research in the area of community-oriented jazz festivals as a means of ensuring the sustainability of festivals.

References

Acorn Consulting Partnership. 2008. "Developing a Niche Tourism Market Database for the Caribbean: 20 Niche Market Profiles." http://www.onecaribbean.org/content/files/OverivewCaribbeanNicheMarkets.pdf.

Amsden, Benoni L., Richard C. Stedman, and Linda E. Kruger. 2011. "The Creation and Maintenance of Sense of Place in a Tourism-Dependent Community." *Leisure Sciences* 33 (1): 32–51.

Baxter, P., and S. Jack. 2008. "Qualitative Case Study Methodology: Study Design and Implementation for Novice Researchers." *The Qualitative Report* 13 (4): 544–59.

Barbados Free Press. 2010. "Barbados Jazz Festival Cancelled. Barbados Tourism Authority Last to Know".http://barbadosfreepress.wordpress.com/2010/12/04/barbados-jazz-festival-cancelled-barbados-tourism-authority-last-to-know/.

Bell, David, and Kate Oakley. 2015. *Cultural Policy*. New York: Routledge.

Bethel, N. 2014. "The Economic Impact of Junkanoo in the Bahamas." *International Journal of Bahamian Studies* 20 (1): 13–26. Retrieved from http://journals.sfu.ca/cob/index.php/files/article/view/206/270.

Burke, Suzanne. 2007. "The Evolution of the Cultural Policy Regime in the Anglophone Caribbean." *International Journal of Cultural Policy* 13 (2): 169–84.

———. 2013. "Eyes Wide Open: Festival Strategy in the Caribbean." *Caribbean Creatives* 5: 21–24.

Carlsen, J., and T.D. Andersson. 2011. "Strategic SWOT Analysis of Public, Private and Not-for-Profit Festival Organisations." *International Journal of Event and Festival Management* 2 (1): 83–97. https://doi.org/10.1108/17582951111116632.

Chaitoo, Ramesh. 2013. "The Entertainment Sector in CARICOM: Key Challenges and Proposals for Action." Inter-American Development Bank. https://publications.iadb.org/en/publication/11860/entertainment-sector-caricom-key-challenges-and-proposals-action.

Clayton, Anthony, Nikolaos Karagiannis, and Jessica M. Bailey. 2015. "Sustainable Development of Caribbean Tourism." In *Public Administration and Policy in the Caribbean*, 337–56.

Curtis, Rebecca Anne. 2010. "Australia's Capital of Jazz? The (Re)Creation of Place, Music and Community at the Wangaratta Jazz Festival. *Australian Geographer* 41 (1): 101–16.

Douglas, Norman, Ngaire Douglas, and Derrett, R. 2001. *Special Interest Tourism*. Sydney: John Wiley and Sons.

Dowrich-Phillips, L. 2016. "Jazz for the People." *Caribbean Beat* 139. https://www.caribbean-beat.com/issue-139/word-of-mouth#axzz7ygwXqxTi.

———, L. 2018. "St Lucia Jazz Festival Returns to Its Roots with Pure Jazz." Loop News, 17 April 2018. https://tt.loopnews.com/content/st-lucia-jazz-festival-returns-its-roots-pure-jazz.

Frisby, W., and D. Getz. 1989. "Festival Management: A Case Study Perspective." *Journal of Travel Research* 28 (1): 7–11.

Getz, D. 2005. *Event Management and Event Tourism*. New York: Cognizant Commuoration.

———. 2008. "Event Tourism: Definition, Evolution and Research." *Tourism Management* 29:403–28.

Hall, C.M. 1992. *Hallmark Tourist Events: Impacts, Management, and Planning*. London: Belhaven Press.

Jamaica Observer. 2010. "No Barbados Jazz Festival." https://www.jamaicaobserver.com/entertainment/no-barbados-jazz-festival/.

Jazz News. 2006. "14th Annual Barbados Jazz Festival." http://home.nestor.minsk.by/jazz/news/2006/12/2103.html.

Khan, P. 2006. *Challenges and Opportunities Presented by Growth of the Tourism Industry in the Caribbean: Implications for Poverty Alleviation*, Report Prepared for the International Development Research Centre (IDRC), Uruguay.

Kotler, P., D.H. Haider, and I. Rein. 1993. *Marketing Places: Attracting Investment, Industry and Tourism to Cities, States and Nations*. New York: Free Press.

Kuuder, C.J., R. Adongo, and J. Abanga. 2012. "The Socio-Cultural Significance of the Kakube Festival of the Dagara of Nandom Traditional Area in Ghana." *Ghana Journal of Development Studies* 9 (2): 103–24.

Laurent, Edwin. n.d. "Jazz in St Lucia." *Caribbean Intelligence*. Accessed 19 May 2016. http://www.caribbeanintelligence.com/content/jazz-st-lucia.

Lee, Jenny, Gerard Kyle, and David Scott. 2012. "The Mediating Effect of Place Attachment on the Relationship between Festival Satisfaction and Loyalty to the Festival Hosting Destination." *Journal of Travel Research* 51 (6): 754–67.

MacLeod, Nicola E. 2006. "The Placeless Festival: Identity and Place in the Post-Modern Festival." In *Festivals, Tourism and Social Change: Remaking Worlds*, edited by Picard and Robinson, 222–37. Tonawanda, NY: Channel View Publications.

Meyers, Dorothea. 2006. "Caribbean Tourism, Local Sourcing and Enterprise Development: Review of the Literature." Pro-Poor Tourism Partnership Working Paper 8, 2016.

MyVueNews.com. 2010. "Barbados Jazz Festival 2011 Cancelled." https://www.myvuenews.com/barbados-jazz-festival-2011-cancelled/.

Nurse, K. 2003. "Festival Tourism in the Caribbean: An Economic Impact Assessment." Paper presented at the Fifth Annual Caribbean

Conference on Sustainable Tourism Development, 9–12 September 2003, Basseterre, St Kitts and Nevis. https://www.academia.edu/3436909/Festival_tourism_in_the_Caribbean_an_economic_impact_assessment.

———, A. Demas., J. Tull, B. Paddington, W. O'Young, M. Gray, H. Hoagland, and M. Reis. 2007. *The Cultural Industries in CARICOM*. Bridgetown: Caribbean Regional Negotiating Machinery.

———, and A. Nicholls. 2011. "Enhancing Data Collection in the Creative Industries Sector in CARIFORUM." https://www.academia.edu/3436218/Enhancing_Data_Collection_in_the_Creative_Industries_Sector_in_CARIFORUM.

Pro-Poor Tourism and Travel Foundation. 2006. "Making Tourism Count for the Local Economy in the Caribbean: Guidelines for Good Practice." https://cdn.odi.org/media/documents/3013.pdf.

Quinn, Bernadette. 2013. *Key Concepts in Event Management*. London: Sage.

Rivera, Manuel A., Kelly J. Semrad, and Robertico Croes. 2016. "The Internationalization Benefits of a Music Festival: The Case of the Curaçao North Sea Jazz Festival." *Tourism Economics* 22 (5): 1087–1103. https://doi.org/10.5367/te.2015.0485.

Smith, C., and P. Jenner. 1998. "The Impact of Festivals and Special Events on Tourism, Occasional Studies." *Travel and Tourism Analyst* 4: 73–91.

South Florida Caribbean News. 2006. "BET J, Barbados Partner to Promote January Dance." 15 November 2006. http://sflcn.com/bet-j-barbados-partner-to-promote-january-jazz/.

Southplanet. n.d. "St Lucia Jazz Festival." Accessed 19 May 2016. http://www.spla.pro/en/file.recurring-event.st-lucia-jazz-festival.512.html.

Williams, Sharon. 2016. "Jazz Decentralized." St Lucia Online. http://www.slucia.com/visions/jazz.html.

St Lucia Tourist Board (SLTB). 2007a. "Evolution of the Other Jazz Events." Accessed 25 April 2007. http://stluciajazz.org/jazz_articles/evolution.asp.

———. 2007b. "St Lucia Jazz 2005: 14 Years and Counting." Accessed April 25, 2007. http://stluciajazz.org/jazz_articles/history.asp.

———. 2007c. "St Lucia Jazz Story – A Perspective." Accessed 25 April 2007. http://stluciajazz.org/jazz_articles/feststory.asp.

———. 2016. "Saint Lucia Jazz & Arts Festival History." Accessed 4 May 2016. http://stluciajazz.org/festivalhistory/.

Stevenson, Deborah, David Rowe, and Kieryn McKay. 2010. "Convergence in British Cultural Policy: The Social, the Cultural, and the Economic." *Journal of Arts Management, Law, and Society* 40 (4): 248–65.

The Barbados Jazz Festival. 2007. Available at http://barbadosjazzfestival.com/ (accessed on 25 April 2007).

Thompson, Rhonda. 2010. "Hurt by Lack of BTA Deal." Nation News, 19 December 2010. https://www.nationnews.com/2010/12/19/hurt-by-lack-of-bta-deal/.

Tull, J. 2017. Caribbean Festival Arts: Exploring Praxis for the Future. *Caribbean Quarterly* 63 (2–3): 291–303. https://doi.org/10.1080/00086495.2017.1352278.

United Nations World Tourism Organization (UNWTO). 2007. *A Practical Guide to Tourism Destination Management*. Madrid: United Nations World Tourism Organization.

Walker, T.B. 2019. "Sustainable Tourism and the Role of Festivals in the Caribbean – Case of the St. Lucia Jazz (& Arts) Festival." *Tourism Recreation Research* 44:258–68.

Yin, R.K. 2012. *Applications of Case Study Research*. Los Angeles: Sage.

7.
Food Tourism in the Caribbean: The Case for Slow Food and Slowness in Travel

Therez B. Walker

Introduction

Defining the Caribbean is often problematic because it is often a matter of perspective and of context (Hedges et al. 2019; Williams and Bunkley-Williams 2021). However, the Caribbean is commonly known as one of the most culturally diverse regions in the world for the same reason. The geography and insular nature of the Caribbean also makes it a collection of idyllic 3S (sun, sea and sand) tourism destinations, much the same way that history and political influences have determined the growth and specialization of tourism in the region. Nonetheless, while the region is traditionally known for its beach offerings with an abundance of 3S resources (Matthews et al. 2021), the Caribbean is inherently, also home to diverse, vibrant and exceedingly delightful food (Lewis and Lewis 2012; Montero 2014). The region is demographically diverse, and Caribbean cuisine is a unique amalgamation of flavours, ingredients and other influences that expresses the history, heritage and culture of the Caribbean (Okumus et al. 2013; Rhiney, Walker and Tomlinson 2015). In addition to foods native to the Americas, many types of ingredients now found in the region were introduced by various ethnic groups, such as Europeans, Africans and Asians. These global influences, in combination with the preparation methods and techniques that they brought to the region, have played a monumental role in defining the evolution of contemporary Caribbean cuisine that is a fusion of African, Creole, Cajun, Amerindian, European, Latin American, South Asian, Chinese and Middle Eastern influences, adding to the indigenous characteristics of each island.

The Caribbean is a unique yet diverse region and this is apparent in the dynamic culture and variety of cuisine that can be found throughout the islands of the region. This chapter will further explore current opportunities that exist for Caribbean small island developing states (SIDS) as it relates to developing a food tourism niche. This chapter will explore food production and consumption and the producer–consumer relationship that is ultimately linked to local culture and identity. Food is expressive of local culture and, where tourism is concerned, this extends to the elements of food such as agriculture and food production that are also expressive of the local environment. The academic discourse has emphasized how backward economic linkages are essential for the tourism industry to effectively contribute to the well-being of residents (Jeyacheya and Hampton 2020). Yet, historical forces in the Caribbean have supported the growth of tourism and a decline in agricultural production (Sheller 2021).

The Slow Food movement will be explored throughout this chapter as a practical approach to food tourism development within the local context, as it promotes the social economy through stakeholder participation and various forms of agritourism. The Slow Food movement is currently present in several Caribbean countries and sets a supportive framework for food tourism in the region. Likewise, Slow Food provides a globally recognized brand that further enhances the competitive marketing of a destination. Ultimately, the goal of destination marketing and branding is to optimize tourism impacts and achieve strategic objectives for all stakeholders (Koo, Mendes Filho and Buhalis 2019). Nonetheless, one determining factor used by potential visitors in choosing one destination over another is a positive image, according to Hahm and Severt (2018).

The Slow Food model is the quintessential positive brand image. The philosophy behind the movement emphasizes sustainability and stakeholder involvement within that process. Guided by progressive elements of Slow Food, food tourism can be seen as a tool for destination development. Here, food tourism presents pertinent considerations for ways in which the tourism industry can be extended to offer an enhanced experience, reduce environmental impact, empower communities and stimulate the local economy. It also presents an important opportunity for destination marketing and branding as the relationship between food and tourism can prove beneficial in establishing a strong identity in the tourism marketplace.

Slow Food Tourism and Slowness in Travel

Slow Food, with its origins in Italy, was formed in the mid 1980s. This occurred in Bra, a small Italian town, when Carlo Petrini and a group of food writers, chefs and other activists protested against the introduction of American-style, fast-food chains, most notably McDonalds. Petrini quite successfully founded an association to "sell" the world a package of history, nature, wine and cuisine, and he emphasized gastronomic education in a revolutionary new agro-culinary program (Laudan 2004, 139). Miele and Murdoch (2002) provided a history of protest that led to the founding of Slow Food when concerns grew about the potential impact of fast food on traditional food establishments that have a close connection to the local food production system. The protest was held in a very Italian manner and protesters demanded slow food to replace fast food as they ate penne pasta in front of the offending fast-food restaurant (Chrzan 2004).

Today, Slow Food is an international non-profit organization of people with the intent to cultivate common cultural and gastronomic interests (Lee 2021). The organization is based on resistance as well as collective consumer action. The movement also seeks to defend local traditions, good food, gastronomic pleasure and a slower pace of life. It has now grown into a large organization with over 1 million supporters and one hundred thousand members in 160 countries. They are all dedicated to the protection of foods linked to particular localities and cultural traditions (Hsu 2014; Leitch 2000,105; Slow Food n.d.a). It is important to note that the aim of the Slow Food movement is to promote eco-gastronomy, and it is also referred to as a gastronomic and ecological movement (Nilsson et al. 2011; Tam 2008; Werner, Griese and Bosse 2020). By focusing on eco-gastronomy, Slow Food recognizes that the best place to preserve biological and cultural diversity is on the plates of consumers, and it does this by featuring foods and their producers and by finding new markets for traditional foods (Pollan 2003). The movement has expanded considerably and is also present in several SIDS.

At the same time, enjoying a slow pace of life is symbolic of many Caribbean islands. This extends to slowness in travel where relaxation and rejuvenation in the sun, sea and sand are some of the things that an island getaway in the Caribbean call to mind. Research has revealed that travellers' to island destinations expect to forget about the stress of everyday life and have memorable and relaxed experiences (Moon and Han 2018, 79). Therefore, since the concept of slowing down is a common part of island life, adoption of the Slow Food movement and its underlying philosophy will allow visitors the opportunity to experience a sense of place by connecting with local people, food and culture as they slow down to enjoy all that the destination has to offer. Interestingly, the Slow Food movement has already been adopted by twelve SIDS (Slow Food n.d.a; Walker and Lee 2021). This has facilitated growth and development, especially where focus has been placed on additional themes such as Slow Fish. In particular, Slow Fish Caribe actively engages a network of Slow Food members in the wider Caribbean region and some attention has been placed on invasive species in Caribbean waters such as the lionfish. Slow Food Barbados works in communities across the island under a number of central themes, including educational gardens, Slow Fish and a chefs' alliance, which is a global Slow Food initiative where locally based chefs promote good quality and sustainably produced local food. It has allowed the small island of Barbados to change menus to support the local food system, improve food security and build stronger producer-consumer relationships (Slow Food Barbados n.d.). The Slow Foods logo is a snail that slowly and calmly eats its way through life, and the movement awards a Snail of Approval to establishments that pursue and practice Slow Food values. In Barbados, when residents or visitors to the island choose a restaurant that is awarded with the Slow Food Barbados Snail of Approval, they know they are consuming quality food that is mostly local and sustainably raised and grown. This essentially guides consumers towards a better national food system. In Barbados, the Slow Food movement also organizes and participates in frequent events and soup drives across the island, where new categories of producers are emerging, such as cheese producers. Slow Food Barbados, therefore, is an example of this untapped, ready-made market for locally sourced Caribbean food and is positioned to be a pioneer in officially certifying and promoting Slow Food travel in one of the most idyllic tourism regions in the world.

Many countries in the Caribbean have already identified specific agricultural commodities that have a competitive advantage and are aware of the significant opportunities that exist within tourism for trade in authentic craft, souvenirs, and natural beauty and wellness products, especially as it relates to the rapidly growing spa sector (Harvey 2010). Slowness in travel may even extend to the slow city network to include additional stakeholders that supply goods and services to the dynamic tourism industry. Furthermore, several researchers have provided an exploration of the potential impact of slowness in travel and tourism from a small island perspective (Conway and Timms 2010, 2012; Harvey 2010, 19; Walker 2020;

Walker and Lee 2021). In light of this, the influence of the Slow Food movement in Caribbean SIDS has the potential to further enhance food production, security and quality while also preserving local traditions and food biodiversity. Likewise, within the overall agricultural system, Slow Food acts as an important guardian of global agrobiodiversity, which is being eroded by conventional production (Lotti 2010, 71).

Concepts like slow cheese, slow wine and slow meat, among others, have all emerged as a part of the Slow Food movement along with a global network of farmers' markets. Slow Food has also evolved and launched several concepts and institutions such as the Ark of Taste, sometimes referred to as the "Noah Principle", that focuses on agricultural biodiversity and catalogues endangered foods, plants, animal breeds, meats, grains, herbs, cheeses and fruits. In similar fashion, Slow Food Presidia is another concept within the movement that engages producers in sustaining quality production and traditional processing methods, safeguarding local animal breeds and plant varieties, and building new facilities for food production (Slow Food n.d.b). The growth of the global movement most recently has introduced a new theme, Slow Food Travel, which offers a model for tourism. Here, slowness in travel encourages unique exchanges between food producers who benefit from the dynamic tourism industry.

The Slow Food movement and, by extension its network of producers, fisherfolk, hotels, restaurants, chefs and other producers, allows for a sustainable food tourism destination and essentially maximizes the positive impact on local food (Fusté-Forné and Jamal 2020; Hendrikx et al. 2016). Contemporary forces have led to the emergence of consumer trends towards the quality of food rather than the experience of dining out (Miele and Murdoch 2002, 313). Therefore, by specifically offering this model of sustainable tourism that allows for interactions with local food producers and chefs, Slow Food Travel effectively facilitates the process of stakeholder collaboration as various stakeholders maximize the tourism multiplier effect while preserving local food biodiversity and having a positive impact on local food production at the same time (Lee, Scott and Packer 2014; Slow Food n.d.c).

Slow Food Travel aims to make visitors aware of the preservation of food biodiversity by bringing them closer to the authenticity and uniqueness of local cultures and identities through gastronomy. Slow Food Travel can have significant benefits for destinations that embrace it. The Slow Food Travel model and its underlying philosophy directly and indirectly support community-based tourism and with this, a dynamic host of initiatives can materialize such as farm to table, farm to fork and tree to table tours and Airbnb stays, in addition to other experiences. This ultimately leads to a paradigm shift for responsible travel, where visitors create a positive impact on the host community as they stay longer at the destination and engage in the slower pace that is typical of the everyday lifestyle in island destinations. Consequently, visitors to Slow Food Travel destinations are able to encounter Art of Taste products and participate in various Slow Food activities while meeting Slow Food Presidia producers across the globe. Essentially, Slow Food can be best defined as a composite and diversified international network of initiatives (Peano, Migliorini and Sottile 2014; Sassatelli and Davolio 2010). Slow Food members across the world can essentially visit Slow Food events and activities in any country and the network does an effective job in sharing information and knowledge across locales and regions. The focus here is on value added experiences.

From a sustainable development perspective, the Slow City (Cittàslow) movement was established out of the Slow Food movement and has materialized as a progressive approach to sustainability and local governance for small communities. As a grassroots movement, people are at the heart of this approach. They commit to improving quality of life and experience for residents and visitors alike by not only accentuating the authentic cultural aspects of a destination but also the unique culinary and artistic local traditions of communities (Baldemir, Kaya and Sahin 2013; Walker, Lee and Li 2021). The concept behind Slow City is simple. It emphasizes good living, which promotes the quality of the local environment and gastronomic resources, while also preserving slowness (where it already exists) and promoting it where there is little of it (Hatipoglu 2015; Munjal, Sharma and Menon 2016). Fittingly, for the modern traveller, small islands remain popular destinations for holiday makers who seek adventure along with this slower pace of life (Harrison 2001, 10). Slowness and authentic experiences have been gaining in appeal in recent years for various reasons, and in the Caribbean, where there is a "laid back" atmosphere, the slow philosophy allows visitors to enjoy the simple pleasures of life in a place that already features this. Slow cities working along with Slow Food in various parts of the world seek to emphasize the importance of local identity by connecting agriculture with the local economy and local food festivals and by promoting local distinctiveness through small market towns and networking and cooperation that encourage the formation of co-ops for local businesses that invest in skill building (Mayer and Knox 2006, 2009; Lin 2020). Although slow cities limit the population size of small towns to fifty thousand, which may be ideal for SIDS, Slow Food does not include such size limitations and the global network provides many lessons for emerging sustainable tourism destinations. The focus here is on the social economy. Walker and Lee (2021) provided a useful analysis of the potential benefits for slow cities in SIDS across the globe.

Moreover, this connection with Slow Food Travel has the potential for a sustainable impact on Caribbean SIDS as it relates to the visibility of local cuisine. Slow Food Barbados, for example, has focused on various initiatives and provides a buyer's guide that is valuable in building and encouraging producer-consumer relationships. Slow Food in the wider Caribbean network collectively has placed emphasis on capacity building and knowledge sharing as more and more countries join the network. While several scholars have critiqued the Slow Food movement in various locations (Chrzan

Figure 7.1: Slow Food and Slowness in Travel

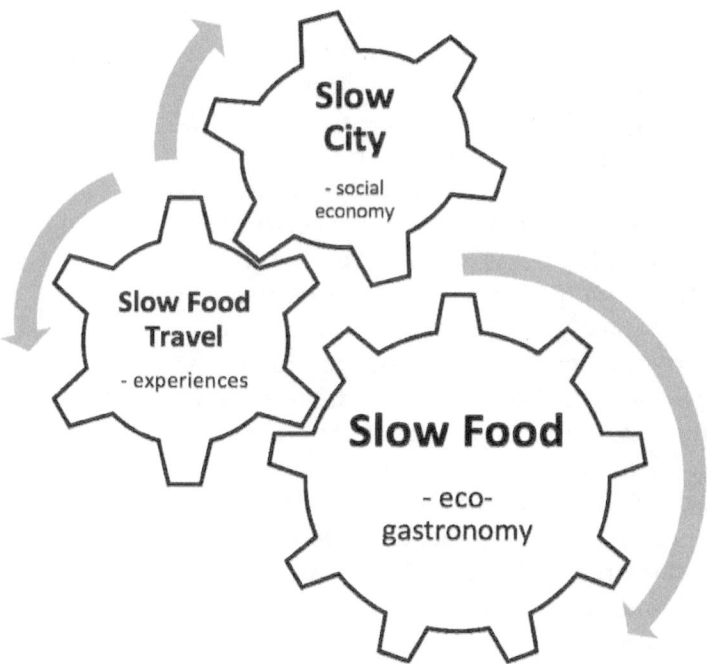

2004; De Grazia 2005; Jones et al. 2003; Laudan 2004; Paxson 2005; Sassatelli and Davolio 2010), the arguments focus on issues relating to the formality of structure for its grassroots activities, consumer trends, elitism and so forth. The rhetoric rebounds to its brand recognition, amongst producers, chefs, restaurateurs and gastronomes in particular. It is for this reason, that within the scope of SIDS, Slow Food and slowness in travel is being evaluated as a supportive framework for developing a food tourism niche in this chapter.

Food Tourism

Ellis et al. (2018) provided a comprehensive look at food tourism and other commonly and interchangeably used terms such as culinary tourism and gastronomic tourism. The researchers concluded that there is a preference to use terminology that places value on the relationship between food and culture. Here the consumer focus becomes that central element to understand the demand and supply relationship. Food tourism includes learning about food, culture and the overall experience of consuming food at the destination. A popular definition for food tourism is tourism that includes visits to primary, secondary and other producers of food, festivals, farmers markets, and other locations for food tasting or to experience the various elements of food production (Hall and Sharples 2003, 10). This definition suggests that the desire to taste or experience a particular type of food must be the major motivation for travel, and this is upheld by other researchers (Hall 2006; Ellis et al. 2018). There are three components to food tourism, according to Du Rand and Heath (2006) and they include agriculture (product), culture (history and authenticity) and tourism (infrastructure and services), which when combined create the food tourism experience.

Over the past decade, many countries have been developing their tourism industry, and tourism can be seen not only as a leisure activity but also one where visitors to a destination get the opportunity to learn about and understand its unique culture and heritage. In addition to a variety of attractions, visitors are also interested in local cuisine, as food provides one of the most authentic elements of the travel experience. Since Bélisle's (1983) exploration of the relationship between food and tourism, research in food where the social and cultural aspects of food in tourism destinations are highlighted has been increasing. Issues related to sustainability and the socio-economic impacts of local communities have also been emphasized and food has become fundamental to the challenge of sustainability, as it is also central to our sense of identity. Here, cuisine can be taken to mean the process where we transform raw materials either with the intent to eat them or, as Fischler (1988) noted, from a state of nature to a state of culture. Research has also discussed the cultural meaning behind food, the importance that local cuisine plays and how the distance between producer and consumer is getting larger, resulting in an increasing sense of unease with how food is produced today (Pietrykowski 2004; Pollan 2003).

There are also changing lifestyle and consumer trends that provide an opportunity from which tourism destinations can benefit. Essentially, the role of food in the local economy is being emphasized in the academic discourse while issues of taste, quality and freshness are being recognized as important, just as what, why and how we eat says something about ourselves, the society we live in and the places we visit (du Rand and Heath 2006; Hall and Sharples 2003). Food tourism has traditionally been developed according to the availability and types of food, taste and cultural aspirations that exists at the destination (Miele and Murdoch 2002, 315). However, another important aspect to mention is how food tourism also increases the income of many stakeholders such as chefs, restauranteurs, butchers, farmers and other producers (Ellis et al. 2018; Hall and Mitchell 2001; Hall 2006). This has a wider reach for the tourism and hospitality industry in terms of direct and indirect employment.

In recent years, issues of industrial agriculture are also being increasingly highlighted in the academic discourse across disciplines. With this, consumer trends to organic labels, farm to table, and the increasing membership actively engaging with innovative and progressive initiatives such as Slow Food and the slow movement give credence to changing consumer dynamics. Coincidentally, Slow Food incorporates food tourism and issues of sustainability. From this perspective, food tourism can be a driving force for farmers and other producers to rethink their production activity, take diversification into account and actively explore opportunities to add value to their products (Sidali, Spiller and Schulze 2011). Additionally, Slow Food and the underlying philosophy behind the movement has been effective in raising the profile of a number of issues, particularly the importance of locally produced, in-season food and the transformation of local farmers' markets and direct food purchases from producers and growers into a leisure commodity (Fullagar, Markwell and Wilson 2012).

The slow movement, the concept of slow food, the organization Slow Food and the many other themes born out of the slow philosophy (such as slow tourism, slow food travel and slow city) have been received with interest among academics of various disciplines (Heitmann, Robinson and Povey 2011; Leer 2020). Yet existing research has not so far explored how the slow philosophy and by extension Slow Food can affect the production and promotion of food tourism in small island destinations. This is important for several reasons. Firstly, there are positive impacts of food tourism on the environment, society and the social economy. Secondly, the slow philosophy complements a Caribbean lifestyle, where slowing down and escaping the realities of a fast-paced life in the metropolis allows visitors to disconnect and focus on the pleasures of local cuisine and culture. This is a key consideration for Caribbean SIDS, as it provides a unique position for small island destinations that already enjoy a slow ethos to encourage slowness in travel and a sense of place while vacationing. Nonetheless, while slowness in travel is well suited to Caribbean small islands, the majority of existing research on the slow movement has been conducted in European and Asian countries. For instance, the movement has been studied in Italy as an example of economic resilience (Di Gregorio 2017), while in Taiwan, research has focused on slowness in travel and transportation (Lin 2017). More specifically, Snyder, Hu and Zheng (2018) addressed slow food across places such as Europe, the United States of America and China by investigating practical cases that range from education projects to initiatives that support farmers to stakeholder participation in the consultation of legislation. This is significant because Slow Food supports the promotion of a socially and environmentally conscious stance towards consumption and seeks to preserve local foods and cuisines by creating and strengthening producer-consumer networks (Pietrykowski 2004). It also encourages slowness and makes a case to understand the concept of "mindfulness at the table", as this is Slow Food's most effective tactic in the face of global agribusiness (Dunlap 2012, 43). Furthermore, The Slow Food organization is seen as a consumer and producer advocate with an extensive network of members that includes farmers, chefs and other producers in the food system. This also includes consumers in every Slow Food location who appreciate various initiatives and food-related activities where they live and visit.

Food Tourism and the Caribbean

Tourism development in the Caribbean is marked by post-war development factors of decolonization and the remarkable transformation of the global tourism industry that also coincided with favourable restructuring and infrastructure developments (McElroy 2003). Various economic arguments offer insights on how tourism development in small islands has merely shifted the burden of dependence from one form of production (agriculture) to another (experiences). However the move is not surprising when the few economic alternatives are considered in addition to the fact that visitor expenditure contributes significantly to the gross domestic product of Caribbean islands (Duval and Wilkinson 2004). In theory, tourism creates an incentive for increased local food production, yet the majority of the food consumed in the Caribbean tourism industry is imported, according to Belisle (1983), and early research has emphasized the need for more research on the impact of tourism on food production in the Caribbean. Today, this remains the same, as policymakers in small islands have been particularly concerned with maximizing returns due to significant loss of revenue from food imports (Hall and Sharples 2003, 4).

In highlighting the importance of food as an input in the tourism sector, Jeyacheya and Hampton (2020) made a case for backward linkages as a way of enhancing tourism benefits. Similarly, Harvey (2010) addressed the decline in agriculture for the growth of tourism and examined the development of agritourism as a productive and fully integrated linkage between the agrifood sector. However, it is important to note that while exploring the potential to strengthen agritourism in the Caribbean, Rhiney, Walker and Tomlinson (2015) identified various case studies of Caribbean agritourism and outlined challenges faced. Yet they concluded that since the link between agriculture and tourism in the Caribbean is weak, it is important to capitalize on the cultural assets of the region to enhance visitor experience through activities such as farm-based tours and the development of alternative forms of tourism. The slow pace of island life further complements the underlying philosophy of the slow movement and encourages the social interactions necessary for the positive impacts of sustainable tourism to be realized. Tourism that is based upon the agricultural economy is referred to as agritourism (Pezzi, Faggian and Reid 2021) and visitors to tourism places and spaces may choose to interact with residents of the host community through farm stays and exchanges, tours, farmers markets, festivals or other types of initiatives and events.

Empirical evidence illustrates that Slow Food has been successful in its initiatives around the world (Chung et al. 2017). The philosophy of the movement has practical implications that promote eco-gastronomy (Payandeh et al. 2020) and raises the visibility of local food in tourism destinations. While the agricultural economy is just one element of Slow Food, it also introduces knowledge sharing that promotes and supports the local processes of food production, which contribute to the all-encompassing experience of food tourism. Additionally, agritourism by itself as a niche is a unique form of entrepreneurship that is linked to a destination's existing natural resources and economic and cultural base (Van Sandt, Thilmany and Hill 2021). This introduces not only sustainability but sustainable food tourism at the destination and further enriches the destination for the typical visitor (Gürsoy 2021). Local food therefore provides opportunities to maximize the multiplier as it relates to tourism. Furthermore, research by Montanari and Staniscia (2009) also supported this relationship between food and tourism and discussed its potential for sustainable local development that can benefit marginalized communities in a meaningful way.

Essentially a shorter commodity chain between producer and consumer allows for more accountability to the consumer, and promoting an eating experience that is based on locality can only prove beneficial to the local community. Slow Food is mainly concerned with the "slow philosophy", of which gastronomy is only one component, yet its approach is reflective of one where consumers are encouraged to recognize their potential to recreate the local agricultural system (Dunlap 2012). Several researchers have discussed the history of Slow Food. It was born out of a revolution that defends the right to pleasure, preserves culinary traditions, promotes sustainable agricultural practices and guides culinary tourists by highlighting authentic spaces and places (Frost and Laing 2014; Frontefrancesco and Corvo 2019). Slow Food advocates that food consumers should be convinced of food's value as they find pleasure in the flavours, traditional practices and cuisines that come with eating good-tasting and sustainably produced local food (Chrzan 2004, 120).

Caribbean SIDS may build on these opportunities to create local markets and seek to protect as well as promote sustainable food systems. Slow Food already does this by focusing on biodiversity and sustainable agricultural practices to support gastronomy. The philosophy of the movement emphasizes how typical products and local cuisine are the key aspects of cultural distinctiveness (Miele and Murdoch 2002, 318). Slow Food also attempts to preserve local foods, products and ingredients that run the risk of nostalgia and potential isolation (Donati 2005; Shneider 2008). Where Caribbean SIDS are concerned, there is an untapped, ready-made market for locally sourced foods and research indicates a preference by visitors to have experiences that are authentic and linked to local foods, culture and heritage while at the destination (Harvey 2010). Authenticity here becomes another opportunity for Caribbean SIDS to reflect on changing consumer dynamics. This is timely, as authenticity is becoming a significant focus for the tourism academic discourse.

Essentially, SIDS are limited in how they can compete in the global tourism landscape, yet research by Punnett and Morrison (2006) has identified niche markets and a model for producer-consumer links that will allow various stakeholders to access high margin markets. This broadens the scope in which local communities can provide continuous and high-quality local products in the dynamic tourism system, as opposed to the traditionally high level of imports that are commonplace in Caribbean economies. This not only adds to the authenticity of the destination but also enhances the overall destination experience. The further focus on fresh, local in-season ingredients and traditional cooking methods that Slow Food promotes ensures a stronger claim to the unique and diverse taste of the Caribbean. This extends to visitor experience and quality of life regarding indicators for sustainable tourism in small islands.

Discussion

By identifying and exploring a unique and emerging approach to sustainability and local governance, this chapter has significant practical implications. This chapter seeks to emphasize the potential impact of an innovative and inclusive approach to sustainability and local governance on the sustainable tourism agenda of island economies in the Caribbean. The considerations explored throughout help to explain the Slow Food phenomenon and its role in food tourism and destination marketing. The marketing of the food tourism product in the Caribbean can benefit from strategies that satisfy the changing needs of consumers and position the region as a socially responsible tourism destination. By focusing on socially desirable practices and outcomes, small islands can implement inclusive approaches that align with the philosophy of the movement and not only contribute to promoting economic linkages and stakeholder cooperation but also offer a strong and established brand image. The timing of this chapter is also important as the slow movement has been steadily gaining the attention of the academic community across several areas. By examining the Slow Food movement and its potential impact on food tourism in the Caribbean, this chapter serves as a foundation for creating an effective planning and management framework for aspiring slow destinations.

The movement certainly excites and provides opportunities for both members and non-members. It celebrates local foods and champions a wide range of almost forgotten tastes and smells (Jung, Ineson and Miller 2014; Tam 2008) and even traditional forms of food preparation and cooking. The slow movement espouses consuming meals at a leisurely pace and in convivial company (Jones et al. 2003). The question going forward should be whether a gastronomic movement like Slow Food, which was originally created to stimulate food tourism, can continue to deliver on the much grander ambitions of its advocates (Laudan 2004). For a region such as the Caribbean, this chapter seeks to explore whether this can translate into a model for promoting food tourism in small places and spaces in a region that is practically synonymous with slowing down. Over the last decade, Slow Food has facilitated a level of international networking that has allowed for more intense collaboration with grassroots civil society organizations at the forefront of development projects, particularly in Africa, Latin America and the Caribbean (Sassatelli and Davolio

Figure 7.2: Impact of Scalable Community Initiatives on Small Island Destinations

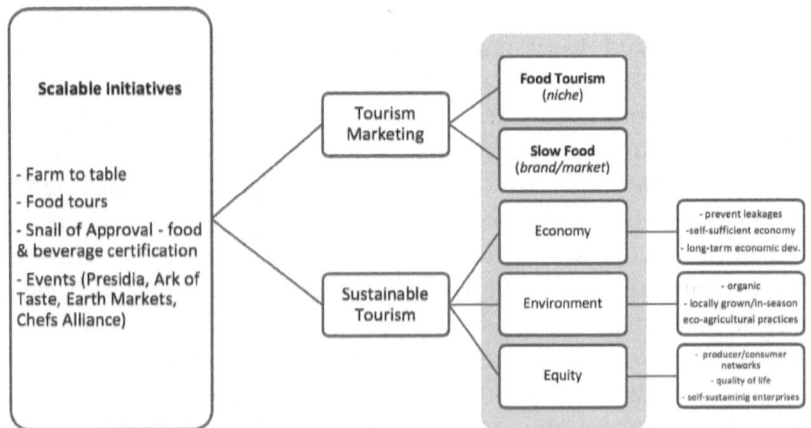

2010, 211). The Slow Food Latin America and the Caribbean network, like many other Slow Food networks, do collaborate and share in taste education through various initiatives. From the perspective of travel and tourism, Slow Food and slowness in travel may extend to experiences (slow food travel) and the social economy (slow city), which all serve as catalysts that SIDS can maximize.

The benefits and impacts of developing the food tourism niche are significant. This, coupled with the advantages of self-sustaining enterprises and the influence of association with the brand Slow Food, further extends and exists around the producer-consumer network of local communities (Leer 2020). To fully realize the role of Slow Food in developing the food tourism niche in the Caribbean, there are several factors to be considered, such as the need for effective stakeholder cooperation and collaboration. This analysis accepts the view put forward by Jamal and Stronza (2009) where the authors concluded that stakeholder arrangements operating amid informal arrangements can be effective. This is as it relates to grassroots movements such as Slow Food, where a coordinated action is necessary for coalition building and collaborative arrangements to be realized. It is equally important that there is a clear and transparent process of evaluating development and full community participation of all stakeholders is enabled (Choi and Sirakaya 2006; Moscardo 2019; Van Niekerk and Getz 2019). This must be a facilitating factor when the sustainable tourism agenda wants to reflect the values and vision of stakeholders.

Other considerations for effective producer-consumer networks will require flexibility according to the unique context. Walker and Lee (2021) mention several potential barriers to adopting such an approach for small islands such as knowledge sharing and awareness, since local attributes, like being a marginalized location, or historical factors may have an influence on the seamless adaptability. While barriers may not be obvious, it is important to note that some approaches are successful in some contexts and not in others. Stakeholder challenges and the business climate in Caribbean small islands may also add to these barriers. This exploration also considers Caribbean SIDS as a group, yet in reality each island has a unique offering and developmental agendas would need to align with local stakeholders and resources at the destination. Realizing the discussed impacts of slowness in travel on food tourism in the Caribbean is therefore strongly reliant on operational stakeholder cooperation and collaboration.

The advent of slow food travel and slow cities, all consistent with the slow philosophy, leads to tourists actively engaging with a wider range of stakeholder groups and both receive mutual benefits that are different from the traditional economic and social model. Essentially, the aim should be to identify the dynamic aspects of the social economy in order to clearly identify spaces and places that can encourage a self-sustaining and inclusive form of economic life. Slow Food is a model of gastronomy that seeks to relocate food as the centre of human culture. Broadway (2015), as well as Schneider (2008) discussed how its model focuses on both the biological and cultural aspects of food production and consumption. This chapter also agrees with Schneider (2008), who argued that the Slow Food model links to older and familiar models of gastronomy like that of *The Physiology of Taste* by Jean Anthelme Brillat-Savarin (1986), as this model embodies not only the role of organic agriculture, preparation methods and taste, but also the cultural and economic dimensions of food. Here, Slow Food ambitiously exemplifies how globalism and even tourism itself can be exploited to protect the local cultures and traditions that are threatened by them. Slow Food and, by extension, slowness in travel, presents and facilitates an effective way for destinations to document their uniqueness. Destinations can use the producer-consumer network to highlight their local and regional stock of gastronomic assets with the Slow Food's vision of social and cultural values in the social economy (Pietrykowski 2004, 316; Williams et al. 2015).

When considering the practicability of the approach or the applicability of developing the food tourism niche, however, it is likewise significant to note contemporary consumer dynamics, as mentioned previously in this chapter. The elements of food tourism and Slow Food are similar, therefore they may work independently or together. The fundamental features of Slow Food offer a ready-made market of producers and consumers for a food tourism niche. Harvey (2010) reported that 86 per cent of travellers to the Caribbean from the United Kingdom source market seek out unique and memorable food and drink opportunities. This has led to an increasing number of chefs in the Caribbean partnering with local farms for a range of initiatives. They are experimenting with exotic tropical flavours and colours within typical Caribbean foods. Local stakeholders have also been able to add increasingly and innovatively to the value chain and build food processing linkages. Slow Food producers, restauranteurs and other stakeholders are able to share knowledge about local unique food, cuisines, producers and traditional production methods with consumers, and this adds value to the tourism product for consumers by enhancing visitor experience. It also adds value for host communities in SIDS based on the well-documented vulnerabilities of small islands (Apostolopoulos and Gayle 2002; Briguglio 1995; Kerr 2005; Scheyvens and Momsen 2008; Weaver 1995). The tourism literature has made notable references to the positive impact of the tourism industry on SIDS. Furthermore, small countries have made strong economic progress from the tourism industry compared to larger ones (Pratt 2015; Streeten 1993), yet for small islands with tight kinship networks and a strong sense of identity (Graci and Dodds 2010), smallness can also facilitate a more coordinated approach to sustainability by making it easier to adapt, innovate and remain flexible (Croes 2006). The slow pace of life that remains part of the Caribbean island lifestyle also makes slowness in travel a reality, left only to be put into practice by adopting sustainable initiatives that promote a sense of place, reflecting a better quality of life for residents and increased visitor experience.

Figure 7.3: Slow Food and Food Tourism Relationship

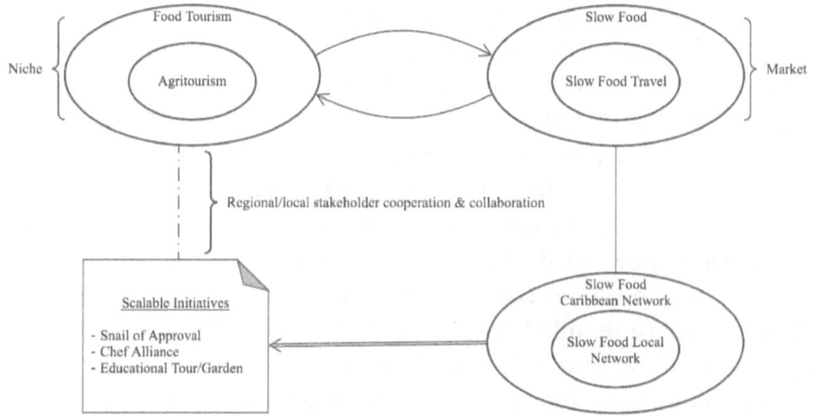

Tourism Planning and Future Research

The analysis presented in this chapter accepts the realities of agritourism in small islands (Addinsall et al. 2016; Anderson 2017; Hepburn 2013; Thomas, Moore and Edwards 2018). Research has revealed that there is dissatisfaction with the local food network in the Caribbean. If sectoral linkages that benefit communities are to be achieved, emphasis needs to be placed on boosting production capacity, increasing local food production and improving the way that local food is supplied and marketed (Rhiney 2011). This exploration of Slow Food, slowness in travel and food tourism in the Caribbean takes these barriers into consideration also while pointing to opportunities. It is for this reason that this chapter recommends a practical approach to leveraging the global success of Slow Food initiatives to support food tourism using regional and local Slow Food networks (Lin 2020; Jung et al. 2015; Lee, Packer and Scott 2015). Here, challenges of supply and demand and the producer-consumer interface will need to be addressed by continuous adaptation and innovation within the local food network. Islands may identify competitive advantages and foster a cooperative environment where key stakeholders can collaborate effectively and innovate within these small yet tight networks, which will allow for flexibility. Building on and learning from local Slow Food initiatives may provide opportunities for pilot projects that can be later scaled within or outside of the producer-consumer network. This can be aligned with existing agritourism or food tourism hotspots for visibility and should be developed to capture as many stakeholders across the dynamic industry as possible.

Effective stakeholder participation and collaboration is central to this approach and, while this chapter explores a framework for stakeholder participation, the relationship between stakeholders and effective collaboration is more complex than the literature presented in this chapter has recognized. Further research will help to clarify the relationship between various actors and provide further awareness in how local attributes, market forces and public policy decisions may influence the success of initiatives related to Slow Food tourism. A more detailed assessment of Slow Food initiatives in the Caribbean will provide additional insights and, in order to overcome the knowledge gaps for prospective slow destinations, primary data will prove useful in capturing the views of the food tourism market. Insights from existing agritourism and food tourism hotspots can give a deeper understanding of the possibilities and challenges of such an approach. It will also offer an informed way forward from isolated pilot projects to scalable initiatives.

References

Addinsall, C., P. Scherrer, B. Weiler, and K. Glencross. 2016. "An Ecologically and Socially Inclusive Model of Agritourism to Support Smallholder Livelihoods in the South Pacific." *Asia Pacific Journal of Tourism Research* 22 (3): 301–15.

Anderson, K. 2017. "Tourism and Global Logistics Hub Development in the Caribbean: Will there be a Symbiotic Relationship?" *Worldwide Hospitality and Tourism Themes* 9:105–15.

Apostolopoulos, Y., and D.J. Gayle, eds. 2002. *Island Tourism and Sustainable Development: Caribbean, Pacific, and Mediterranean Experiences.* Westport, CT: Greenwood Publishing Group.

Baldemir, E., F. Kaya, and T.K. Sahin. 2013. "A Management Strategy within Sustainable City Context: Cittaslow." *Procedia – Social and Behavioral Sciences* 99:75–84.

Bélisle, F.J. 1983. "Tourism and Food Production in the Caribbean." *Annals of Tourism Research* 10 (4): 497–513.

Briguglio, L. 1995. "Small Island Developing States and their Economic Vulnerabilities." *World Development* 23 (9): 1615–32.

Brillat-Savarin, J.A. 1986. *The Physiology of Taste.* Translated by M.F.K. Fisher. New York: Heritage Press.

Broadway, M. 2015. "Implementing the Slow Life in Southwest Ireland: A Case Study of Clonakilty and Local Food." *Geographical Review* 105 (2): 216–34.

Choi, H.C., and E. Sirakaya. 2006. "Sustainability Indicators for Managing Community Tourism." *Tourism Management* 27:1274–89.

Chrzan, J. 2004. "Slow Food: What, Why, and to Where?" *Food, Culture and Society* 7 (2): 117–32.

Chung, J.Y., J.S. Kim, C. Lee, and M.J. Kim. 2017. "Slow-Food-Seeking Behaviour, Authentic Experience, and Perceived Slow Value of a Slow-Life Festival." *Current Issues in Tourism* 21 (2): 123–27.https://doi.org/10.1080/13683500.2017.1326470.

Conway, D., and B.F. Timms. 2010. "Re-branding Alternative Tourism in the Caribbean: The Case for 'Slow Tourism'." *Tourism and Hospitality Research* 10 (4): 329–44.

———. 2012. "Are Slow Travel and Slow Tourism Misfits, Compadres or Different Genres?" *Tourism Recreation Research* 37 (1): 71–76.

Croes, R.R. 2006. "A Paradigm Shift to a New Strategy for Small Island Economies: Embracing Demand Side Economics for Value Enhancement and Long-Term Economic Stability." *Tourism Management* 27 (3): 453–65.

De Grazia V. 2005. *Irresistible Empire. America's Advance through Twentieth-Century Europe.* Cambridge: Belknap Press.

Di Gregorio, D. 2017. "Place-based Business Models for Resilient Local Economies: Cases from Italian Slow Food, Agritourism and the *Albergo Diffuso.*" *Journal of Enterprising Communities: People and Places in the Global Economy* 11 (1): 113–128. https://doi.org/10.1108/JEC-02-2015-0016.

Donati, K. 2005. "The Pleasure of Diversity in Slow Food's Ethics of

Taste." *Food, Culture and Society* 8 (2): 227–42.
Dunlap, R. 2012. "Recreating Culture: Slow Food as a Leisure Education Movement." *World Leisure Journal* 54 (1): 38–47.
Du Rand, G.E., and E. Heath. 2006. "Towards a Framework for Food Tourism as an Element of Destination Marketing." *Current Issues in Tourism* 9 (3): 206–34.
Duval, D.T., and P.F. Wilkinson. 2004. "Tourism Development in the Caribbean: Meaning and Influences." In *Tourism in the Caribbean: Trends, Development, Prospects*, edited by D.T. Duval, 59–80. London and New York: Routledge.
Ellis, A., E. Park, S. Kim, and I. Yeoman. 2018. "What is Food Tourism?" *Tourism Management* 68:250–63.
Fischler, C. 1988. "Food, Self and Identity." *Social Science Information* 27 (2): 275–92.
Fontefrancesco M.F., and P. Corvo. 2019. "Slow Food: History and Activity of a Global Food Movement Toward SDG2." In *Zero Hunger. Encyclopedia of the UN Sustainable Development Goals*, edited by W. Leal Filho, A. Azul, L. Brandli, P. Özuyar, and Wall. Cham: Springer.
Frost, W., and J. Laing. 2014. "Communicating Persuasive Messages through Slow Food Festivals." *Journal of Vacation Marketing* 19 (1): 67–74.
Fullagar, S., K. Markwell, and E. Wilson. 2012. *Slow Tourism: Experiences and Mobilities*. Bristol: Channel View Publications.
Fusté-Forné, F., and T. Jamal. 2020. "Slow Food Tourism: An Ethical Microtrend for the Anthropocene." *Journal of Tourism Futures* 6 (3): 227–32. https://doi.org/10.1108/JTF-10-2019-0120
Graci, S., and R. Dodds. 2010. *Sustainable Tourism in Island Destinations*. London: Earthscan.
Gürsoy, I.T. 2021. "Slow Food Justice and Tourism: Tracing Karakılçık Bread in Seferihisar, Turkey." *Journal of Sustainable Tourism*, 29 (2–3): 467–87. https://doi.org/10.1080/09669582.2020.1770772.
Hall, C.M. 2006. "Introduction: Culinary Tourism and Regional Development: From Slow Food to Slow Tourism?" *Tourism Review International* 9: 303–5.
———, and L. Sharples. 2003. "The Consumption of Experiences or the Experience of Consumption? An Introduction to the Tourism of Taste." In *Food Tourism around the World*, edited by C.M. Hall, L. Sharples, R. Mitchell, N. Macionis, and B. Cambourne, 1–24. New York: Routledge.
———, and R. Mitchell. 2001. "Wine and Food Tourism." In *Special Interest Tourism*, edited by Norman Douglas, Ngaire Douglas and Ros Derrett, 307–29. Sydney: John Wiley and Sons.
Hahm, J., and K. Severt. 2018. "Importance of Destination Marketing on Image and Familiarity." *Journal of Hospitality and Tourism Insights* 1 (1): 37–53.
Harrison, D. 2001. "Islands, Image and Tourism." *Tourism Recreation Research* 26 (3): 9–14.
Harvey, E.C. 2010. "Strategic Plan for Regional Development (SPRD)." Background Study. Regional Agrotourism Policy. https://caricom.org/documents/9838-eharvey_agrotourism_study_final.pdf.

Hatipoglu, B. 2015. "'Cittaslow': Quality of Life and Visitor Experience." *Tourism Planning and Development* 12 (1): 20–36.

Hedges, S.B., R. Powell, R.W. Henderson, S. Hanson, and J.C. Murphy. 2019. "Definition of the Caribbean Islands Biogeographic Region, with Checklist and Recommendations for Standardized Common Names of Amphibians and Reptiles." *Caribbean Herpetology* 67:1–53.

Heitmann, S., P. Robinson, and G. Povey. 2011. "Slow Food, Slow Cities and Slow Tourism." In *Research Themes for Tourism*, edited by P. Robinson, S. Heitmann, and P. Dieke, 114–27. Wallingford: CAB International.

Hendrikx, B., S. Dormans, A. Lagendijk, and M. Thelwall. 2016. Understanding the Geographical Development of Social Movements: a Web-link Analysis of Slow Food. *Global Networks* 17 (1): 47–67. https://doi.org/10.1111/glob.12153.

Hepburn, E. 2013. "Investigating the Understanding, Interest and Options for Agri-Tourism to Promote Food Security in the Bahamas." Proceedings of the 30th West Indies Agricultural Economics Conference, 30 June–6 July 2013. Port of Spain, Trinidad. https://ideas.repec.org/p/ags/cars13/242079.html.

Hsu, E.L. 2014. "The Slow Food Movement and Time Shortage: Beyond the Dichotomy of Fast or Slow." *Journal of Sociology* 53 (3): 1–15.

Jamal, T., and A. Stronza. 2009. "Collaboration Theory and Tourism Practice in Protected Areas: Stakeholders, Structuring and Sustainability." *Journal of Sustainable Tourism* 17 (2):169–89.

Jeyacheya, J., and M.P. Hampton. 2020. "Wishful Thinking or Wise Policy? Theorising Tourism-Led Inclusive Growth: Supply Chains and Host Communities." *World Development* 131. https://doi.org/10.1016/j.worlddev.2020.104960.

Jones, J., P. Shears., D. Hillier, D. Comfort, and J. Lowell. 2003. "Return to Traditional Values? A Case Study of Slow Food." *British Food Journal* 105 (4/5): 297–304.

Jung, T., E. Ineson, M. Kim, and M. Yap. 2015. "Influence of Festival Attribute Qualities on Slow Food Tourists' Experience, Satisfaction Level and Revisit Intention: The Case of the Mold Food and Drink Festival." *Journal of Vacation Marketing* 21:277–88.

Jung, T.H., E.M. Ineson, and A. Miller. 2014. "The Slow Food Movement and Sustainable Tourism Development: A Case Study of Mold, Wales." *International Journal of Culture, Tourism and Hospitality Research* 8 (4): 432–45.

Kerr, S.A. 2005. "What is Small Island Sustainable Development About." *Ocean and Coastal Management* 48:503–24.

Koo, C., L. Mendes Filho, and D. Buhalis. 2019. "Smart Tourism and Competitive Advantage for Stakeholders." *Tourism Review* 74 (1): 1–4.

Laudan, R. 2004. "Slow Food: The French Terroir Strategy, and Culinary Modernism." *Food, Culture and Society* 7 (2): 133–44.

Lee, K., N. Scott, and J. Packer. 2014. "Habitus and Food Lifestyle: In-destination Activity Participation of Slow Food Members." *Annals of Tourism Research* 48:207–20. https://doi.org/10.1016/j.annals.2014.06.009.

Lee, K., J. Packer, and N. Scott. 2015. "Travel Lifestyle Preferences and Destination Activity Choices of Slow Food Members and Non-Members." *Tourism Management* 46:1–10.

Lee, K.H. 2021. "Slow Food Movement." In *The Routledge Handbook of Gastronomic Tourism*, edited by S. K. Dixit, 377–84. New York: Routledge.

Leer, J. 2020. "Designing Sustainable Food Experiences: Rethinking Sustainable Food Tourism." *International Journal of Food Design* 5 (1&2): 65–82.

Leitch, A. 2000. "The Social Life of Lardo." *The Asia Pacific Journal of Anthropology* 1 (1): 103–18.

Lewis, S., and C. Lewis. 2012. *A Taste of Paradise: A Feast of Authentic Caribbean Cuisine and Refreshing Tropical Beverages for Health and Vitality*. Carabelle, Florida: Psy Press.

Lin, L. 2017. "Industrial Tourists' Behavioral Intention Toward Slow Travel in Taiwan." *Journal of Sustainable Tourism* 25 (3): 379–96. https://doi.org/10.1080/09669582.2016.1213848.

Lin, Y. 2020. "Sustainable Food, Ethical Consumption and Responsible Innovation: Insights from the Slow Food and 'Low Carbon Food' Movements in Taiwan." *Food, Culture and Society* 23 (2): 155–72. https://doi.org/10.1080/15528014.2019.1682885.

Lotti, A. 2010. "The Commoditization of Products and Taste: Slow Food and the Conservation of Agrobiodiversity." *Agriculture and Human Values* 27:71–83.

Matthews, L., D. Scott, J. Andrey, R. Mahon, A. Trotman, R. Burrowes and A. Charles. 2021. "Developing Climate Services for Caribbean Tourism: A Comparative Analysis of Climate Push and Pull Influences using Climate Indices." *Current Issues in Tourism* 24 (11): 1576–94.

Mayer, H., and P. Knox. 2006. "Slow Cities: Sustainable Places in a Fast World." *Journal of Urban Affairs* 28 (4): 321–34.

———. 2009. "Pace of Life and Quality of Life: The Slow City Charter." In *Community Quality-of-Life Indicators: Best Cases III*, edited by M. J. Sirgy, R. Phillips and D. R. Rahtz, 21–40. New York: Springer Science and Business Media.

McElroy, J.L. 2003. "Tourism Development in Small Islands Across the World." *Geografiska Annaler: Series B, Human Geography* 85 (4): 231–42. https://doi.org/10.1111/j.0435-3684.2003.00145.x.

Miele, M., and J. Murdoch. 2002. "The Practical Aesthetics of Traditional Cuisines: Slow Food in Tuscany." *Sociologia Ruralis* 42 (4): 313–338. https://doi.org/10.1111/1467-9523.00219.

Montanari, A., and B. Staniscia. 2009. "Culinary Tourism as a Tool for Regional Re-Equilibrium." *European Planning Studies* 17 (10):1463–83.

Montero, C.G. 2014. "Tourism, Cuisine, and the Consumption of Culture in the Caribbean." In *The Routledge History of Food*, edited by C. Helstosky, 291–312. London and New York: Routledge.

Moon, H., and H. Han. 2018. "Destination Attributes Influencing Chinese Travelers' Perceptions of T Experience Quality and Intentions for Island Tourism: A Case of Jeju Island." *Tourism Management Perspectives* 28:71–82.

Moscardo, G. 2019. Rethinking the Role and Practice of Destination Community Involvement in Tourism Planning. In *Tourism Policy and Planning Implementation: Issues and Challenges*, edited by K. Andriotis, D. Stylidis, and A. Weidenfeld, 36–52. New York: Routledge.

Munjal, S., S. Sharma, and P. Menon. 2016. "Moving Towards 'Slow Food', the New Frontier of Culinary Innovation in India The Vedatya Experience." *Worldwide Hospitality and Tourism Themes* 8 (4): 444–60.

Nilsson, H.J., A.C. Svärd,, Å. Widarsson, and T. Wirell. 2011. "'Cittáslow' Eco-Gastronomic Heritage as a Tool for Destination Development." *Current Issues in Tourism* 14 (4): 373–86.

Okumus, F., G. Kock, M.G. Scantlebury, and B. Okumus. 2013. "Using Local Cuisines when Promoting Small Caribbean Island Destinations." *Journal of Travel and Tourism Marketing* 30 (4): 410–29.

Paxson, H. 2005. "Slow Food in a Fat Society: Satisfying Ethical Appetites." *Gastronomica* 5 (1): 14–18.

Payandeh, E., M.S. Allahyari, M.F. Fontefrancesco, and J. Surujlale. 2020. "Good vs. Fair and Clean: An Analysis of Slow Food Principles Toward Gastronomy Tourism in Northern Iran." *Journal of Culinary Science and Technology* 20 (1): 51–70. https://doi.org/10.1080/15428052.2020.1808136.

Peano, C., P. Migliorini, and F. Sottile. 2014. "A Methodology for the Sustainability Assessment of Agri-Food Systems: An Application to the Slow Food Presidia Project." *Ecology and Society* 19 (4): 24. http://dx.doi.org/10.5751/ES-06972-190424.

Pezzi, M., A. Faggian, and N. Reid. 2021. *Agritourism, Wine Tourism, and Craft Beer Tourism: Local Responses to Peripherality Through Tourism Niches*. New York: Routledge.

Pietrykowski, B. 2004. "You are What You Eat: The Social Economy of the Slow Food Movement." *Review of Social Economy* 62 (3): 307–321.

Pollan, M. 2003. "Cruising on the Ark of Taste." *Mother Jones* (Mane): 75–77.

Pratt, S. 2015. "The Economic Impact of Tourism in SIDS." *Annals of Tourism Research* 52:148–60.

Punnett, B.J., and A. Morrison. 2006. Niche Markets and Small Caribbean Producers: A Match Made in Heaven? *Journal of Small Business and Entrepreneurship* 19 (4): 341–53.

Rhiney, K. 2011. Agritourism Linkages in Jamaica: Case Study of the Negril All-Inclusive Hotel Subsector. In *Tourism and Agriculture: New Geographies of Consumption, Production and Rural Restructuring*, edited by R.M. Torres and J. H. Momsen, 119–39. New York: Routledge.

———, T. Walker, and J. Tomlinson. 2015. "Study on Agribusiness Development – Strengthening Agritourism Potential in the Caribbean." The Technical Centre for Agricultural and Rural Cooperation and the Inter-American Institute for Cooperation on Agriculture. https://www.ceintelligence.com/files/documents/AgritourismReportPrintReadyDraftJune18.pdf.

Sassatelli, R., and F. Davolio. 2010. "Consumption, Pleasure and Politics:

Slow Food and the Politico-Aesthetic Problematization of Food." *Journal of Consumer Culture* 10 (2): 202–32.

Scheyvens, R., and J. Momsen. 2008. "Tourism in Small Island States: From Vulnerability to Strengths." *Journal of Sustainable Tourism* 16 (5): 491–510.

Schneider, S. 2008. "Good, Clean, Fair: The Rhetoric of the Slow Food Movement." *College English* 70 (4): 384–402.

Sheller, M. 2021. "Reconstructing Tourism in the Caribbean: Connecting Pandemic Recovery, Climate Resilience and Sustainable Tourism through Mobility Justice." *Journal of Sustainable Tourism* 29 (9): 1436–49.

Sidali, K.L., A. Spiller, and B. Schulze, eds. 2011. *Food, Agri-Culture and Tourism: Linking Local Gastronomy and Rural Tourism: Interdisciplinary Perspectives.* Berlin: Springer.

Slow Food. n.d. "About us, Our History." Accessed 24 June 2021. https://www.slowfood.com/about-us/our-history/.

———. n.d. "Slow Food Presidia." Accessed 21 August 2021. https://www.fondazioneslowfood.com/en/what-we-do/slow-food-presidia/.

———. n.d. "Slow Food Travel." Accessed 21 August 2021. https://www.slowfood.com/what-we-do/themes/slow-food-travel/.

Slow Food Barbados. n.d. "Our Initiatives." Accessed 21 August 2021. https://www.slowfoodbarbados.org/our-initiatives.

Snyder, F., Z. Hu, and X. Zheng. 2018. "Slow Food in Europe, the USA and China: A Comparative Perspective." *Peking University School of Transnational Law Research Paper* 18-6. https://dx.doi.org/10.2139/ssrn.3167906.

Streeten, P. 1993. "The Special Problems of Small Countries." *World Development* 21 (2): 197–202.

Tam, D. 2008. "Slow Journeys: What Does It Mean to Go Slow?" *Food, Culture and Society* 11 (2): 207–18.

Thomas, A., A. Moore, and E. Edwards. 2018. "Feeding Island Dreams: Exploring the Relationship between Food Security and Agritourism in the Caribbean." *Island Studies Journal* 13 (2): 145–62.

Van Niekerk, M., and D. Getz. 2019. *Event Stakeholders: Theory and Methods for Event Management and Tourism.* Oxford: Goodfellow Publishers.

Van Sandt, A., D. Thilmany, and R. Hill. 2021. "Targeting Agritourism to Leverage the Unique Natural Resource Base and Heritage of the Rural West." In *Agritourism, Wine Tourism, and Craft Beer Tourism: Local Responses to Peripherality Through Tourism Niche*, edited by M. Pezzi, A. Faggian, and N. Reid, 15–30. New York: Routledge.

Walker, T.B. 2020. "A Review of Sustainability, Tourism and the Marketing Opportunity for Adopting the Cittaàslow Model in Pacific Small Islands." *Tourism Review International* 23 (3–4): 99–114.

———, and T.J. Lee. 2021. "Contributions to Sustainable Tourism in Small Islands: An Analysis of the Cittaàslow Movement." *Tourism Geographies* 23 (3): 415–35.

———, T.J. Lee, and C. Li. 2021. "Sustainable Development for Small

Island Tourism: Developing Slow Tourism in the Caribbean." *Journal of Travel and Tourism Marketing* 38 (1): 1–15.

Weaver, D.B. 1995. "Alternative Tourism in Montserrat." *Tourism Management* 16 (8): 593–604.

Werner, K., K. Griese, and C. Bosse. 2020. "The Role of Slow Events for Sustainable Destination Development: A Conceptual and Empirical Review." *Journal of Sustainable Tourism* 29 (11–12): 1913–31. https://doi.org/10.1080/09669582.2020.1800021.

Williams, L., J. Germov, S. Fuller, and M. Freij. 2015. "A Taste of Ethical Consumption at a Slow Food Festival." *Appetite* 91:321–28. https://doi.org/10.1016/j.appet.2015.04.066.

Williams, E.H., and L. Bunkley-Williams. 2021. "What and Where is the Caribbean? A Modern Definition." *The Florida Geographer* 52 (1): 3–28.

8.
Examining the Case of Volcano Tourism in Montserrat, British West Indies

Ineta R. West-Gerald

Introduction

Vacations, holidays, annual leave, whatever you call them on your side of the world, chances are you want to use them to travel, usually abroad, to take a break and experience something new. Tourism options are as extensive as the world is vast and offer something for everyone. No surprise then that sun-lust to sun-plus is the new rave. Most people often associate a dream vacation in the Caribbean with sun, sea and sand. Individuals from many of the wealthier nations such as Europe, the United States of America and Canada often opt for foreign travel, usually in regions with a warmer climate. However, many persons, particularly Millennials, Generations Y and Z, are looking for more than just the sun or visiting a sandy beach; they now want more out of their vacation. Many countries have recognized this trend and have started to think outside the box about ways to increase their appeal, stay ahead of the curve and be more competitive.

Adventure tourism has long been attractive to tourists, with many tourists visiting the over fifteen hundred active volcanoes worldwide (Cooper and Cooper 2015). Many people find volcanoes fascinating because of their unpredictability and unique landforms (Cooper and Cooper 2015) and as such, countries like Iceland and Italy have capitalized on this interest. Notably, when Iceland's volcano famously erupted in 2010, "the Eyjafjallajökull eruption led to a booming economy" (Troxler 2020) and the country saw an increase in visitors who wanted to get up close and personal with that natural wonder.

Travelling to a destination to fulfil a bucket list wish will always be an intriguing proposition. This gives travellers an opportunity to fulfil a long-term dream that sometimes feels unattainable but, when achieved, makes it even more rewarding. So why the hype about volcano tourism? Awe-inspiring, breathtaking and beautiful but deadly are some of the words used to describe volcanoes – natural geological formations which can erupt and cause much distress, including social and scientific upheaval for many. However, for others, a volcanic eruption presents the perfect backdrop to study and understand the dynamic process. For yet others, it is the place to be to enjoy these truly awesome, natural phenomena. This chapter seeks to examine the case of volcano tourism in Montserrat and why this niche is gaining popularity and can perhaps be used to diversify the markets of other Caribbean islands with volcanoes.

The Caribbean has long been promoted as a sun, sea and sand destination for obvious reasons, as noted in chapter one. It has been blessed with near perfect year-round temperatures and beautiful beaches. But the Caribbean has so much more to offer, including different cultures, food, history and traditions, to name a few. In analysing this niche, it is important to highlight the motivation for travel and the recent travel trends that are emerging due to changes in tastes and perceptions. According to Poon (1993), travellers are seeking more personalized and experiential holidays and outdoor activities as well as health and wellness and eco-tourism activities, including volcano activities.

Competition from Other Destinations

Most Caribbean islands offer the sun, sea and sand element, and many also have volcanoes. What then makes Montserrat stand out from the crowd? Montserrat is a quaint, relaxed, modern-day Pompeii fused with Afro-Irish charm. However, there is competition from other volcanic destinations, often claiming to have the most active or most recent volcanic activity, thus increasing their visibility which makes them more topical and thus allowing them to trend more readily. The last volcanic eruption in Montserrat occurred in 2010. However, while the volcano remains active, much of the hype about the volcano ended shortly after 2010.

St Vincent's volcano erupted in 2021 and has been trending, soon to be replaced by another that is seen as more current and perhaps more captivating. However, St Vincent will stand to benefit in the long term based on how they wish to pursue volcano tourism. On the other hand, St Lucia also has an active volcano and boasts the world's only drive-in volcano, which sets them apart. It is noted therefore that what is important is how the destination continues to stay ahead of the curve while its volcano goes through the different phases. Understanding what motivates travellers and how to adapt to changes is paramount. As Crouch and Ritchie (2006) put it, competition between destinations is important as it plays a critical role in shaping the global tourism industry. This is also critical in shaping the local economy. Competition increases creativity and creativity is required to satisfy changing tastes. Tourism destinations are therefore becoming more competitive as more and more destinations are looking to tourism as a new economic generator, replacing agriculture, mining and manufacturing.

Literature Review

What is Volcano Tourism?

Cooper and Erfurt-Cooper (2010) define volcano tourism as the exploration and study of active volcanic and geothermal landforms and processes. This includes visits to dormant and extinct volcanic regions where remnants of activity attract visitors with an interest in geological heritage. They added that when combined with a special geodiversity, volcano tourism offers an extensive range of outdoor activities including the opportunity for education about geoheritage as well as an insight into volcanoes' significant value for regional culture, religion and history. They further added that the importance of volcanic and geothermal environments to the tourism sector have been recognized with the development of volcano-based national parks and, more recently, national and global geoparks.

The examples given here imply that volcanic tourism is not new. Indeed, volcanic and geothermal activity have attracted tourists across locations for centuries, as in the case of Mt. Vesuvius, which erupted in Italy in AD 79 and engulfed the city of Pompeii and which continues to attract visitors even today. Other countries, such as Japan, Hawaii, the Philippines, the United States of America, Iceland and many others, attract millions of visitors per year to witness these natural spectacles.

Types of Volcanoes

Each year, volcanic eruptions occur in different countries across the globe. They are unpredictable and can cause loss of life and livelihoods. Grattan and Torrence (2007) highlighted the negative impacts of volcanoes on communities including physical, economic, social, cultural and environmental consequences affecting climate and ecology.

Volcanoes are either active, dormant or extinct. An active volcano is one that is presently erupting or is expected to erupt. A dormant volcano is one that is not erupting or predicted to erupt in the near future. An extinct volcano is one which has not erupted for thousands of years, and there is no possibility of another eruption (Erfurt-Cooper and Cooper 2010). There are four types of volcanoes – cinder cones, composite [stratovolcanoes], shield volcanoes and lava domes. All of these types of volcanoes are different and are known to have attracted visitors.

In the Caribbean region there are nineteen active volcanoes, seven of which are in Dominica, two within and one off the cost of Grenada, one in Guadeloupe, one in Martinique, one in Montserrat, one in Nevis, one in St Kitts, one in Saba, one in St Lucia, one in St Vincent and one in St Eustatius (https://www.caribbeanandco.com/active-volcanoes-in-the-caribbean/"Active Volcanoes In The Caribbean | Caribbean & Co.(caribbeanandco.com)). These nineteen volcanoes are of different types. The volcano on Montserrat is a stratovolcano, a conical buildup of many layers of hardened lava with periodic explosive eruptions, including pyroclastic flows (a fast-moving current of hot gas and volcanic matter) (MVO n.d.).

Motivation and Volcano Tourism

Island tourism is important to visitors as islands are considered exotic, attractive, appealing and different. Butler (1993) argues that island appeal may relate to the feeling of separateness and difference that islands have. When pursuing leisure, people desire what is different, and different climates, physical environments and cultures increase the attractiveness of islands as tourism destinations.

With volcanic eruptions so dangerous and destructive, it remains intriguing to determine the motivation to travel to volcanic destinations. Travelling to experience the thrill of volcanoes has been booming most recently because of social media. Visitors seek out photogenic areas which they capture and post online so that others can view their enviable videos and photos on Facebook, YouTube and Instagram, whether they are similarly motivated or not.

Different types of volcanoes and their levels of activity will attract different types of visitors. What motivates this type of travel is related to push factors, which Gnoth (1997) describes as internal motives or forces that cause tourists to seek activities to reduce their needs, and pull factors, which link to destination-generated forces and the knowledge that tourists have about a destination. Several articles point to the push and pull factors of volcano tourism and highlight the demographics of this market segment, including age and gender, as key to determining who these visitors are and how they are motivated to to travel. Robinson (1970) argues that there are seven reasons why people are motivated to travel in general. Four of those reasons link with this chapter: relaxation and refreshment of body and mind, health, pleasure, and curiosity and culture. Geologic heritage linked to culture and natural heritage, including landscapes, formations and geological sites, tie in with volcano tourism and are added reasons for people to travel as highlighted by Robinson (1970), and Erfurt-Cooper and Cooper (2010) cemented this and added that people are motivated to visit volcanic and geothermal areas for sightseeing, scientific interest, photography, field research and curiosity as well as for documentaries, collection of data and collection of rocks (if permitted). They may also visit on educational trips, guided tours or study tours. They added that understanding volcano tourists, including their motivations, is an important step towards explaining why individuals participate in leisure and recreational activities in volcanic environments.

The element of risk does not seem to deter people from visiting destinations with volcanoes, which becomes evident when people camp at the bases of volcanoes to get a first-hand view of these geological phenomena or even take a fly-over tour of active volcanoes.

Changes in Consumer Tastes Shape Travel Trends

A notable change in travel tastes and trends has been emerging for a number of years. As people are becoming better educated and gaining more travel experience, their taste also changes. Plummer (1989) explains that many developed Western nations are in the midst of a change in their basic value structures, perhaps even a paradigm shift or reordering of the way they see the world around them. There is greater value placed on experience, which in turn is promoting the growth of travel, lifelong education, the arts and sports (Plummer 1989, 13). This general tendency towards changes in lifestyle has implications for special interest tourism in general and for educational travel in particular. As summarized by Schwaninger (1989), there is a decrease of physically and culturally passive forms of vacations in favour of more active pastimes, a shift towards custom-made holidays and an emergence of new specialized markets and market segments.

Poon (1993, 92), a leading commentator on future trends in tourism, predicted the emergence of "new" tourism over "old" tourism.

She foresaw the movement away from sun-lust and towards sun-plus tourism, environmental pressures, technology and changing consumer tastes. Similarly, Krippendorf (1987, 39) suggested that the travel market would emphasize the environmental and social context within which tourism occurs and the humanization of travel. Since then, the evidence has supported Krippendorf's (1987) analysis of changing consumer patterns, which have given rise to new patterns in holiday taking. Helber (1988, 21) also reported a trend towards "experience oriented" holidays with an emphasis on action, adventure, fantasy, nostalgia and exotic experiences.

From all accounts, volcano tourism is linked to many new tourism trends, which many scholars described as active, special interest and educational. However, there is a level of risk associated with this niche.

Risks as Part of Adventure Travel

When there is adventure there will always be risks, and one could argue that visiting an active volcano carries significant risks due to their unpredictability. Natural disasters have very destructive properties and a major impact on the local economies of small islands (Strobl 2012). Risk, which is identified as the possibility of danger, injury or loss, is associated with any natural disaster. Volcanic risks are real and differ from volcanic hazards. Risk management is important to mitigate and reduce these risks. Wilson and Crouch (1987, 267) stated that "the essence of risk assessment is the application of past mistakes (and deliberate actions) in an attempt to prevent new mistakes in new situations". Managing risks therefore allows adventure tourism to thrive by reducing the risk to a level that visitors and authorities are comfortable with so that they are willing to participate in these activities.

Why Seek Risk in Tourism?

Adventure travel is categorized as the deliberate seeking of risk and danger, and Morgan (1998) claimed that tourists seeking adventure holidays are often drawn to activities that involve risk, excitement, fun and challenge. This challenge is an important motivator in outdoor recreation and is regarded as an important factor in risk recreation (Iso-Ahola 1980; Johnston 1987). Challenge in this sense can be related to the concept of flow, or that special feeling (adrenaline rush) that occurs when the abilities of the individual meet the demands of an activity or situation (Hall 1992). Johnston (1987, 152) argues that it is the desire to experience flow that provides the central motivation for individuals wanting to participate in adventure activities.

Volcanoes are unpredictable and the potential for disaster is very real. Visitors risk experiencing unexpected eruptions, pyroclastic flows, toxic gas, lava flows and mud flows. However, visitors knowingly visit these dangerous areas in their quest to satisfy their curiosity, signalling the need for risk prevention programmes. It can be summed up therefore that adventure seekers are generally risk takers but, while this is so, they often require safety, which points to the need to manage the adventure tourism experience and take into account participants' safety, skills and abilities.

The Montserrat Concept

Background

Montserrat is a British Overseas Territory and is part of the Lesser Antilles Chain in the Leeward Islands, located in the Caribbean. It was once the playground of a number of celebrities, including Sting, Paul McCartney, members of Dire Straits, Stevie Wonder and a host of others who visited the island to record their music in the early 1980s at the famed Montserrat Air Studios. It has near perfect year-round temperatures but is also known for the active Soufrière Hills volcano and its eruptions. The island is located 27 miles (43 kilometres) southwest of Antigua and 30 miles (50 kilometres) northwest of Guadeloupe. The island is mountainous and volcanic in origin and covers an area of only 39 square miles (102 square kilometres). In addition to the active Soufriere Hills Volcano in the south, there are three extinct volcanic centres: the Silver Hills and the Centre Hills in the north of the island and the South Soufriere Hills at its southern tip. The island's vegetation ranges from rainforest to coastal scrub and woodland with a variety of flora and fauna, including one endemic species of bird, the Montserrat oriole, which is the national bird of Montserrat.

Due to the landscape of the island, Montserrat's tourism product is based mainly on attractive scenery with soaring mountainscapes, ebony sand beaches, virgin forests and an unspoilt environment. Montserrat has been promoted as the Emerald Isle of the Caribbean because of its links with and similar coastline to Ireland. Its tourism appeal is based on its greenery and is describe as the "quintessence of the way the Caribbean ued to be", uncrowded, unspoilt and laid back. Because of this, less emphasis has been placed on the typical sun, sea and sand narrative of most Caribbean islands, emphasizing more nature-related activities 2015–25 (Tourism Intelligence International, 2019).

The Disaster and Its Effects on the Island

Like many other Caribbean islands, Montserrat has experienced a number of disasters, the most recent of which are Hurricane Hugo in 1989 and the eruption of the Soufrière Hills volcano in the southern part of the island it began in 1995. Following a three and a half year period of occasional earthquake swarms observed from 1992 (Ambeh and Lynch 1996), the first visible signs of volcanic unrest occurred on 18 July 1995 with a small phreatic steam and ash eruption at Soufrière Hills (MVO n.d.). This unusual activity prompted a team of scientists from the Seismic Research Unit (SRU) based in Trinidad to visit Montserrat. They carried out inspections and discovered a volcanic event (MVO n.d.). Known as a potentially active volcano from the 1930s, Soufriere Hills has since been monitored remotely from the UK and then from the Seismic Research Unit (SRU) based in Trinidad. However, this unusual activity prompted the deployment of a team of SRU volcanologists in Montserrat, followed by visits of many other scientists mostly from the the United Kingdom and the United States.

Shortly after the volcanic activity started, the Montserrat Volcano Observatory (MVO), which now houses a team of scientists who monitor the volcano twenty-four hours a day, was established. A Volcanic Risk Map was developed and published, dividing the island into zones that were classified as safe, unsafe, danger and exclusion. This also included Maritime zones (MVO n.d.). There were several iterations of the Risk Map over the years with the zones later changing to northern, daytime entry (central) and exclusion. A new Hazard Level System was developed in 2014 and is currently in use (MVO n.d.)

The authorities also implemented an early warning siren system to warn the public of imminent danger and provided regular volcanic updates on the local radio station.

The eruptions prompted a number of early evacuations to the northern part of the island in 1995, the first of which were from the eastern and southern villages and Plymouth, the capital. These evacuations were short-lived as residents were allowed to return to their homes five months later. This was again disrupted by a series of eruptions. Major pyroclastic flows accompanied by heavy ash, the release of stones or projectiles, gas and lahars (mud flows)

Figure 8.1: Volcanic Hazard Zones – Montserrat, 2014

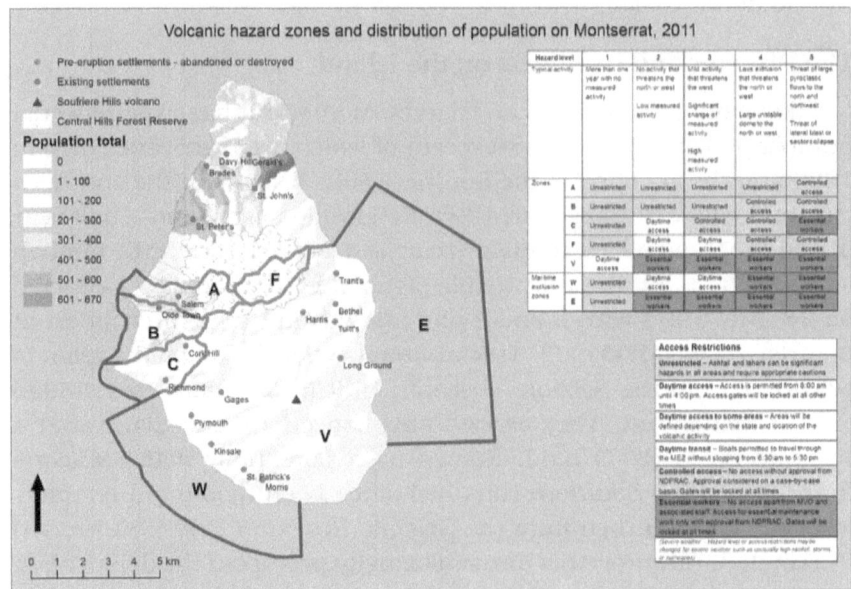

Source: Montserrat Volcano Observatory n.d.

accompanied by lightning and thunder destroyed nine villages, including Plymouth, the capital. The airport was destroyed on 21 September 1997 and, on 26 December 1997, a large pyroclastic flow destroyed the southwestern sector of the island (MVO n.d.). Again in 2003, the largest recorded collapse of an active volcanic dome occurred at Soufrière Hills, when about 210 million cubic meters (275 million cubic yards) of dome rock slid away over an eighteen-hour period. This event triggered large pyroclastic flows that swept into the sea causing new land to form and thus increasing the size of the island.

During these periods of activity, the mountain also went through a phase of glowing, which many classified as a truly memorable and awe-inspiring spectacle. The glowing of the lava dome is referred to as incandescent and occurs as a result of materials pushing to the surface of the dome (MVO n.d.). It is the first years (1995–97) of the eruption that had the most impacts on Montserrat's society – its economy, demographics and also on the landscape and accessible areas. The Soufriere Hills last dome collapse and explosion occurred in 2010. While there are currently no explosive events, the volcano continues to be active with occasional gas and steam and has been for the past twenty-eight years.

Figure 8.2: Volcanic Eruption

Photo credit: MVO n.d.

The Effects of the Volcano on the Tourism Sector in the Early Years

The series of volcanic eruptions from 1995 to 2010 caused destruction to parts of the island. This resulted in the island receiving a lot of attention and publicity, both negative and positive, which significantly affected the tourism industry for several years.

Tourism plays an important role in the national economy as an earner of foreign exchange. It was estimated to contribute approximately 25 per cent to gross domestic product annually in 1993 and generated approximately EC$52m (US$19.3m) (Montserrat Tourist Board 1994). The island was also enjoying a steady growth of arrivals at an average rate of 17 per cent annually since 1992, with just over thirty-six thousand visitors by the end of 1994 (Ministry of Finance and Economic Development 1995). Unemployment was also at its lowest, and the small business sector was making a significant contribution to the development of the island. With the onset of volcanic activity in 1995, the island began to experience a reversal to this trend. As of 31 December 1995, overall visitor arrivals decreased by 18.4 per cent as compared to 1994 (Ministry of Finance and Economic Development 1996). Later figures showed the decrease of tourism expenditure from US$25m in 1995 to US$3.6m in 1997, a drop of 86 per cent (Ministry of Finance and Economic Development 1998).

The accommodation sector offered 1,417 rooms of various types and categories with emphasis on villas and apartments. This made up 79 per cent of total room capacity with the traditional full-service hotels accounting for only 8 per cent of room stock (Gernott 1994) Many of these accommodations remain inaccessible due to their location in the Exclusion or Day Time Entry Zones. Restaurants were destroyed as were many man-made and natural sites, including the Belham Valley Golf Course, the Great Alps Waterfall, Galways Soufrière and Hot Water Pond, which was once used to provide mineral baths and valuable hiking and biking trails. Scores of homes and landmarks lay buried under upwards of thirty feet of ash in some areas. The destruction of Plymouth led to the coining of the descriptor the modern-day Pompeii, with the disaster being likened to the eruption of Mount Vesuvius in Italy in AD 79 and its effects on Pompeii. Both ports of entry to the city were inaccessible, which prompted new modes of transport into and out of the island, including a high-speed ferry and helicopter service (Montserrat Tourist Board 1997).

British Embassies and High Commissions issued warnings about travelling to Montserrat, which led to airlines, tour operators and cruise companies taking Montserrat off their reservations systems (Montserrat Tourist Board 1997). The eruptions rendered two-thirds of the island a maritime exclusion zone, which extends one mile offshore. This led to mass migration of the population where more than seven thousand residents left the island to settle in other Caribbean islands, the United States or the United Kingdom.

Motivation for Visiting the Island before the Eruptions

In the past, Montserrat was marketed to soft adventure enthusiasts who enjoyed hiking, biking, birding, diving and golfing. This was based on the attributes the island possessed. According to the Montserrat Visitor Survey (1993/1994), the peace and quiet, its outstanding natural attractions and the friendliness of the population were visitors' main reasons for choosing Montserrat. Other reasons, such as sightseeing and sun, sea and sand were also influential in the decision-making process. Additionally, the island is located off the beaten track, making it a unique holiday getaway and adding to its appeal. The main market for Montserrat was the United States, with the Caribbean following closely behind, followed by the United Kingdom, Canada, Europe and the rest of the world. The cruise market also accounted for about 50 per cent of the market (Gernott 1994).

Reasons for Visiting the Island Post Volcanic Eruptions

Motivation for travelling to a destination differs from individual to individual. Primary research carried out by the author five years after the volcanic eruptions started in 1995 to determine the motives for travelling to the island at that time revealed several interesting findings (West 2000/2001). A small sample of thirty questionnaires was randomly distributed to visitors to Montserrat at ports of entry and accommodations during Christmas 2000 and early January 2001, of which twenty-five questionnaires were completed and returned.

One of the questions targeted the factors involved in the decision to visit Montserrat. Respondents rated "visiting friends and relatives" the highest, followed by "previous visit", then "peace and quiet", followed by "attractions" then "volcano tourism" and finally "sun and beaches". These responses might be due to the number of repeat visitors to the island, many of whom were of the "visiting friends and relatives" market who would have been familiar with the island and much of the activities already available. This might also be attributed to the fact that Montserrat is not a typical sun, sea and sand destination.

The same question was asked of people visiting a Caribbean destination in general and a very different response was noted. The majority of people rated "sun and beaches" the highest, followed closely by "natural attractions" then "other cultures and traditions", followed by "volcano tourism" and ending with "peace and quiet". It is important to note that even at that time, a small percentage of respondents regarded volcano tourism as a reason to visit the Caribbean. The same is true for the respondents who mentioned that the volcano was a deciding factor in travelling to Montserrat.

Persons were also asked if they had any fears about visiting Montserrat while the volcano was active and only 26 per cent of respondents had some reservations about visiting the island, while 74 per cent of respondents indicated that they were not very fearful about visiting the island at that time. This is important to note as later in the research, 100 per cent of participants indicated that they would recommend Montserrat as a holiday destination, even while the volcano was active.

Only a small sample of day trippers completed the questionnaire due to their short visit to the island. Because of this, it was difficult to measure the level of interest in volcano tourism from this market segment. However, the statistics point to a growing number of day trippers who travel to the island for a few hours mainly to view the volcano (Ministry of Finance and Economic Development 2001). During the period May 2010–June 2011, an Exit Survey Report was completed by the Montserrat Tourist Board. The survey revealed that "climate" and "beaches" were again rated the highest factors in the decision to visit Montserrat, followed by "volcano tourism" and "nature". Respondents were also asked to rate five main activities on the island they participated in during their stay. "Volcano viewing" was rated the highest, followed by "bird watching" and "festival and event", then "hiking" and ending with "diving and snorkelling". This suggests that while the volcano was not the deciding factor to visit the island, which might be due to the lack of positive promotions of that niche at the time, it was still considered a leading activity.

While it appears that tastes are changing from sun-lust to sun-plus (Poon 1993), travellers still regard the sun and beaches as important motivators. This might be due to a number of things like age of respondents, or they might be attributed to the push and pull factors identified by Dann (1981) and Gnoth (1997). Pull factors, positive attributes of an island like Montserrat with a relatively good climate all year round, beaches, beautiful landscapes and an active volcano, can help to entice people to visit the destination, along with push factors such as the poor climate in the source markets (United States, Canada and Europe). It follows therefore that the motive to travel to a Caribbean island might be linked to one or more aspect of conflicting desires, needs, tastes and dislikes, as identified by Wahab (1975).

Montserrat's Unique Selling Proposition

The Soufrière Hills volcano was identified by stakeholders as Montserrat's unique selling proposition during a planning workshop used to develop the Montserrat Tourism Strategy 2019–22. However, even before this was officially documented, visitors to the island already saw this as an emerging niche, as pointed out in the 2010

Survey (West 2011), which revealed that the volcano was the second most influential factor for visiting the island. It is also considered one of the most striking elements of Montserrat. What makes it so unique is the fact that the island is quite small, yet many people commune and live with the volcano, which makes real the concept of being one with nature. A wide cross section of the population has witnessed the eruptions and are able to provide real life accounts of the devastation to this day. Furthermore, the volcano has been active for more than twenty-eight years. During the explosive phases there were many reports and stories documented by renowned journalists. Montserrat was featured in publications like *National Geographic*, *Lonely Planet*, CNN, NBC and the *Independent*, to name a few. While there was some sensationalism in the reporting, many positive reviews and information circled about the island, helping to put Montserrat on the map.

Volcano Tourism on Montserrat

There are documents that point to the benefits of volcanoes and volcano tourism for many destinations, as previously highlighted. While visitor numbers to Montserrat are quite small, there is real potential for growth. As with all other destinations, visitor arrivals have declined dramatically due to the COVID-19 pandemic, however, with trends pointing to volcano tourism as a growing niche; the future looks bright for Montserrat post COVID-19, even while the volcano has moved out of its explosive stage.

The Volcano: An Opportunity for Growth

With residents confined to the northern third of the island, the least populated part of the island before the volcanic activity, the government of Montserrat saw the need to develop this area. Surface works on roads and drainage infrastructure were carried out throughout the northern part of the the island (Sustainable Development Plan). A new airport was opened in July 2005 to accommodate small Islander and Twin Otter aircrafts and a small jetty was constructed which provided services for cargo and pleasure crafts. An area for commerce was developed for banking and shopping in Brades and homes and government buildings were also constructed. A school was converted into a hospital and homes for the elderly were built. More schools were built along with restaurants and visitor accommodation.

One of the most important buildings to be constructed was the MVO, which is used to monitor the volcano. The volcano is monitored twenty-four hours a day, seven days a week and provides a level of comfort and safety to residents and visitors alike. Scientists work collaboratively with the Seismic Research Centre in Trinidad and Tobago and other scientists worldwide and provide weekly activity reports. They also carry out research and education and have been instrumental in the staging of several successful Volcano Conferences on Montserrat, which have hosted a multitude of like-minded geologists, scientists and educators.

The MVO also has a small gift shop and theatre where a twenty-minute video of volcanic eruptions is shown to visitors. Volcano viewings are also possible from the MVO and from various other safe vantage points across the island. The MVO was instrumental in creating the Mountain Aglow Project, a component of the Disaster Passed Project that focusses on the recent eruptions of the Soufrière Hills volcano. It highlights the impact of the volcano on the lives of Montserratians reflected in memories, stories, poetry and songs over the past twenty-five-plus years. There is a nine-foot-high mobile conical model of the volcano where stories, photos and videos are showcased. As part of the Curating Crises project, the MVO has led the creation of four community mural paintings across the island aimed at raising volcanic risk awareness while showing the relationship between Montserratians and the volcanic landscape.

Plymouth: The Buried City Dubbed the Modern Day Pompeii

One of the most chilling experiences that can be had on a visit to Montserrat an exploration of Plymouth, the capital city that was devastated by pyroclastic flows that buried buildings and roads more than thirty feet deep. It is eerily reminiscent of the ancient city of Pompeii. To ensure visitor safety, the government of Montserrat, through its tourism division, developed a certification programme. All tour guides and taxi drivers must be certified before entering Plymouth. A collaborative effort between the MVO, Disaster Management Coordination Agency and the police department, the programme covers story-telling, vehicle testing, safety and access routes.

As a way to manage and protect the area, consideration has been given to making parts of Plymouth a geopark, though this requires further research before a decision can be made. In addition, there are several new beaches that have opened which were not visible before but occurred as a result of pyroclastic flows causing sand build up that extended the shoreline and increased the size of the island. Amenities on some of the new land include a beach bar, toilet facilities, a golfing range and more.

Volcano Interpretation Centre

A Volcano Interpretation Centre to be constructed later this year is intended to convey the social elements of the volcano through the creation of user-friendly and immersive exhibits for all users. This will be an iconic building and will add to Montserrat's product offerings.

By-Products of the Volcano

Mining and export of volcanic material has been done and will continue in the foreseeable future.

Geo-Thermal Exploration

Three testing wells have been dug for the exploration of geothermal renewable energy. Two of these wells have been successfully flow tested proving the existence of a high temperature reservoir. Further exploration is due to be carried out on this project.

The table below shows that tourism arrivals to the island have been increasing steadily from 2010 onwards. There was a notable increase of 26.5 per cent in tourism arrivals in 2012 as compared to 2011. This was attributed to the fiftieth anniversary of the festival that was celebrated at that time. In 2020, the island was poised for further growth as a number of cruise ships, including *Windstar, Silversea, SeaDream* and others, had included Montserrat in their itinerary for more than two years (Montserrat Tourism Division 2021). The addition of a high-speed ferry from Antigua and a quarterly ferry service from Guadeloupe also added to the product, increasing day

Table 8.1: Montserrat Tourism Data – 2010–20

	Montserrat Tourism Data 2010–2020										
	2010	2011	2012	2013	2014	2015	2016	2017	2018	2019	2020
Visitors	7,707	8,506	10,756	9,085	10,737	13,275	13,555	18,570	18,338	20,956	8,300
Expenditure EC$m	15.1	14.0	19.0	18.3	22.2	22.9	22.9	25.4	26.8	27.0	13.8

Source: Statistics Department 2020

visitors to the island, many of whom are interested in the Buried City Tour. Further, the annual St Patrick's Festival in March each year has been overwhelmingly successful. Additionally, with the roll out of the Tourism Strategy in 2019 and funding from the European Union to further develop the product and promote the island, it has been projected that tourism arrivals will increase by more than 7 per cent each year.

Challenges Encountered

While there are notable opportunities for growth, as highlighted above, there are some challenges that the island is currently facing, in addition to the risk of eruption. The migration of more than 50 per cent of the population had a negative impact on the island which may have contributed to its slow economic growth. This led to brain drain across the island and, as a result, there are few skilled people remaining.

There was insufficient funding for some capital projects, for example, the new airport that was constructed is only able to facilitate small islander and twin-otter aircrafts. The temporary jetty that was built in Little Bay has some drawbacks, which are especially noticeable during rough seas. These facilities have limited access to the island, which negatively affects the tourism industry.

The volcano is still active and, while volcanic activity is currently low, there is always the possibility that it will erupt again. Eruptions can affect air quality. Poor air quality particularly affects vulnerable people with breathing difficulties, but can also disrupt flights, leading to cancellations if there is ash in the atmosphere. The loss of arable farmland following the eruptions has been challenging for some farmers who have had to purchase or lease new land, much of which is sloping and more difficult to cultivate. Non-nationals from neighbouring islands living in Montserrat have brought their own cultures, altering the core culture of the island. This is very noticeable in schools where many teachers are non-Montserratians and where some children sometimes have difficulty understanding their various accents.

A Brief Overview of La Soufrière Volcano in St Vincent and the Grenadines

St Vincent and the Grenadines is located in the Eastern Caribbean to the west of Barbados and, like Montserrat, is blessed with beautiful scenery and fertile land, providing the perfect canvas for a number of outdoor activities including hiking, biking, walking and volcano adventure. The La Soufrière volcano is a stratovolcano located on St Vincent and that has had five explosive eruptions since 1718. The most recent major eruption took place on 9 April 2021, with additional eruptions taking place throughout the month. The eruption caused severe destruction and disruption with a significant loss of infrastructure that left many people homeless. The ash from the eruptions reached neighbouring islands and caused some airports to close, rooftops to crumble and intense breathing difficulties for some (Nash 2021). Consider that the eruptions took place during the COVID-19 pandemic, rendering it a double whammy for the destination.

St Vincent's primary industry is tourism. Its green and mountainous landscape drew visitors to the island even before the volcano eruption. The tourism sector spiralled drastically as a result of the COVID-19 pandemic, which was compounded by global travel bans. This was further exacerbated when the volcano erupted and wiped out the green landscape that had drawn visitors to the island. Since the eruptions, there have been recovery efforts to relaunch yacht tourism. The Volcano Experience was being promoted to yachters as a way to see the volcano from a safe distance (Kendy 2021). Unfortunately, at the time of writing there were no available tourism statistics to compare to the April 2021 eruptions, which was possibly due to the COVID-19 pandemic).

Conclusion

A number of destinations benefit from volcano tourism, including Hawaii, the Philippines, Iceland, Italy and others. While erupting volcanoes are extremely destructive and have caused numerous hardships to destinations, many countries have turned these negative impacts into positives. Pompeii welcomes approximately 2.5 million tourists per year, is the third most visited city in Italy and is ranked as the 48th most visited destination in the world (Pompeii Sites n.d.). Italy promotes Pompeii as a living lab by showcasing the devastation in a very poignant way. Much of the city of Pompeii has remained intact following the eruption of Mount Vesuvius and visitors are able to get a glimpse into what it looked like pre-79 AD. The site of Pompeii provides visitors with a wealth of information including the social, economic, cultural, religious and political lives of the residents who once occupied the area.

Volcanoes are here to stay and their beauty and intrigue will keep tourists wanting to explore more. While they are being promoted and while access is being granted to tourists, it is paramount that the very real risks are measured and mitigated as much as possible. Currently, Montserrat has a number of risk reduction measures in place, including monitoring the volcano on a twenty-four-hour basis, an early warning siren system and signage that are used to warn people of imminent danger, helicopter fly-overs and monitoring by scientists, and continued outreach and notices provided via various media.

These measures require continuous testing and improving to keep both locals and visitors safe. Nonetheless, a small island such as Montserrat, and perhaps the rest of the Caribbean, will be competing with larger countries that are better placed and more able to promote these natural phenomena. For this reason, it is important for the volcanic islands in the region to work collaboratively by promoting a Volcano Heritage Trail where visitors are afforded the opportunity to visit several island destinations that are geographically close but culturally unique. Such an opportunity will provide visitors with more value for money in exchange for more enriching experiences. Finally, more research is required to determine how small Caribbean islands can further benefit from these natural phenomena safely.

References

Butler, R.W. 1993. "Tourism Development in Small Islands." In *The Development Process in Small Islands States*, edited by Douglas G. Lockhart, David Drakakis-Smith and John Schembri, 71–91. London: Roarthscan.

Cooper, P., and M. Cooper. 2015. *Volcano and Geothermal Tourism: Sustainable Geo-Resources for Leisure and Recreation*. London: Earthscan.

Crouch, G., and J.R. Brent Ritchie. 2006. "Destination Competitiveness." In *International Handbook on the Economics of Tourism*, edited by Larry Dwyer and Peter Forsyth, 419–33. Cheltenham, UK: Edward Elgar Publishing.

Dann, G.M.S. 1981. "Tourist Motives in Appraisal." *Annals of Tourism Research* 8 (2): 187–219.

Erfurt-Cooper, P., and M. Cooper, eds. 2010. *Volcano and Geothermal Tourism: Sustainable Geo-Resources for Leisure and Recreation*. London: Earthscan.

Gernott, O. 1994. *Montserrat Visitor Survey 1993/1994*. Barbados: Caribbean Tourism Organization.

Gnoth, J. 1997. "Tourism Motivation and Expectation Formation." *Annals of Tourism Research* 24 (2): 283–304. https://doi.org/10.1016/S0160-7383(97)80002-3.

Grattan, J., and R. Torrence. 2007. "Beyond Gloom and Doom. The Long-Term Consequences of Volcanic Disasters." In *Living Under* the Shadow: The Cultural Impacts of Volcanic Eruptions, edited by J. Grattan and R. Torrence. Walnut Creek: Left Coast Press.

Hall, C.M. 1992. *Hallmark Tourist Events: Impacts, Management and Planning*. London: Belhaven Press.

Helber, L.E. 1988. "The Roles of Government in Planning in Tourism with Special Regard for the Cultural and Environmental Impact of Tourism." In *The Roles of Government in the Development of Tourism as an Economic Resource, Seminar Series* (1) : 17–23.

Holden, A. 2005. *Tourism Studies and the Social Sciences*. London: Routledge

Iso-Ahola, S.E. 1980. *The Social Psychology of Leisure and Recreation*. Dubuque, IA: William C. Brown. https://books.google.co.uk/books/about/The_Social_Psychology_of_Leisure_and_Rec.html?id=rNSBAAAAMAAJ&redir_esc=y.

Johnston, M. 1987. "Risk in Mountain Recreation: Challenge or Danger?" In *Geography and Society in a Global Context*, edited by R. Le Heron, M. Roche and M. Shepherd, 148–53. New Zealand Geographical Society Conference Series No. 14, Massey University, Palmerston North. https://library.unitech.ac.pg/cgi-bin/koha/opac-detail.pl?biblionumber=51508.

Kendy. 2021. "St Vincent Govt Plans Tourism Recovery." *NationNews*, 13 May 2021. https://www.nationnews.com/2021/05/13/st-vincent-govt-plans-tourism-recovery/.

Krippendorf, J. 1987. *The Holiday Makers*. London: Heinemann.

Ministry of Finance and Economic Development. 1994. Statistical Report. Montserrat Statistics Department.

———. 1995. Statistical Report. Montserrat Statistics Department.

———. 1996. Statistical Report. Montserrat Statistics Department.

———. 1998. Statistical Report. Montserrat Statistics Department.

———. 2001. Statistical Report. Montserrat Statistics Department.

Montserrat Volcano Observatory (MVO). n.d. http://www.mvo.ms/.

Morgan, D. 1998. "The Adventure Tourism Experience on Water: Perceptions of Risk and Competence and the Role of the Operator." Unpublished Master's thesis, Lincoln University. https://journals.sagepub.com/doi/10.1177/1468797604057323.

Morgan, D., and M. Fluker. 2006. "Risk Management for Australian Commercial Adventure Tourism Operations." In *Tourism, Security and Safety: From Theory to Practice*, edited by Yoel Mansfield and Abraham Pizam, 153–68. Burlington, MA: Elsevier Butterworth-Heinemann.

Nash, Cheryl. 2021. "La Soufrière Eruption: What has the Impact been on St Vincent and the Grenadines?" *The Boar*, 12 May 2021. https://theboar.org/2021/05/la-soufriere-eruption-impact-on-st-vincent-and-the-grenadines/.

Phillips, S.G., and E. Emmanuel. 2008. "Ministry of Economic Development and Trade – Montserrat Sustainable Development Plan, 2008-2020." Mapco Printers Ltd, Kingston, Jamaica.

Plummer J.T. 1989. "Changing Values." *The Futurist*, 23 (1): 8–13.

Pompeii Sites. n.d. "Visitor Data." http://pompeiisites.org/en/

archaeological-park-of-pompeii/visitor-data/.
Poon, A. 1993. *Tourism, Technology and Competitive Strategies.* Wallingford, UK: CAB Intern McIntosh.
Schwaninger, M. 1989. "Trends in Leisure and Tourism for 2000–2010: Scenario with Consequences for Planners." In *Tourism Marketing and Management Handbook*, edited by Stephen F. Witt and Luiz Moutinho, 599–605.
Strobl, E. 2012. "The Economic Growth Impact of Natural Disasters in Developing Countries: Evidence from Hurricane Strikes in the Central American and Caribbean Regions." *Journal of Development Economics*, 97 (1): 130–41.
Tourism Intelligence International. 2019. "Montserrat Tourism Strategy 2019–2022."
Troxler, S. 2020. "Eyjafjallajökull: The Volcano That Erupted Icelandic Tourism." EHL Insights. https://hospitalityinsights.ehl.edu/iceland-tourism-boom.
Wahab, S. 1975. *Wahab on Tourism Management.* London: Tourism International Press.
West, I.R. 2000/2001. "Could Montserrat Continue to Market Itself as a Tourism Destination, Given the On-Going Volcanic Situation?" Unpublished Bachelor's dissertation. University of Derby, UK.
———. 2011. *Montserrat Tourist Board Stayover Visitor Survey – Exit Survey Report – June 2010 – May 2011.*
Wilson R., and E. Crouch. 1987. "Risk Assessment and Comparisons: An Introduction." *New Series* 236 (4799): 267–70. https://www.jstor.org/stable/–May2011.

9.
Unlocking the Potential of Diaspora Tourism in Trinidad and Tobago

Andre Phillips

Introduction

Tourism is considered a potential earner of hard currency and a substantial source of employment for several Caribbean countries. Many countries in the region subscribe to market segmentation of tourism products to increase benefits to each destination from conventional tourists. Diaspora engagement pursued through a tourism strategy enables a transfer of resources, investments, skills and predictability of travel that outweigh the gains accrued from conventional tourists.

Human beings are motivated to visit their countries of origin by a natural desire to interact with their homeland. Recent studies have commonly referred to this physical engagement between host and home countries as diaspora tourism or diasporic tourism (Huang, Haller and Ramshaw 2013; Nurse and Kirton 2014; Tichaawa 2017).

Diaspora tourism can have significant economic, socio-cultural and political benefits and therefore, like other forms of diaspora engagement such as remittances, investments and technology transfers (Schyvens 2007), deserves more serious consideration. For example, diaspora tourism can boost agriculture and agro-processing, given that tourists from the diaspora are more likely than other international travellers to have or make connections with the local economy (Agunias and Newland 2012). Diaspora tourists tend to have a profile similar to that of cultural tourists in that they invest more in indigenous goods and services. Consequently, diaspora tourism may allow for higher levels of capital (profit) retention within the regional economy compared with traditional mass tourism, all-inclusive hotels and cruise ships (Nurse and Kirton 2014).

According to Newland and Taylor (2010), diaspora tourism includes a broad spectrum of return visits, incorporating medical tourism, business-related tourism, heritage or "roots" tourism, exposure or "brithright" tours, education tourism, VIP tours and peak experience tours. These represent an amalgam of tourism niches, most of which are hardly disaggregated in tourism data, especially within Caribbean countries. The common denominator in all these forms is travel to the homeland. Other elements that impact the definition of diaspora tourism include notions of nostalgia, place and kinship ties as ventilated by researchers such as Scheyvens (2007) and Wagner (2008). Roberts (2012) added two other elements that must be identifiable in defining the diaspora tourism: international and intraregional migration and the formation of social and economic networks to facilitate the sharing of information, goods and resources.

This study examines the extent to which diaspora tourism can contribute to the development of sustainable tourism in Trinidad and Tobago. The research objectives focused on identifying triggers for homeland visits and analysing the patterns of homeland visits by persons of Trinidad and Tobago birth and parentage. It also examines the potential contribution of homeland visits to the sustainable development of Trinidad and Tobago's tourism industry. Finally, it provides recommendations for practitioners and policymakers for boosting homeland visits to Trinidad and Tobago and maximizing the impact of these visits on the sustainable development of the country's tourism industry.

The Trinidad and Tobago Diaspora

Before Trinidad and Tobago achieved independence in 1962, a wave of emigration to Panama occurred as opportunities opened up for work on the Panama Canal at the turn of the twentieth century. Most of the labourers eventually moved north to settle in different American cities. Another wave of emigration to England occurred during the 1950s, as local inhabitants who felt the need to improve educational and earning opportunities took advantage of England encouraging its colonies to assist in its post-war rebuilding efforts. Outside of these waves, inhabitants of Trinidad and Tobago were attracted to the United States and Canada during the second half of the twentieth century. A steady rate of departures for greener pastures became evident from the 1960s, when British immigration policies were more adverse favourable for Caribbean people (Richmond 1987). In the ensuing decades, more people left Trinidad and Tobago's shores seeking a better life in North America. In 2013, one estimation of the number of Trinidad and Tobago migrants in the metropolitan countries was three hundred and sixty-four thousand, of which two hundred and forty-nine thousand lived in the United States and seventy-six lived in Canada (UNICEF 2013). Another estimation was that there were two hundred and twenty thousand Trinidad and Tobago nationals in the United States in 2014, based on the US 2018.

Economic Profile of Trinidad and Tobago

The twin-island nation of Trinidad and Tobago is categorized as a high income country by the World Bank and has one of the highest levels of gross domestic product (GDP) per capita in the Americas, in terms of purchasing power parity (Oxford Business Group 2020). Trinidad and Tobago is the largest producer of oil and gas in the Caribbean: its energy sector accounts for approximately 35 per cent of industries (Lewis and Jordan 2008). Like many other hydrocarbon producing nations, Trinidad and Tobago faced an economic slowdown beginning in mid-2014 due to soft global demand.

In many respects, Trinidad and Tobago is viewed as a country with untapped tourism potential (WTTC 2017). The National Development Strategy for 2030 reinforces this expectation by acknowledging the integral role tourism can play to increase jobs and foreign exchange inflows. The economic data on tourism impacts within Trinidad and Tobago confirms a widely held view in the Caribbean that the tourism industry creates more jobs per dollar invested when compared with other industries (CDB 2017). This is highlighted in Trinidad and Tobago, where tourism and hospitality rank fourth in terms of the labour force, behind construction, manufacturing and agriculture, though the sector contributes less than 2 per cent of GDP (Trinidad and Tobago Ministry of Finance 2020).

Trinidad and Tobago ranks in the top ten for Caribbean Tourism Organization member states, with the highest stayover visitor arrivals despite the fact that its tourism industry has the lowest share of national GDP of the member states, continuously recording between 1 and 2 per cent. Trinidad and Tobago is thought to have the most diverse leisure and nature-oriented experiences, which are on par with the best performing destinations in the Caribbean (ACS 2014). The Caribbean Tourism Organization acknowledges that cultural and heritage niches are strongest in Trinidad in particular, and eco-tourism, along with the traditional sun, sea and sand offering, accentuate the attributes of Tobago, Trinidad's much smaller sister island.

In 2019, Trinidad and Tobago had a total of 7,731 rooms available for visitor accommodation. Trinidad provided 49.0 per cent (or 3,788 rooms), and Tobago 51.0 per cent (or 3,943 rooms). Data for 2019 indicates that the occupancy rate in Trinidad expanded to 62.1 per cent from the 59.8 per cent recorded in 2018 (Trinidad and Tobago Ministry of Finance 2020). Data on the occupancy rate in Tobago was unavailable for 2019.

Tobago is the tourist haven of Trinidad and Tobago, with substantial appeal to international visitors from the United Kingdom and Europe in addition to domestic visitors from its larger neighbouring island. Following the 2008 global financial crisis, the island recorded a drastic reduction in visitor arrivals, which continued for many years, as can be seen in table 9.1. The current statistics show that visitor arrivals declined to 388,756 in 2019 from a position of 439,000 in 2015. Trinidad and Tobago's situation contrasts with other Caribbean destinations, which recorded annual growth rates of visitor arrivals ranging from 3 to 12 per cent in the same period of 2010–19. This is even more apparent when reviewing market segments for stayover visitors in most regional destinations. Arrivals from the United States, United Kingdom and Europe have trended upwards in other Caribbean destinations, in contrast to a downward pattern observed in Trinidad and Tobago tourism.

Table 9.1: Trinidad and Tobago International Stayover Annual Arrivals

2015	2016	2017	2018	2019
439,749	408,782	394,650	375,485	388,756

Source: Trinidad and Tobago Ministry of Finance (2020)

Table 9.2: Comparison of US-Born and Trinidad and Tobago-Born Stayover Visitors for the Period 2013–17

Year	Total no. surveyed	No. born in Trinidad and Tobago	No. born in US	% of Trinidad and Tobago born to overall US residents
2013	1182	609	443	51.5
2014	1834	980	604	53.4
2015	1376	709	462	53.4
2016	4694	2516	1539	55.9
2017	3209	1702	1097	53.0

Source: Trinidad and Tobago CSO (2017)

An estimated 45 per cent of international stayover visitors are from the United States followed by the United Kingdom and Canada, which together account for a smaller contribution than the United States.

The data presented in table 9.2 illustrates the significant diaspora component of stayover arrivals from the United States of America. Visitors denoted as Trinidad and Tobago-born account for between 50 and 55 per cent of arrivals. These are dual citizens who use US passports and are recorded as foreign visitors. However, it is likely that dual citizens resident in the United States of America who use local passports on entry will be captured as Trinidad and Tobago residents.

The state of the Trinidad and Tobago tourism industry warrants a new strategy that recognizes the importance of the diaspora visitor in the survival and growth of a more sustainable tourism product in Trinidad and Tobago.

Literature Review

The contemporary definition of diaspora underpinning this study denotes migrants and their descendants who maintain strong sentimental and material links with their countries of origin (Duval 2003; Newland 2010). In this case, the diaspora refers to migrants settled permanently in countries other than those they were born in, but who are aware of their country of origin and who continue to maintain patriotic links with their country of origin.

It is an emerging view that the diaspora is not a substitute term for migrants. Instead, it refers to a subset of migrants whose transnational activities and affinity distinguish them from migrants who have very little interaction with their home countries. This distinction was underscored in research on Scottish-Canadians, which found that country of origin does not by itself delineate diaspora. On the contrary, second- and third-generation migrants born in host countries may have a stronger emotional sense of belonging and commitment to their parents' homelands (Gaudry 2007). Other researchers support this difference in homeland connection between diaspora and migrant (Plaza 2008).

Despite the diversity of diasporic experiences, one characteristic that people in a diaspora have in common is a connection to both their country of origin and their host society, reaffirming the observation that when this occurs the nation state becomes blurred by transnational identity (Plaza 2008). Coles and Timothy (2004) used he term "hyphenated community", which rfers to "the semantic coupling of the homeland and the hst state" in labels such as Irish-Americans and Scottish-Canadians. The hyphenation reflects how immigrants must compromise and negotiate between different nationalities and ethnicities. Moreover, the migration experience allows one to move between regions and across national boundaries. Because diasporic populations are often spread to several destinations, transnational connections also exist between diasporas in different host societies. These transnational connections increasingly trigger diaspora travel, which also expands tourism studies.

The concept of transnationalism focuses on the cultivation and development of activities spanning national borders (Plaza 2008; Vertovec 1999). The International Organization for Migration referred to transnationalism as a process whereby people establish and maintain socio-cultural connections across geopolitical borders (IOM 2013). It aligns with the definition by Vertovec (1999, 447) stating that "transnationalism refers to multiple ties and interactions that link people and their institutions across the borders of nation-states".

Sustainability and Diaspora Tourism

The potential of diaspora tourism to advance a more sustainable tourism receives minimal treatment in literature, but its impact is gaining momentum and stimulating interest. Telfer and Sharpley (2007) advocated that tourism's compatibility with sustainable development can be assessed in terms of fundamental principles, development objectives and sustainability objectives. This study reveals how the diaspora tourist can more easily advance the sustainable tourism agenda than any other segment of stayover visitor traffic in tourist destinations.

Diaspora tourists contribute to most of the pillars of sustainable tourism, particularly the sustainability of cultural heritage, traditions and sites. This is identifiable from key empirical research on the diaspora of countries in Africa and in the Caribbean and Pacific regions (Nurse 2011; Scheyvens 2007; Tichaawa 2017). It should be noted that migrants who make home visits are typically conscious of their environment, cultural heritage, living standards and human development. Research shows that first-generation migrants are more inclined to support initiatives that preserve customs and traditions of the homeland (Scheyvens 2007; Tichaawa 2017; Wagner 2008). Trinidad and Tobago's diasporic communities, particularly in the United States, participate in numerous events that help to sustain an image of home. When overseas diasporic communities return home on short visits, they are inclined to seek out authentic customs and traditions that bring them cultural fulfilment. The synthesis between tourism and sustainable development is most recognizable in Caribbean countries and the diaspora is contributes significantly to this (CTO 2018).

When members of the diaspora visit their homeland, they engage in activities, often at the community level, that span inter-sectoral linkages (Nurse and Kirton 2014). In its policy guidance (CTO 2008), the Caribbean Tourism Organization spoke to the need to strengthen links between tourism and other economic sectors, and fostering diaspora activities will support this policy implerative. Nurse and Kirton (2014) identified strong links between operators in the agricultural and creative sectors of Jamaica and members of the diaspora who own businesses in the United Kingdom.

Impact and Challenges of Diaspora Tourism

Many studies around the world have shown that when members of the diaspora visit their homelands, also known as sending countries, they engage in activities that benefit their communities of birth and origin politically, socially, economically and environmentally. The empirical work of Scheyvens (2007), Nurse (2011) and Huang, Haller and Ramshaw (2013) in Samoa, Suriname and China, respectively, elucidated the intertwined relationship between tourism, transnationalism and diaspora. Regular engagement with the homeland generates travel motivations that align with Plaza's (2008) references to a transnational lifestyle, Portes, Guarnizo, and Haller's (2002) characteristics of socio-cultural transnationalism and the relational driver espoused by Vertovec (1999).

Socio-Cultural Benefits to the Diaspora Tourist

Travel to the homeland helps members of diasporic communities evaluate themselves, resolve their personal identity conflicts and connect with their predecessors (Newland and Taylor 2010). Homeland visits contribute to maintaining cultural identity, sustaining or creating connections to one's cultural roots, discovering oneself and resolving personal identity crises (Duval 2003; Powers 2011; Iarmolenko and Kerstetter 2015). These issues align with the tenets of socio-cultural transnationalism espoused by Portes, Guarnizo, and Haller (2002).

The "roots" theme is especially strong among dispossessed diasporas or those who have a very distant and disassociated migration history and who are given to reimagining the homeland (Powers 2011). Pilgrimage and birthright tours such as the Sankofa tour experience in Ghana help migrants to rediscover connections with their homeland (Powers 2011). Other researchers investigated second- third-generation members of the diaspora, who express satisfaction and derive a sense of home and belonging while experiencing cultural immersion (Huang, Haller and Ramshaw 2013; Iarmolenko and Kerstetter 2015).

Diaspora Tourist Contribution to an Economy

Several researchers have concluded that members of the diaspora contribute to homeland development on homeland visits because of the nature of their travel, their comsumption practices and their asset expansion.

Diaspora tourists contribute significantly both to the number of annual stayover arrivals in Caribbean destinations and to the percentage of total arrivals. Guyana has a high dependence on diaspora tourism, with members of the diaspora comprising an estimated 70 per cent of total tourist arrivals to that country (Wenner and Johnny 2015). The share of diaspora tourism in Jamaica is estimated to be between 30 and 35 per cent. Members of the diaspora account for more than 30 per cent tourist arrivals in Trinidad and Tobago (captured in the Trinidad and Tobago data as arrivals visiting friends and relatives) since 2013. In absolute terms, Jamaica, with two million tourist arrivals annually, hosts more members of the diaspora than any other English-speaking country in the Caribbean (WTTC 2017). Trinidad welcomes four hundred thousand diaspora tourists annually, compared with Guyana's two hundred thousand (WTTC 2017). In terms of travel frequency, the Guyana Tourism Authority estimates 45 per cent of its diaspora tourists return every year. Anecdotal data placed the annual diaspora tourist arrival to Jamaica closer to 70 per cent. No official data is available on Trinidad and Tobago.

Within the limited research on diaspora tourism, diaspora tourists display characteristics and travel patterns that are different from the standard tourist with no link to the destination. Diaspora tourists tend to stay longer and make more short-break visits, particularly for events and festivals (Asiedu 2005; Duval 2003; Orozco 2005). Diaspora tourists often transfer monies to family before departure and may have also forwarded barrels of goods via a freighting company to arrive days before their arrival (Nurse 2016).

The consumption practices of diaspora tourists differ from that of all other tourists and they tend to generate high demand for labour intensive or artisanal products (Asiedu 2005; Duval 2003; Poel, Masurel, and Nijkamp 2006; Schyvens 2007). As a consequence, diaspora tourism has the potential to have a favourable impact on local businesses and communities (Tichaawa 2017; Wagner 2008). Diaspora tourists tend to spend more on local goods and services than the average holiday tourist (Newland and Taylor 2010). They are also more likely to purchase a local mobile phone or SIM card, which they are likely to use on several visits. The creative industries are also known to benefit from diasporic tourism in that sales of books, paintings, DVDs, CDs, fashion, crafts and so on tend to peak when there is a major festival that attracts diaspora tourists (Nurse and Kirton 2014). The heritage tourism sector also benefits from the inflow of diaspora tourists.

The observations above indicate that diasporic tourism can foster intersectoral linkages far beyond its impact on the hotel and hospitality sector (Newland 2010). In addition, diasporic tourism, when enhanced by information and communication technologies, can generate investment, exports and employment and create greater opportunities for economic inclusion (Nurse and Kirton 2014). According to Newland and Taylor (2010), diaspora populations scattered around the world can help to open markets for new tourist destinations and goods produced in and associated with the heritage and culture of the country of origin. Unlike international tourists, diaspora tourists are more likely to stay in local accommodation, patronize local food establishments and buy local goods and make more connections with the local economy (Aguinas and Newland 2012). As a consequence, diaspora spending infuses the local economy and spawns a multiplier effect within the destination (Phillips 2018).

Diaspora tourism is less subject to seasonality compared to other types of tourism and has the potential to expand across more of the country's geography. Indeed, diaspora tourists tend to travel to less visited sites (secondary sites) and participate in more cultural events (Powers 2011). In this regard, Newland and Taylor (2010) asserted that diaspora tourism assists greatly in the development of the homeland by attracting not only tourists but also investors, consumers and volunteers from the diaspora. In this respect, Orozco (2005) claimed that diaspora and migrant populations are heavy consumers of homeland products and goods, particularly food products and artisanal goods, which he referreostalgic home country goods".

The tourist sector also provides opportunities for diasporic populations to invest in tourism facilities and to open new and perhaps lesser-known tourist destinations to wider audiences (Newland and Taylor 2010). Research has also shown that diaspora tourists are more likely to invest in the construction of second homes, especially in Caribbean destinations (Mortley 2011). Nurse (2011) also suggested that diaspora tourism has become a facilitator of investment in the area of medical tourism. For example, in the last few years, Suriname has witnessed a steady growth in the number of medical tourism investments, specifically pertaining to physical care hotel facilities, rehabilitative surgery, physiotherapy and other related services (Nurse 2011). These transnational practices foster more job opportunities in the construction sector and property management. All these possibilities portend for Trinidad and Tobago, where there is a need to appreciate the diaspora tourism's capacity to contribute to the diversification of the economy.

Challenges in Expanding the Role of Diaspora Tourism

The heterogeneous nature of diasporas is commonly identified as a key challenge in exploiting the potential of diaspora tourism. Phillips (2018) cited the need to size and incentivize diaspora subgroups, which are denoted as the lived diaspora, ancestral diaspora and the more emergent affinity diaspora as postulated by Butler (2003). Other complexities identified by Newland and Taylor (2010) focus on supporting research, training, and policy development for diaspora tourism, trade and heritage sites; supporting diaspora-specific marketing and branding efforts; and identifying opportunities for high value-added trade and tourism investments.

Furthermore, destination promotion agencies need to engage in product development strategies meant to enhance tourism competitiveness in order to generate an increased annual average spend per tourist, either by attracting high spending tourists or even by lowering the seasonality factor (WTTC 2017).

Methodology

This study examines the relationship between the Trinidad and Tobago diaspora and tourism activities in Trinidad and Tobago with a focus on triggers, patterns and benefits of diaspora engagement when homeland trips are pursued. A qualitative methodological approach was adopted with a phenomenological research strategy, embracing the semi-structured interview data collection method. Twenty-five US residents of Trinidad and Tobago birth or parentage were interviewed using non-synchronous methods combined with face-to-face interviews at various locations. Three key informant interviews were also conducted: two with senior personnel in government departments – an immigration official and a statistician – and one with a Carnival entrepreneur who produces costumes for celebrations in Trinidad and the United States of America.

The use of semi-structured interviews in this study is consistent with phenomenological orientation and data collection methods. To maintain consistency, responses were elicited using an interview protocol as a starting point, but the interviewer took care to ensure that respondents were able to give wide-ranging responses without being constrained by a rigid interview protocol. Before any interview began, respondents were informed that the goal of the interview was to elicit feedback on how the respondents exhibited connection to home in their normal lives, how those efforts influenced homeward travel and the specific reason and activities associated with the previous homeland trip as well as to collect demographic data and information about their trips. Respondents were asked to define their homeland attachment practices while in America and about their household income, their spending during the homeland trip and their spending on souvenirs when exiting Trinidad and Tobago. Twenty-five interviews were conducted between June and October 2018. Six face-to-face interviews were conducted, three in the United States and three when the participants journeyed to Trinidad and Tobago. The remaining nineteen respondents were engaged in online interviews using WhatsApp and Skype.

The sampling approach for the Trinidad and Tobago study referenced the preferred definition of diaspora tourism: "An engagement with persons living and working in metropolitan countries or other perceived economic cores whose socialisation, networks, values and heritage link them to communities and kinship ties in their birth country and who travel back to these communities primarily to reconnect with people and place" (Roberts 2012, 121).

Identification and characterization of themes was a process that began early in the study and continued until the final phase. Potential themes were first noted when reading through the transcripts. They then evolved throughout the entire coding process to produce the

final report. Codes were applied to the interview transcripts and were often included under more than one theme. Possible thematic categories were identified, and codes were arranged to illustrate the themes in the best manner. The template analysis process identified four themes as follows:
1. Triggers and patterns of homeland visits
2. Roots and recreation
3. Spending patterns during migrant homeland visits
4. Effects/benefits of migrant homeland visits

It is important to note that the template analysis method enhances analytical rigour by using a quasi-statistical approach where qualitative data is quantized (Saunders, Lewis and Thornhill 2016). This improves the probability that a testable proposition will emerge from the data. Evidently, triggers to homeland visits are predominantly identified in the cultural art forms retained by migrants from Trinidad and Tobago in the United States. Simple tables amplify the frequency of the occurrences that convey the proposition strongly.

Study Findings and Discussion
Triggers for Homeland Visits

The intentions of members of the diaspora to visit their homeland are typically linked to three main pull factors: visiting family, festivals including Carnival, and empowerment initiatives in the homeland. Not surprisingly, the presence of family ties is mentioned by a significant proportion of respondents (66 per cent) as being the main reason for their return. This finding supports those of several researchers (Nurse 2011; Poel, Masurel and Nijkamp 2006; Tichaawa 2017; Wagner 2008) who suggested that because diaspora tourists often have family and friends living at their original place of birth, they tend to visit their homeland in order to reaffirm and strengthen their roots and identities. Nurse (2011) emphasized that such ties are strong reasons to travel. Evidently, diaspora involvement in culturally oriented practices in the United States, which are entrenched in Trinidad and Tobago society, typically undergird homeland visit intentions. Table 9.3 outlines the categories of activities that migrants and their children typically pursue in the United States of America.

The findings confirm that diverse activities are pursued to sustain connections with home. The views expressed by a majority of the respondents who travel to Trinidad and Tobago annually or occasionally (approximately two-thirds of respondents) suggest that their home travel is inspired by the need to reintegrate with the homeland vibe. This augurs well for the continued commitment to destination Trinidad and Tobago. Furthermore, the quest for authenticity ensures the continuation of strong visitor traffic for festivals and traditions primarily related to Carnival, Parang, Christmas and Phagwa. The desire for authentic experiences and tastes by Trinidad and Tobago diaspora tourists seems more pervasive than the literature review would suggest.

Table 9.3: Breakdown of Migrant Participation in Transnational Activities in the US

Carnival Participation by Migrants	Steelpan Involvement by Migrants	Volunteer & Philanthropic Activities by Migrants	Other Forms of Homeland Attachment Pursued in the US
14 of 25 are active in US-based carnivals	6 of 25 exhibit active interests	19 of 25 engaged in volunteer and philanthropic activities in the past 2 years	4 of 25 attend Trinidad-styled shows in the US and functions that celebrate national independence

Trip Patterns

The study found that diaspora arrivals are often highest in the periods of Carnival and Christmas, but steady traffic is observed all year round. Nineteen of the twenty-five respondents had journeyed home at least once within a year of this research starting. At least one-third of the respondents confined their travel to summer and autumn seasons in the United States, thus avoiding travelling in winter, the peak of travel by diaspora visitors. Another third of the respondents who undertake two or more visits each year typically make at least one non-peak trip home. This points to a sustainable segment of tourism that reduces the seasonality of travel to Trinidad and Tobago, which is normally associated with conventional tourists.

Typically, a tenth of all annual visitor arrivals are in February. In recent years, December has accounted for almost the same number of visitor arrivals as the Carnival period. The third highest month for visitor traffic is July. There are no popular festivals to explain this, but members of the diaspora are increasing sending their children home for the summer holidays. Over the last five years, Trinidad and Tobago Central Statistical Office data reveals that, on average, international visitors to Trinidad were accompanied by at least one other traveller.

The survey found that 53 per cent of respondents travelled to Trinidad alone, while the remaining 47 per cent were accompanied. This study reinforces anecdotal evidence that the visiting friends and relatives segment of visitors stays in Trinidad and Tobago the longest. Another substantial finding relates to trip planning by the second-generation diaspora, where emphasis is placed on bundling airline and accommodation rates. US-based carriers offer loyalty programmes that improve incentives for domestic and international flights. Points earned on overseas trips are accumulated and used to lower ticket fares on US carriers, namely American Airlines and United Airlines, which offer daily services to Trinidad. The millennial traveller is more inclined to make a homeland trip on a US carrier, with the added benefit of discounted hotel accommodation and vehicle rentals, using points earned in loyalty programmes. In this way, diaspora tourists eliminate the need to use family accommodation on homeland trips.

Spending Patterns During Homeland Visits

The general trend seen in this research study is the diaspora visitors' eagerness to improve living standards in Trinidad and Tobago at household and community levels. A homeland visit involved spending on food, transport, entertainment, shopping (nostalgic purchases) and accommodation, and even spending of a philanthropic nature. The total of these transactions often exceeded USD 1,000 for a two-week stay by a single visitor.

Empirical studies by Orozco (2005), Schyvens (2007), Tichaawa (2017) referred to nostalgia goods purchased by migrants, which extend the parameters of the gift-buying phenomenon. This research denotes a range of items which do not appeal to typical tourists, such as a wide assortment of culinary delights and the raw materials to produce them. As one visitor said: "When I am going back to New York my bags are stuffed with foodstuff. You cannot find our curry in the USA, also local coffee and even Tobago's fine honey and the local seasoning made and bottled by my cousin. These things are hard to find in my city and if you find them, they are very expensive and may not be rich in quality" (Eva, 1 September 2018, New York, United States).

Other purchases range from fabric to steel pan items, that is, nostalgic goods. When this is considered within the context of the lengthier stay of the diaspora visitor, the overall spending of the diaspora visitor tends to exceed the spending of the typical leisure visitor. The study findings reflect a diverse pattern of spending. Typically, almost half of spending during a Trinidad and Tobago visit is directed towards nostalgic shopping or home improvement. Respondents pointed to three specific examples of travellers whose trip expenditure totalled USD 2,000 or more. Nostalgic shopping was the biggest spending category of the longer stay visitor (four weeks), though one respondent focused more on home improvement spending during a one-week visit, while a couple who visited primarily for a funeral recorded an estimated USD 2,000 for their two-week stay. Additionally, the study identified that this expenditure pattern applied to Trinidad and Tobago migrants in both the lower income bracket, that is, under USD 70,000 annually, and the middle-income bracket, which had a ceiling of USD 120,000 annually.

A visit to Tobago, with its host of natural and historical attractions and fantastic beaches on both the Caribbean Sea and the Atlantic Ocean, is seen by most Trinidad-born members of the diaspora as a vacation. This is what influences the "roots and recreation" theme, which reflects a more dichotomous profile of the Trinidad and Tobago diaspora than what is highlighted in the literature review.

The preceding discussion highlights several aspects of congruence between the literature review and the study findings. This research deepens the existing academic literature and adds new dimensions to diaspora tourism literature, including in the areas of tourism planning and social impact. Overall, the key findings unearth some significant characteristics of the Trinidad and Tobago diaspora tourist and highlight dichotomous patterns observed in respondent expectations during homeland visits.

Diaspora homeland visits exert a positive effect on heritage preservation through festivals-related tourism, care for the environment through eco-tourist appeal, and human development through structured and unstructured philanthropic pursuits. Finally, the Trinidad and Tobago diaspora remains well-informed through online radio, social media and connections with friends and family.

Conclusion and Recommendations

The study findings help to cement the potential of diaspora tourist arrivals as the linchpin of visitor traffic to Trinidad and Tobago and a driver of sustainable tourism development. As it related to the former, diaspora tourists undertake homeland visits throughout the year and return more frequently than other tourist types. Relatedly, the diaspora tourist's overall spending per trip typically surpasses that of other tourist types and is considered to have a greater multiplier effect in local Trinidad and Tobago communities. The evidence that diaspora tourism is a driver of sustainable tourism development is borne out by the activities pursued by diaspora tourists during their stay in Trinidad and Tobago and their post-trip activities. A diaspora tourism-led strategy should receive significant and urgent attention by the authorities in Trinidad and Tobago. Components of such a strategy should inform destination promotion, product development, policy research, investments and so on.

Destination promotion agencies should accelerate efforts to devise and initiate promotional strategies to woo members of the diaspora to the homeland while understanding the extent of heterogeneity evident within this tourism niche. Increasing the number and innovativeness of promotions, which may include branching out to streaming radio services, should generate more arrivals to Trinidad and Tobago, especially from the United States, the main source market for the country's visitors. Roots and recreation remain at the forefront of diaspora visit intentions. A cultural immersion offering with authentic elements at its core should fuel a reshaping of product development to boost diaspora arrivals, especially among migrants' children and grandchildren.

Policy research in tourism needs an overhaul to better assess diaspora arrivals and spending data. This is the initial step to a definitive unlocking of diaspora tourism potential. Introducing the Trinidad and Tobago Travel Pass could prove useful in disaggregating diaspora arrivals within total international stayover visitor data. Diaspora interaction on homeland visits strengthens the tourism sector and engenders linkages with construction, agriculture and small business. Firstly, this study confirms diaspora spending on second homes, which often add to the tourism accommodation stock. Secondly, diaspora visitor expenditure boosts local commerce, including purchases that are made for the return trip to the United States. Typically, spending extends across a diverse range of edible and non-edible items (nostalgic shopping) and bolsters annual earnings of micro- and small enterprises within the agro, creative and small manufacturing sectors.

The survey feedback points to substantial diaspora support for festival tourism. Some respondents lament that the smaller festivals in both islands lack effective promotion outside of Trinidad and Tobago. It is observed that some diaspora visits occur around periods when certain smaller festivals are scheduled. The long-standing Point Fortin Borough Day and Tobago Jazz Experience are at the apex of diaspora consideration. Two other festival-oriented initiatives generate interest, but deeper incentives are required for more international appeal – Parang Festival in Paramin, Trinidad, and the Blue Food Festival in Tobago. Evidently, the less frequented festivals require better planning and packaging to appeal more to the Trinidad and Tobago diaspora population, particularly those who reside in the central and western regions of the United States.

Finally, the Trinidad and Tobago diaspora population frequently exhibits interest in empowerment initiatives by pursuing worthwhile endeavours relating to skills transfer during return visits. This study confirms that most respondents use informal channels to share expertise and skills, while exposing residents in Trinidad and Tobago to networks within the United States in ways that are beneficial to home-based individuals and groups. This concept of social remittances often attracts others with no connection to Trinidad and Tobago and appears to be a fertile track for more structured diaspora engagement with homeland authorities in and beyond sustainable tourism.

The latter recommendation typifies the socio-cultural impact associated with diaspora tourism and complements earlier recommendations that reflect the substantial economic impact that Trinidad and Tobago can derive from a purposeful engagement with diaspora tourism. Additionally, the research findings dispel the widely held view among travel organizers that Trinidad and Tobago migrants lack the financial resources to undertake repeat visits at short intervals. More than half of respondents have a household income greater than the median household income. All of these have positive implications for increased homeland visits with the attendant benefits of heritage and environmental preservation, improved community well-being and a boost to local prosperity. For the floundering tourism industry in Trinidad and Tobago, diaspora tourism is a gamechanger, an enabler of economic and socio-cultural benefits fostered through research, collaboration and investment between the Trinidad and Tobago diaspora and the homeland.

References

Association of Caribbean States (ACS). 2014. *Association of Caribbean States: 20 Years Promoting Cooperation in the Greater Caribbean.* Mexico City: Association of Caribbean States. http://www.acs-aec.org/sites/default/files/english_ebook_acs_20_low_res.pdf.

Agunias, Dovelyn Rannveig, and Kathleen Newland. 2012. *Developing a Road Map for Engaging Diasporas in Development: A Handbook for Policymakers and Practitioners in Home and Host Countries.* Geneva: International Organization for Migrations, and Migration Policy Institute. https://publications.iom.int/system/files/pdf/diaspora_handbook_en_for_web_28may2013.pdf.

Asiedu, Alex Boakye. 2005. "Some Benefits of Migrants' Return Visits to Ghana." *Population,* Space and Place 11 (1): 1–11. https://doi.org/10.1002/psp.350.

Butler, Richard. 2003. "Relationships between Tourism and Diasporas Influences and Patterns." *Espace Populations Sociétés* 21 (2): 317–26. https://doi.org/10.3406/espos.2003.2084.

Caribbean Development Bank (CDB). 2017. *Tourism Industry Reform: Strategies for Economic Impact.* Barbados: Caribbean Development Bank.

Coles, Tim, and J. Timothy Dallen, eds. 2004. *Tourism, Diasporas and Space.* London: Routledge.

Caribbean Tourism Organization (CTO). 2008. *Caribbean Sustainable Tourism Policy Framework.* St Michael, Barbados: Caribbean Tourism Organization.

———. 2018. *Caribbean Tourism Statistics Report 2018.* St Michael, Barbados: Caribbean Tourism Organization.

Duval, David Timothy. 2003. "When Hosts Become Guests: Return Visits and Diasporic Identities in a Commonwealth Eastern Caribbean Community." *Current* Issues in Tourism 6 (4): 267–308. https://doi.org/10.1080/13683500308667957.

Gaudry, Lesley Renee. 2007. "What Clan Are You? An Exploration of Heritage and Ancestral Tourism for Canadian Scottish Descendents." M.Sc. thesis, University of Waterloo. https://uwspace.uwaterloo.ca/bitstream/handle/10012/3086/Lesley 0Gaudry%20Thesis.pdf?sequence=1.

Huang, Wei-Jue, William Haller, and Gregory Ramshaw. 2013. "Diaspora Tourism and Homeland Attachment: An Exploratory Analysis." Tourism Analysis 18 (3): 285–96. https://doi.org/10.3727/108354213X13673398610691.

Iarmolenko, Svitlana, and Deborah Kerstetter. 2015. "Potential Predictors of Diaspora Tourism for Ukrainian Immigrants in the USA." *World Leisure Journal* 57 (3): 221–34. https://doi.org/10.1080/16078055.2015.1066604.

International Organization of Migration (IOM). 2013. *Diasporas and Development: Bridging Societies and States.* Geneva:International

Organization of Migration. https://www.iom.int/files/live/sites/iom/files/What-We-Do/idm/workshops/IDM-2013-Diaspora-Ministerial-Conference/DMC_Final_Conference_Report.pdf.

Lewis, A., and Jordan, L. 2008. "Tourism in Trinidad and Tobago: Carving a Niche in a Petroleum-Based Economy." *International Journal of Tourism Research*, 10: 247–57.

Mortley, Natasha Kay. 2011. "Strategic Opportunities from Diaspora Tourism: The Jamaican Perspective." *Canadian Foreign Policy Journal* 17 (2): 171–85. https://doi.org/10.1080/11926422.2011.601616.

Newland, Kathleen, ed. 2010. *Diaporas: New Partners in Global Development Policy*. Washington, DC: Migration Policy Institute.

Newland, Kathleen, and Carylanna Taylor. 2010. *Heritage Tourism and Nostalgia Trade: A Diaspora Niche in the Development Landscape*. Washington DC: Migration Policy Institute.

Nurse, Keith. 2011. "Diasporic Tourism and Investment in Suriname." *Canadian Foreign Policy Journal* 17 (2): 142–54. https://doi.org/10.1080/11926422.2011.602838.

———. 2016. "The Diasporic Economy, Trade and Investment Linkages in the Commonwealth." International Trade Working Paper 2016/09, Commonwealth Secretariat, London. https://doi.org/10.14217/5jm2jfg8c26c-en.

———, and Claremont Kirton. 2014. *Caribbean Diasporic Entrepreneurship Analytical Report*. Washington, DC: Inter-American Development Bank.

Orozco, Manuel. 2005. *Diasporas, Development and Transnational Integration: Ghanaians in the U.S., U.K. and Germany*. Washington, DC: Institute for the Study of International Migration and Inter-American Dialogue.

Oxford Business Group. 2020. *The Report: Trinidad and Tobago 2021*. London: Oxford Business Group.

Phillips, Andre. 2018. "Diaspora Engagement – New Imperative for Tourism Growth in Trinidad and Tobago with Implications for the Caribbean." In *Dynamics of Diaspora Engagement in the Caribbean: People, Policy, Practice*, edited by George K. Danns, Ivelaw Lloyd Griffith, and Fitzgerald Yaw, 134–44. Georgetown: University of Guyana Press.

Plaza, Dwaine. 2008. "Transnational Return Migration to the English-Speaking Caribbean." *Revue Européenne des Migrations Internationales* 24 (1): 115–37. https://doi.org/10.4000/remi.4317.

Poel, Pauline, Enno Masurel, and Peter Nijkamp. 2006. "The Importance of Friends and Relations in Tourist Behaviour: A Case Study of Heterogenity in Surinam." In *Tourism and Regional Development*, edited by Maria Giaoutzi and Peter Nijkamp, 219–38. Aldershot: Ashgate Publishing.

Portes, Alejandro, Luis Eduardo Guarnizo, and William J. Haller. 2002. "Transnational Entrepreneurs: An Alternative Form of Immigrant Economic Adaptation." *American Sociological Review* 67 (2): 278–98. https://doi.org/10.2307/3088896.

Powers, Jillian L. 2011. "Reimaging the Imagined Community: Homeland Tourism and the Role of Place." *The American Behavioral Scientist* 55 (10): 1362–78. https://doi.org/10.1177/0002764211409380.

Richmond, Anthony H. 1987. "Caribbean Immigrants in Britain and Canada: Socio-Demographic Aspects." *Revue Européenne des Migrations Internationales* 3 (3): 129–50. https://doi.org/10.3406/remi.1987.1148.

Roberts, Sherma. 2012. "Assessing the Potential of Diaspora Tourism." *Journal of Eastern Caribbean Studies* 37 (3/4): 115–33.

Saunders, Mark, Phillip Lewis, and Adrian Thornhill. 2016. *Research Methods for Business Students*. 7th ed. New York: Prentice Hall.

Scheyvens, Regina. 2007. "Poor Cousins No More: Valuing the Development Potential of Diaspora Tourism." *Progress in Development Studies* 7 (4): 307–25. https://doi.org/10.1177/146499340700700403.

Telfer, David J., and Richard Sharpley. 2007. *Tourism and Development in the Developing World*. London: Routledge.

Tichaawa, Tembi. 2017. "The Nature of Diasporic Tourism in Cameroon: An Opportunity for Tourism Development." *African Journal of Hospitality, Tourism and Leisure* 6 (2): 1–18.

Trinidad and Tobago Central Statistical Office (CSO). 2017. *Survey of Departing Visitors 2017*. Port of Spain, Trinidad and Tobago: Central Statistical Office.

Trinidad and Tobago Ministry of Finance. 2020. *Review of the Economy 2020*. Port of Spain, Trinidad and Tobago: Ministry of Finance.

United Nations International Children's Emergency Fund (UNICEF). 2013. "Trinidad and Tobago Migration Profiles." https://esa.un.org/miggmgprofiles/indicators/files/TrinidadTobago.pdf.

Vertovec, Stephen. 1999. "Conceiving and Researching Transnationalism." *Ethnic and Racial Studies* 22 (2): 447–62. https://doi.org/10.1080/014198799329558.

Wagner, Lauren. 2008. "Diasporic Visitor, Diasporic Tourist: Post-Migrant Generation Moroccans on Holiday at 'Home' in Morocco." *Civilisations* 57: 191–205. https://doi.org/10.4000/civilisations.1396.

Wenner, Mark D., and Teneisha Johnny. 2015. *Tourism and Ecotourism Development in Guyana: Issues and Challenges and the Critical Path Forward*. Washington, DC: Inter-American Development Bank.

World Travel and Tourism Council (WTTC). 2017. *Travel and Tourism Economic Impact 2017 Caribbean*. London: World Travel and Tourism Council.

10.
Medical Tourism: An Examination of Caymankind

Belinda Blessitt Vincent

Introduction

The medical tourism market is described as one of the most dynamic sectors in the economy (Veslova 2017). The Centers for Disease Control and Prevention defined medical tourism as when a person travels to another country for medical care (CDC n.d.). However, Kelley (2013) noted that there is no universally agreed definition. Some countries count foreign patients who visit hospitals while staying in the country, while others count the entry of individual patients into the country. Some countries record nationality and not residence. He identified medical travellers using a formula that removes expatriates seeking care in their country of residence and subtracting emergency cases (where medical care was not planned but instead necessitated by an emergency) from all international inpatients receiving care, he was able to identify medical travellers. Kelley (2013) defined medical tourism as the practice of tourists electing to travel across international borders to receive some form of medical treatment in a country outside of their place of primary residence. For this chapter, we will use this definition proposed by Kelley (2013).

In the 2021 Allied Market Research report (Sanjivan and Sahil 2020), the volume of the global medical tourism market in 2019 was 23,042,900 patients, projected to reach 70,358,610 patients by 2027. This number represents a compound annual growth rate of 15 per cent between 2019 and 2027. In the same report, the forecast for the global market for medical tourism in 2019 was US$104.68 billion and was projected to reach US$273.72 billion by 2027, representing a compound annual growth rate of 15 per cent between 2019 and 2027. This demand for medical tourism is attributed to the high cost of health care in many developed countries. In the McKinsey 2017

Consumer Health Insights survey, affordability of health care was highlighted as a pressing concern for many consumers (Cordina et al. 2018). Vesolova (2017) also identified the significant difference in the level of health care as one of the factors that lead patients to seek these services abroad at a lower cost and in a timely manner.

Some of the drivers of medical tourism were access to the most advanced technology (40 per cent), better quality of care (32 per cent), faster access (15 per cent), lower cost of care (9 per cent) for medically necessary procedures, and lower cost of care (4 per cent) for discretionary procedures (Kelley 2013). These factors are affected by "macro policy issues such as the individual freedom of persons to seek treatment overseas, lack of binding legal frameworks on medical tourism, crossborder arrangements (such as immigration and trade agreements), and patient ethical and privacy issues" (Xu et al. 2021, 2).

The number of medical tourists and destinations providing medical services increases every year. According to Precy and Malini (2016), medical tourism, people travelling to developing countries for treatment and leisure, is increasing. The Medical Tourism Index considers three factors: destination environment, medical tourism industry and the quality of facilities and services, and destinations' attractiveness. From 2014 to 2015, it assessed twenty-five countries as medical tourism destinations. This was expanded to forty-one destinations across five regions in its 2016–17 assessment, and to forty-six countries in its 2020–21 assessment (MTI 2021). Interestingly, several Central American and Caribbean countries (Costa Rica, Dominican Republic and Jamaica) are on these lists. The main destinations for medical tourism are in Asia (India, Thailand and Singapore) (Xu et al. 2021). However, the Caribbean and Central America have developed a reputation as successful health service exporters and emerging medical tourism destinations (Johnston and Crooks 2013).

Medical tourism has taken on "reverse globalization" in the Caribbean. Patients from developed countries seek medical treatments in developing countries such as Cuba, Dominican Republic, Barbados and the Cayman Islands (Connell 2013). Cost, access, quality of service and delivery are the main drivers. The Caribbean region's traditional sun, sea and sand mass tourism formula is easily replicated, so many countries diversify their tourism products to remain globally competitive (Chambers and McIntosh 2008). Countries like the Bahamas, Barbados and Jamaica have identified medical tourism as a new niche product with the potential for future development (Chambers and McIntosh 2008; Connell 2013).

In the Cayman Islands, the Health Practice (Amendment) Bill, 2010 was adopted to amend the Health Practice Law (2005 revision) to make provision for tourism services. This Bill sought to establish a special registration category for incidental and connected purposes (The Health Practice [Amendment] Bill G25, S4 2010). Clause 3 of the Bill inserted a new section 7A into the principal law, conferring the right for persons to provide medical tourism service on the island. The term "medical tourism services", as defined by the law, "includes inpatient and ambulatory medical and surgical services provided to individuals who have travelled to the Islands for the purpose of obtaining health care" (The Health Practice [Amendment] Bill, G25, S4 2010, 5).

Since then, several amendments have been made to the Health Practice Law (2005 revision), now the Health Practice Act (2021 Revision). Of importance is Section 7A (3): "a medical tourism provider shall not operate a medical tourism facility without a certificate issued under this Act authorising the operation of the health care facility at which the relevant medical tourism services are provided" (Health Practice Act (2021 Revision) G12, S2 2021, 6).

These include specialist clinics such as Cayman Fertility Centre and Health City Cayman Islands hospital (HCCI). In 2021, NovoClinic Ltd received designation as a medical tourism provider and a medical tourism facility under section 7A (1) and (2) of the Health Practice Act (2021 revision). New to the list of medical tourism facilities is AsterCayman Medcity, a proposed medical tourism project and a collaboration between Aster DM Healthcare and the Cayman Islands government.

Even as medical tourism develops in the Caribbean region, Spencer and Tarlow (2021) warned that the COVID-19 pandemic will change the nature of tourism itself. They noted that a "health crisis quickly becomes a tourism crisis...People who are frightened do not travel" (77). The multinational crisis that is COVID-19 has affected the social and economic framework of the Caribbean region (Spencer and Tarlow 2021). It is imperative that the government and tourism stakeholders reimagine Caribbean tourism (including medical tourism) and develop pandemic protocols to guarantee the health and safety of visitors. Spencer and Tarlow (2021) suggested having health protocols in place that account for the visitor's entire journey, from when they leave home to when they return home.

In the Cayman Islands, such protocols were put in place by the government with a five-phase border reopening plan. This five-phase approach aims "to safely reopen the country while locally managing the risk of transmission by maximising vaccination rates and continued surveillance testing" (Cayman Islands Government n.d.). Regulations were made by Cabinet under the Public Health Act (2021 Revision) for the prevention, control and suppression of COVID-19. The Control of Covid-19 (Travel) (No. 2) Regulations 2022 came into effect as of 8 April 2022. These new regulations now permit any vaccinated person to travel to the Cayman Islands without being subject to quarantine on arrival (Cayman Islands Government n.d.).

Medical Tourism in the Cayman Islands

Medical tourism is a growing niche in the Cayman Islands, with private hospitals and several speciality clinics offering patient care and medical services to international clients. To understand the evolution of medical tourism in Cayman, its current state and its linkages to wellness tourism, this study will conduct a critical assessment of its development, its competition, how it is marketed, promoted and financed, the risks it poses (if any), and the role of the government. The aim is to develop a case study-based understanding of medical tourism in the Cayman Islands from the perspectives of those participate in its development. To this end, this study explores three of these facilities with a significant emphasis on HCCI, the pioneer in medical tourism in the Cayman Islands.

In 2014, Dr Devi Prasad Shetty, famed heart surgeon and physician to Mother Teresa, established HCCI in Grand Cayman. This private medically advanced tertiary hospital offers high-quality, low-cost medicine and attracts patients from the Caribbean, the United States and Latin America.

CaymanSpine at NovoClinic is a speciality clinic for motion surgery in the spine. The clinic is operated by a group of board-certified and fellowship-trained spine surgeons who specialize in motion surgery. According to its website, CaymanSpine offers motion solutions unavailable in the United States (CaymanSpine 2020).

Cayman Fertility Centre is a full service in vitro fertilization clinic that opened in early 2019 in Grand Cayman. It serves patients across the Cayman Islands, United States of America and the northern Caribbean. It is "a sister clinic to the world-renowned Barbados Fertility Centre, a JCI [Joint Commission International] accredited centre of excellence for IVF with over 19 years experience in helping couples achieve their dream of a family" (Cayman Fertility Centre 2020).

The Cayman Islands Government

The government of the Cayman Islands has supported medical tourism from the outset. The Health Practice (Amendment) Bill, 2010 was adopted to amend the Health Practice Law (2005 revision) to make provisions regarding medical tourism services. To date, approximately ten facilities are offering medical tourism services. The government gave HCCI US$800 million in a broad effort to create jobs and diversify the Cayman economy (Harkins 2014). In late 2020, the former government led by Premier Alden McLaughlin announced plans for a new US$350 million, five-hundred-bed hospital in Grand Cayman, called Aster Cayman Medcity. The Premier stated that this new facility would have "an immense impact on Cayman's economy, [give] opportunities for Caymanians, not just in the construction of the facility, but the operation of the facility, educational opportunities, and access to some of the best health care in the world" (Connolly 2020).

The government's support for its tourism product has also boosted medical tourism. Additional airlift from North America and hotel and condominium development projects have improved connectivity and accommodation offerings to the medical tourist and made access to the islands' medical tourism services easier. Like many islands, the government is interested in diversifying its products and boosting its economy. The former Premier McLaughlin explained, "in usual non-pandemic times, the field of healthcare is recession-proof, and expanding the islands' medical tourism capacity will mean Cayman will not have to rely solely on its two main economic pillars of tourism and financial services" (Connolly 2020).

Literature Review

There is much literature and many early studies on medical tourism in Europe and Asia. However, there is a dearth of literature on medical tourism in the Caribbean and Latin American regions. Nevertheless, medical tourism is an evolving niche in Caribbean tourism, with Cuba pioneering medical tourism in the early nineties (Connell 2013) and other small nation-states following its lead. This study on medical tourism in the Cayman Islands will add to this literature and generate interest in further research in this area.

Government's Role

Many Caribbean nations are embracing this new niche of medical tourism. They are "touting the potential economic benefits of developing a medical tourism sector, publicly demonstrating this interest in press releases, speeches, and through attendance at international medical tourism trade shows" (Johnston and Crooks 2013, 251). According to Veselova (2017), the development of medical tourism as an industry is the government's responsibility. Veselova (2017) argued that this industry is impacted by the technological level of national medicine, special legislation and shared infrastructure development. If the government does not systematically develop these resources, there will be no medical tourism.

However, Criollo Oquero (2021), in an article titled "Puerto Rico Medical Tourism Stuck in the Sand", wrote that the private sector believes that the government is hindering the growth potential of medical tourism. In this article, the president of the Puerto Rico Hospital Association, Jaime Plá, suggested the underdevelopment of medical tourism is because the government sees itself as the "absolute custodian of medical tourism" (10). The government's desire to control the industry rather than facilitate it is an additional stumbling block to the development of this industry. Plá theorized that medical tourism would have a more significant economic potential for the island if the government worked with the private sector instead of controlling the activities.

Some posited that for countries to realize the full potential of the medical tourism industry, the government needs to have a strategic plan (Sharma, Sharma and Padroo 2016). In India, the government's commitment to medical tourism included subsidies, concessions, government panels and government insurance schemes (Sharma, Sharma and Padroo 2016). In South Korea, the government encouraged medical tourism by creating a medical visa system (Xu et al. 2021). This system made it easier for the medical tourist to enter South Korea and access its health care system. The South Korean government also developed medical malpractice insurance policies covering both domestic and foreign patients.

Even so, proponents of medical tourism still believe that the government efforts in South Korea are insufficient when compared with its competitors. Low awareness and lack of good public relations, inadequate infrastructure to support medical tourism services, lack of integrated support systems, overregulation that hinders medical tourism activation and intensified competition from competitors were some weaknesses identified in the report (Xu et al. 2021). The report recommended new policies such as extensive deregulation, open investment, developing remote medical services, expanding the number of beds for foreign patients and attracting foreign patients through insurance companies.

Benefits vs Costs

Supporters of medical tourism argue that medical tourism will: (1) improve the local quality of medical care since there will be more investment in the tertiary health care sector, (2) stem the brain drain and increase the number of health care workers locally, and (3) improve the economy through increased employment and opportunity to earn foreign exchange (Johnston and Crooks 2013). For patients, the advantages are cost effectiveness and affordability. For others, it is immediate treatment, high quality health care and the availability of medical experts. Anonymity, privacy and travel opportunities are also benefits for patients seeking medical tourism services.

Medical tourism offers tremendous potential for developing countries because of its low cost advantage. In India, complicated medical procedures are being performed at only a tenth of what they would cost in industrialized countries. The government, the tourism ministry and various agencies promote health and medical tourism as a growth sector. It has provided an economic boost to India and has realized financial benefits, upwards of US$2 billion in 2015 (Sharma, Sharma and Padroo 2016). In Malaysia, medical tourism was identified as a tool for economic development by the national government and as a potential economic growth engine for medical and non-medical sectors (Klijs et al. 2016).

People engage in medical tourism for cost savings, availability of certain drugs, treatments not offered in their home country and alternative medical care (Hart, Slater and Kavan 2018). The main advantages of medical tourism are the low cost of treatment, attractive travel packages, skilled medical personnel, weighed against long waiting hours for treatment and high costs for medical care in patients' own countries (Precy and Malini 2016).

Having health insurance to cover these treatments is also a viable benefit, and companies offering insurance products for medical travel services will have a competitive advantage. Some writers see insurance as a catalyst for growth and an important stakeholder in medical tourism. Precy and Malini (2016) noted that "medical tourism insurance products are an emerging part of the health tourism industry" (7). According to Mittal (2017), having insurance enables patients from other countries to make quick decisions, access quality health care services, reduce out of pocket expenditures and cover post-operation expenses and follow up treatments. Some health insurance companies are promoting medical tourism as an alternative to high medical costs in the home country. Some medical procedures can cost up to eighty times more in the home country than in the destination country. According to estimates by McKinsey and Co., the rise of medical tourism has resulted in annual savings on health-related expenses that amount to nearly US$20 billion (Precy and Malini 2016). To tackle this problem, some insurance companies are developing models that cover medical treatments in any country, including models between the United States and Latin American and Caribbean countries (Mittal 2017).

Many patients turn to medical tourism even if their insurance does not cover specific medical procedures, certain experimental treatments or drugs that are not approved in their home country (Hart, Slater, and Kavan 2018). More companies in the insurance industry (CIGNA, Aetna and Blue Cross) are paying attention to medical tourism, and some are considering pilot programmes that will offer partial travel medical insurance. According to Precy and Malini (2016), "medical tourism which was previously the territory of the uninsured and the underinsured is now considered by industry" (7).

Another benefit for some medical tourists is the potential tax benefits derived from incurring medical expenses abroad (Hart, Slater and Kavan 2018). In the United States, the rules and regulations for the taxpayer seeking medical services in the United States also apply to taxpayers seeking medical services abroad. The medical tourist needs to understand what is considered an allowable medical expense and what medical costs qualify for tax benefits.

In countries like Malaysia, "rural-urban brain drain of medical professionals and diversion of resources essential for public health care to private health care" have been identified as high costs of medical tourism (Klijs et al. 2016, 3). There is also the issue of environmental health equity in small nation-states, such as those in the Caribbean. There are concerns that with population growth and increased demand for services, there may be a significant impact on the social and natural environments. There may be limited economic benefits for locals if infrastructure and linkages are not fully developed, leading to reduced access to health services as costs go up (Johnston and Crooks 2013).

Another concern is the government's use of public resources to incentivize developers. In a 2015 Auditor's General Report on the HCCI deal, the auditor reported that the agreement committed the government to US$800 million in tax, duty and fee concessions and introduced obligations for infrastructure upgrading and expenditure (Pollard, Jenkins and Youngman 2015).

Cohen (2012) raised legal and ethical concerns with medical tourism. What baseline is used to evaluate the quality of care? What are the procedures concerning medical malpractice? What law regulates medical error, the home country or the destination country? Should medical malpractice be considered a non-waivable right, or should patients be allowed to choose to do without in order to get better priced procedures? Does medical tourism have "negative effects on access to medical care by the destination country poor, and if so, do those effects impose normative duties on the home country or international bodies to try and prevent or correct them?" (Cohen 2012, 11).

One concern about surgeries and medical procedures performed overseas is follow-up care. Patients need to know how follow-up care will be handled, especially if complications arise. In his book, *The Globalisation of Health Care: Legal and Ethical Issues*, Cohen (2013) cited twenty-seven case reports of medical tourists who died following cosmetic surgery or bariatric surgery. He offers several recommendations to protect medical tourists from the risk of harm. The American Medical Association noted that many tourists receive quality care. However, there are always safety and quality issues, so physicians need to be aware of the implications of medical tourism for individual patients and the community (AMA n.d.).

There are also ethical issues surrounding circumvention tourism, a sub-type of medical tourism where the motivation is travelling to another destination in order to avoid a domestic prohibition a particular medical service (Cohen 2018). In 2018, the American Medical Association adopted new ethical guidance on medical tourism; these policies will help guide physicians on the implications of medical tourism and their patient responsibilities (AM n.d.).

Medical and Wellness Tourism

The Global Wellness Institute (n.d.b) defines wellness tourism as travel associated with the pursuit of maintaining or enhancing one's well-being. Wellness tourism is seen as one of the fastest growing trends in Europe (Šuligoj 2020) and is projected to grow an average annual rate of 7.5 per cent through 2022 (The Global Wellness Institute n.d.a). It is common to distinguish between medical and wellness tourism. Medical tourism involves obtaining high-tech medical care in a hospital or medical centre. Wellness tourism refers to a more general pursuit of well-being in a spa or resort environment. Many countries are actively participating in the tourism market to develop medical and wellness tourism by combining new high-tech clinics with resorts (Veselova 2017). Some writers believe that medical tourism should focus on wellness, rejuvenation and healthy living (Chambers and McIntosh 2008). They have opined that health care should be an integral part of a holistic vacation experience.

The Global Wellness Institute (n.d.b) suggested that wellness tourism should not be confused with medical tourism, using a continuum to note the difference. On the left side is medical tourism, treating poor health, injury and illness. The right side is wellness, where individuals try to maintain a healthy lifestyle by reducing stress and enhancing their well-being. Wellness is related to healthy eating, body care and exercise.

The Future of Health Care

As medical tourism grows in the Caribbean, more discussion is needed on environmental equity to balance the benefits and costs for the local populations and the region (Johnston and Crooks 2013). Some writers have suggested that the only way for the Caribbean to compete with the more developed medical tourism markets is to focus on demand and supply authentication (Chambers and McIntosh 2008). These writers propose that the focus should be on the tourist having an experientially authentic experience on the demand side. On the supply side, the focus should be on "providing medical tourism products which are ethical, sincere and legitimate" (931).

Methodology

This case study used qualitative inquiry to explore medical tourism in the Cayman Islands. Data were collected using documentation, in-depth interviews and questionnaires. Five key professionals were intentionally selected using purposive sampling, a government representative, the director of tourism and representatives from three main entities offering medical tourism services in the Cayman Islands.

The COVID-19 protocols prevented the face-to-face interviews that were initially planned, so the data collection method was changed. There were two one-on-one interviews, one was face-to-face and the other was virtual. Interviewees were asked general, open-ended questions. The respondent who did the face-to-face interview also completed the survey. The other respondents provided information via structured open-ended question surveys with follow-up questions via email or telephone. Four people were surveyed, three from the medical facilities and one government representative. There were two survey instruments, one for the entities offering medical tourism services and another for the government representative. Organization documents and secondary data sources offered more information on medical tourism activities and the roles of the entities and government. Using multiple methods to obtain data ensured triangulation. Due to the limited time and COVID-19 pandemic protocols in place, data collection was constrained.

Findings and Discussion

The survey responses were categorised under the following sections: (1) reasons for medical tourism development, (2) marketing and promotion, (3) financing and risks associated with medical tourism, (4) partnership, (5) competitors and competitive advantage, (6) medical tourism and wellness and lifestyle tourism, and (7) other findings. Survey respondents were Respondent 1, representing a speciality clinic (CaymanSpine NovoClinic), Respondent 2, private hospital (HCCI) and Respondent 3, clinic (Cayman Fertility Centre).

A representative from the ministry who knew of the Health Practice Amendment Bill and information relating to the government's work with medical tourism providers over the years also agreed to participate. The survey was sent via email. Before completing the survey, the respondent noted that she was speaking from a personal position and not as the voice of the Cayman Islands government. The government representative was labelled Respondent 4.

Reasons for Medical Tourism Development

All respondents identified the availability of medical experts as the main reason for the active development of medical tourism in the Cayman Islands. Other reasons were cost effectiveness, affordability and the ability to provide immediate treatment. One respondent reported,

> Medical Tourism in the Cayman Islands is on the increase due to the spiralling costs in the USA. This allows high quality physicians to offer services at a fraction of the cost and help fill gaps in other Caribbean and LATAM countries. It should also be noted that wait times in Canada for elective surgeries such as knee and hip replacements have become unacceptable to the point where Canadians are willing to pay out of pocket to gain access to surgeries quicker.

McKinsey's 2017 Consumer Health Insights survey (Cordina et al. 2018) supported this observation about the spiralling costs of health care, where 72 per cent of the respondents expressed concern about at least one type of health care expense. The affordability of health care in the United States continues to be one of the pressing consumer concerns and needs.

Respondent 4 mentioned that standardization is essential for the success of medical tourism. The Joint Commission International accreditation received by HCCI indicates the quality of the tourism services offered in the Cayman Islands. The article *Mapping the Market for Medical Travel* indicated that 40 per cent of all medical travellers sought high quality medical care and paid little attention to the proximity of potential destinations or cost of care (Ehrbeck, Guevara and Mango 2008).

Other reasons were anonymity or privacy, providing an economic boost and increasing employment and country development. Several writers have identified providing employment opportunities as a driver for medical tourism globally and reversing the brain drain, attracting health workers back to their home country (Klijs et al. 2016; Lunt et al. n.d.; Sharma, Sharma and Padroo 2016). In the Caribbean, medical tourism is seen as a new means of creating employment (Connell 2013); this was one of the selling points listed by AsterMed City in its proposal to the Caymanian government. Thompson, one of the local investors, stated that Caymanian employees would be given priority, and over two thousand jobs in direct and indirect roles would be created during construction.

All respondents identified the United States and Canada as the central regions the medical tourists came from. This finding is similar to the findings obtained by Veselova (2017), who indicated that the majority of medical tourists were from Europe and North America, where patients paid high prices for medical services. Medical tourists are also visiting from the Caribbean, United Kingdom, Central and

South America and Africa. One respondent identified cruise lines that were not identified in any of the literature reviewed, providing new research data.

The most popular services used by the medical tourists in the Cayman Islands were spinal disease, orthopaedics, heart disease, stem cell therapy and in vitro fertilization. Like in Cayman, stem cell therapy and fertility treatments are on the rise in Latin American countries and the rest of the world (Holzer and Mastroleo 2019). However, in their research, Holzer and Mastroleo (2019) indicated that even though there is an increased use of innovative practices in some Latin American countries, there are concerns about the lack of international regulations and enforcement of the legal and ethical guidelines governing these services. The entities in the Cayman Islands are regulated. For example, CaymanSpine offers motion solutions not available in the United States but assures their patients that they elevate the standard of care through practice synergies and clinical research.

Although the research indicated that many tourists travelled for cosmetic and weight reduction surgeries (Veslova 2017), the facilities surveyed offered none of these services. Since only three entities were used in this case study, other medical providers could speak to these offerings in further research.

Marketing and Promotion

The respondents' direct marketing and promotional tools are websites, social media, search engine marketing, testimonials and word of mouth. Some entities also use advertisement and public relations. One respondent also used sales channels such as meeting with payers (insurance companies) and governments. More insurance companies are now partnering with medical tourism providers and government agencies to ensure easier access to medical services for the patients and developing models for destinations, including the Caribbean and Latin America (Precy and Malini 2016; Mittal 2017). Harkins (2014) also identified a symbiotic relationship between the government and HCCI, asserting that the government has assisted HCCI in promoting health care to patients.

Financing and Risks Associated with Medical Tourism

Medical facilities have spent over US$1 million to accommodate their medical tourists. One respondent stated, "We have spent over 150 million dollars to set up our hospital and are looking to make an additional 100 million". Respondent 4 stated that concessions and subsidies might be granted to any entity that applies to the Ministry of Finance and Economic Development. An auditor's report confirmed concessions for the HCCI project included US$800 million in customs duty concessions on medical equipment and supplies, an unknown amount in reduced work permit fees, and provision of water at a preferential rate by the Water Authority for an unlimited period. There was also a commitment to upgrade airport facilities to accommodate an expected increase in traffic due to medical tourism (Pollard, Jenkins and Youngman 2015).

AsterMed City, the US$350 million hospital planned for Grand Cayman, has received government support. However, the former Premier indicated at the signing of the agreement that the concessions given would not be like the deal given to HCCI (Connolly 2020). The local Cayman investors have reported that Aster DM Healthcare is the only investor in Aster Cayman MedCity's proposed medical tourism facility (Pollard, Jenkins and Youngman 2015).

Connell (2013) stated that governments are investing in medical tourism, some through a partnership with private investors or offering concessions and other benefits to assist with the development of their nation-states. These investments are being carried out with the hope of creating a new revenue stream, achieving economic growth, creating employment and stimulating foreign exchange flows (Connell 2013; Chambers and McIntosh 2008). As far back as the 1990s, significant investment has been made in medical tourism, with Cuba as the pioneer followed by other Caribbean countries such as the Dominican Republic, which established its medical tourism industry, and St Kitts and Nevis, which invested US$15 million in a medical centre in Nevis (Connell 2013).

The respondents identified risks of medical tourism to the organization and country as non-availability of preoperative and postoperative care, health insurance companies' refusal to pay for overseas treatment, inadequate investment in the health care industry, and additional costs (flights, accommodations) faced by the medical tourist. In follow up interviews with the respondents from the medical facilities, they indicated that preoperative care is usually conducted in the home country. However, postoperative care can be problematic since some tourists return home shortly after completing procedures. Postoperative care is identified as a risk by several writers as well as the American Medical Association. Its Code of Medical Opinion 1.2.13 states, "Substandard surgical care, poor infection control, inadequate screening of blood products, and falsified or outdated medications in lower-income settings of care can pose greater risks than patients would face at home" (AMA, n.d.). The American Medical Association advises physicians to be aware of these risks and their implications for individual patients and the community.

Some patients will return to their home country for postoperative care and may experience complications and other side effects, which become the health care system's responsibility in the patients' home countries (Lunt et al. n.d.). Crooks et al. (2017) identified several public health concerns associated with medical tourism both in the individual's home country and the destination country. They also highlight the risks faced by caregivers who accompany the medical tourist and provide advice on avoiding these risks. Advice included assessing and avoiding exposure to risks, anticipating medical tourist care needs and familiarizing oneself with essential logistics. The American Medical Association also advises physicians to familiarize themselves with issues in medical tourism so that they can make informed decisions and offer follow-up care where possible. The association also recommends that physicians advocate for "appropriate oversight of medical tourism and companies that facilitate it to protect patient safety and promote high-quality care".

Partnership

All three entities have partnered with the government. Respondent 1 noted that the purpose of the partnership was to ensure that there was Health Practice Commission oversight. Respondent 2 stated, "We have partnered with the government to ensure the atmosphere is such to encourage medical tourism". Research findings show that national strategies implemented by governments are supportive of medical tourism (Lunt et al. n.d.). In 1998, amid the Asian Financial Crisis, medical tourism was identified by the national government of Malaysia as a tool for economic development, and investment was made in the development of modern facilities, medical technologies and medical expertise (Klijs et al. 2016). In an OECD study, several national government agencies and policy initiatives have sought to promote medical tourism in their countries; for example, India introduced a new visa category, the Singapore Tourism Board implemented a branding and marketing campaign for its health care services and Poland created the Polish Medical Tourism Chamber of Commerce (Lunt et al. n.d.).

Respondent 4 noted that the role of the government was leadership and governance. Delivering health service to its constituents and providing due diligence through its Health Practice Councils was part of this role. When asked about the future, the respondent stated, "The CIG [Cayman Islands Government] should ensure that the proper due diligence is conducted to prevent any reputational risk/damage to the Cayman Islands. In addition, CIG should ensure that Caymanians are not disenfranchised and prioritize employment if qualified. Also, opportunities exist for CIG to engage the medical tourism partners through public, private partnerships in providing the necessary health care services/expertise not currently readily available".

These responses indicate that the growth and development of medical tourism within the Cayman Islands are dependent on a partnership between the government and the industry stakeholders.

Competitors and Competitive Advantage

The competitors in the field of medical tourism are Caribbean, North American and Latin American countries. Connell (2013) noted that success for Caribbean countries would be difficult to achieve in a crowded market. However, if these countries were to specialize, there might be some competitive advantage. He suggested that having a particular niche is crucial, such as fertility tourism in Barbados, addiction therapy in Antigua, and prostate cancer and spinal surgery in the Bahamas. The three entities in this case study use a niche product approach: fertility, spinal surgery and cardiovascular treatment. As noted by one respondent, "We offer a treatment not available anywhere else in the world". Other advantages were language, the seamless patient pathway, the all-inclusive bundled prices, the substantial cost differential (approximately 50–75 per cent less) and a higher success rate.

Medical Tourism and Wellness and Lifestyle Tourism

The responses concerning the connection between medical tourism and wellness and lifestyle tourism were mixed. Respondents 1 and 4 did not see a connection and suggested that the Department of Tourism might better respond to this query. Respondent 3 suggested the connection is implied through the promotion of healthy relaxation and environment. Respondent 2 noted,

> Wellness can be a segment that stands on its own as our Cayman Islands leisure visitors would be more inclined to pay premiums

for this type of service. (Potentially as add-ons to their vacation or maybe even group wellness trips.) Our core medical tourism is for severe ailments and major life-threatening surgeries. We do offer Executive Health check-ups which lend themselves to wellness; however, the volume in this area is not a significant patient driver from an international perspective due to the overall costs associated with airfare and hotel.

Some destinations attempt to develop both types of tourism by combining their medical clinics with resorts (Veslova 2017). Executive health checks and aftercare services for medical tourists may show an overlap between wellness and medical tourism, but research findings indicate that each product is separate. According to The Global Wellness Institute (n.d.b) while both forms of tourism are dependent on the region's basic tourism and hospitality infrastructure and amenities, the types of visitors, activities, services, businesses and regulations involved are very different.

Other Findings

One respondent described the closure of the borders in March 2020 due to the COVID-19 pandemic as a major obstacle. Currently, only repatriation flights are allowed, and medical tourism has essentially halted.

Health City Cayman Islands (HCCI) Model

Mr Shomari Scott, chief business officer (CBO) of HCCI, was interviewed on the HCCI medical tourism model. He was asked to respond to a statement made by Chandy Abraham, MD, HCCI's facility and medical director, to delegates at the World Medical Tourism and Global Healthcare Congress about the affordability of the services at' HCCI. Dr Abraham said, "We're one of the few hospitals in the world to publish our prices as a bundled flat rate. And that's what you'll pay, nothing more. You get one bill, and you'll never get another bill. It's a model that gets a lot of attention when we talk with other healthcare providers." (Harkins 2014).

The CBO agreed that all surgeries at HCCI are a bundled price, "one price and that is it". He compared a cardiac bypass surgery in New York, costing between US$150,000 and US$200,000, to the same surgery at HCCI, costing between US$22,000 and US$35,000. HCCI can bundle costs because of different efficiencies, (1) the supply chain, going directly to the pharmaceutical companies and manufacturers, (2) physician expertise (employing physicians from India who have conducted a multitude of complex surgeries on a large population), and (3) infection control, with an infection rate that is lower than other hospitals (The CBO stated that HCCI's surgical site infections is 1.41 per cent when compared with the benchmark 2–4 per cent).

HCCI is, therefore, able to produce high quality surgeries at a much lower cost than providers in the United States. The CBO explained that since there is no third party, these efficiencies, "a sum of all parts", lead to savings that are passed on to the patients or their insurance companies. The HCCI model is potentially very disruptive to US health care. According to Govindarajan and Ramamurti (2018), "Even with zero co-pays and deductibles and free travel for the patient and a chaperone for 1–2 weeks, insurers would save a lot of money".

Goodman (2016) posited that quality tends to be higher when patients pay a fixed package price. He notes that US health care makes money on mistakes, but the reverse happens when a facility offers a package. In these instances, the hospital (not the patient) will pay the cost of infection and readmission. This strategy is what HCCI has done, and the quality data support its strategy. Compared with the industry benchmark, its key performance indicators are better and indicate how a hospital can minimize its expenses. For example, the unplanned return rate to theatre within forty-eight hours is 0.88 per cent, while the benchmark for return rate to theatre within 48 hours is 4.6 (WHO). The CBO suggested that having these key performance indicators and Joint Commission International accreditation has instilled trust in the HCCI model and provides reassurance to its medical tourists.

The CBO also noted that such efficiency from a medical tourism perspective allows HCCI to offer its patients the highest level of surgery at a cost that people could access and afford. One of the outcomes of this model is that HCCI has conducted five hundred "free" lifesaving surgeries for children and families based on charitable organizations who can afford US$5,000–$15,000 rather than the US$80,000 that typical high-level surgery would cost. The CBO noted that the number of international patients had been zero for the past six months but, based on the cost-effective and efficient model, the hospital has remained operational.

The CBO explained that the perception that affordability meant a lower quality of care might have been an issue when the facility first opened because the Western world was not familiar with Dr Shetty and Narayana Health. However, over the years, this scepticism has diminished since the facility has provided evidence showing quality care and quality outcomes. In an article in *Harvard Business Review*, Dr Shetty explained that affordable health care can become global. For this to happen, "American policy makers and American think-tanks can look at a model that costs a fraction of what they pay and see that it has similarly good outcomes" (Govindarajan and Ramamurti 2018). At HCCI, the quality measures highlighted were zero mortality rate, accreditation by Joint Commission International and patient testimonials.

The CBO believes that HCCI's presence in the Cayman Islands shows confidence in the economy and that medical tourism is working and will be a pull factor for other facilities entering the market. HCCI is expanding its services to cater to both overseas and local patients. HCCI offers services in Cayman Brac, has a clinic in Camana Bay and will start construction on a 70,000 sq ft seventy-bed hospital with full oncology and neonatology suites. The CBO noted that this would push medical tourism in the Caribbean, since HCCI would be filling a gap, using a medical linear accelerator for radiotherapy and specialized care for neonates.

The CBO explained the importance of partnership with all its stakeholders. Over five years, HCCI has used only US$5.7 million of the US$800 million concessions within the agreement with the government. Concessions were used for purchasing medical equipment and paying a lower percentage for specific permits categories. HCCI partners with the Cayman Islands Health Services Authority and fills gaps such as cardiac care, high level orthopaedic care from car accidents and care from a diagnostic perspective. HCCI is also providing care to locals and, over the last five years, has averted five thousand air ambulance transfers which could have cost between US$20.8 million to US$40 million. Several benefits have been derived from having these surgeries on the island, saving lives and incurring lower costs for patients and insurance companies. HCCI also partners with other physicians and medical providers who refer patients to the facility.

The CBO purported that HCCI is giving back to the community, primarily through its Health Explorer Programme. There have been approximately seventeen thousand student interactions and 109 scholarships for medical pathways. Retirees from overseas are now seeing the Cayman Islands as a retirement option compared to other retirement locations in the United States and Europe because of the high quality of medical services provided on the island.

There was potential for wellness tourism, but HCCI's strength is tertiary care and providing high surgical quality. Within this type of care is a holistic element. HCCI has combined holistic care in its infrastructure, postoperative care services, executive health checks, nutritional counselling and massage.

Destination Health Care

The interview with the Director was to explore a connection between wellness and lifestyle tourism and medical tourism. The director stated that the Department of Tourism is charged with leisure tourism and travel and was not mandated to put marketing support behind medical tourism. The department's principal purpose was to showcase the destination strengths and position all three islands' strengths and quality services. Medical tourism was the central focus of the health service providers, while the department's health strategy focus was related to leisure and related tourism benefits. The department's primary focus is to grow leisure tourism, since 95 per cent of its visitors are leisure tourists. So the emphasis was on conference hosting and facilitation and support for hospitality.

The director explained that her colleagues "struggled with the term medical tourism", and it was believed that this term was too technical and more internal and specific to health personnel and that industry. A new term, "destination health care", was developed from this discussion, ensuring visitors enter an environment where quality health care is accessible if needed.

The director stated that Caymankind in essence is the spirit of the Cayman Islands. The destination is attractive to travellers; it is seen as a place of safety with modern infrastructure, quality facilities, quality care and low COVID-19 related infections. The department's goal is to carve out leisure into a lifestyle platform where wellness is positioned to travelling individuals and groups. Marketing wellness is a priority since it is an extension of the traveller's lifestyle but should not be confused with medical tourism, which follows a different trajectory.

Conclusion

Medical tourism is evolving in the Cayman Islands, with its pioneer medical tourism provider, HCCI, leading the way. Based on projections, this tourism niche will continue to grow as medical tourists demand a more accessible and affordable product. Each entity studied in this case has concretized its speciality. They are determined to be the leaders in the region in their areas of expertise. To attract these international clients, they have targeted distinct markets and use several touchpoints to reach target customers and present their brand favourably. The intent is to attract visitors from their current marketplace, United States, United Kingdom and Canada, and seek new visitors from Latin America and the Caribbean.

The literature shows that the success of medical tourism is contingent on the support and partnership, not control, of the government and other regulatory agencies. The Cayman Islands government seems to be supportive and has encouraged investment in medical tourism projects to diversify the economy and provide employment and new opportunities for its residents. However, as medical tourism expands, the government must ensure that its population's interests are protected and that locals' needs are balanced with the country's economic interests. If there is any perception of an imbalance in providing public health care, with higher costs of medical services to residents and inadequate infrastructure, the growth of this niche will stagnate. It will be in the government's best interest to have a structured approach to medical tourism, develop its resources and include medical tourism policies in its national strategic plan.

Medical tourism should not be confused with wellness tourism and should be viewed on a continuum from poor health to a healthy lifestyle. Is there a linkage between these two products? While there is linkage potential for the two products, they still need to be delineated in their marketing efforts. Clients searching for medical services will not search for wellness and vice versa. The target markets for these products do not see an association between them, so they will travel to the destination and only experience one. This information gap allows stakeholders to change consumers' perceptions and develop a product that offers a holistic experience. The destination must be seen as offering diverse products which can turn first-time visitors into repeat visitors.

The findings from the case indicate that both types of tourism could be embraced by a new concept, "destination health care". Medical tourism has a resultant effect since the destination can be marketed as a healthy and relaxed environment to rejuvenate and rehabilitate. Several writers supported this idea of holistic health and wellness (Vesolova 2017; Chambers and McIntosh 2008) and suggested that countries could market the product as such.

These findings are relevant to the Cayman Islands as they promote their Caymankind tourism product. Embracing medical and wellness tourism under the destination health care banner will allow the target market to see the destination as a holistic vacation experience. The Department of Tourism will need to work with various stakeholders to develop this product and develop consumer learning to see the association. The product should see medical tourists using the destination for postoperative care and future wellness activities. The wellness tourist will know that the destination has the infrastructure to treat medical emergencies that arise while vacationing in the destination. This association will provide the traveller with an authentic holistic experience of Caymankind.

References

American Medical Association (AMA). n.d. "Ethics." Medical Tourism. Accessed 26 September 2021. https://www.ama-assn.org/delivering-care/ethics/medical-tourism.
CaymanSpine. 2020. "World-Class Care." https://caymanspine.com/.
Cayman Fertility Centre. 2020. "Patient Centered Fertility Treatment in Paradise." https://caymanivf.com/.
Cayman Islands Government. 2021. Health Practice Act (2021 Revision), Supplemental 2, Legislation Gazette No. 12, (2021) https://cbc.gov.ky/images/documents/HealthPracticeAct_2021_Revision.pdf.
Cayman Islands Government. n.d. "We Are in Phase 5 Of the Border Reopening Plan." Accessed 18 April 2022. https://www.exploregov.ky/reopening-plan.
Cayman Islands Government. 2010. The Health Practice (Amendment) Bill Supplemental 4, Legislation Gazette No. 25, (2010). http://gazettes.gov.ky/portal/pls/portal/docs/1/115266901.PDF.
Cayman Islands Public Health Act Revision. 2021. G16, S7 (2021).
CDC. n.d. "Travelers Health." Medical Tourism: Travel to Another Country for Medical Care. Accessed 19 April 2021. https://wwwnc.cdc.gov/travel/page/medical-tourism).
Chambers, Donna, and Bryan McIntosh. 2008. "Using Authenticity to Achieve Competitive Advantage in Medical Tourism in the English-Speaking Caribbean." *Third World Quarterly* 29 (5): 919–37. doi:10.1080/01436590802106056.
Cohen, I. Glenn. 2012. "How to Regulate Medical Tourism (And Why It Matters for Bioethics)." *Developing World Bioethics* 12 (1): 9–20. doi:10.1111/j.1471-8847.2012.00317.x.
———. 2013. *The Globalization of Health Care: Legal and Ethical Issues.* New York: Oxford University Press.
Cohen, Glenn. 2018. "Circumvention Medical Tourism and Cutting Edge Medicine: The Case of Mitochondrial Replacement Therapy." *Indiana Journal of Global Legal Studies* 25 (1): 439–62. https://doi.org/10.2979/indjglolegstu.25.1.0439.

Connell, John. 2013. "Medical Tourism in the Caribbean Islands: A Cure for Economies in Crisis?" *Island Studies Journal* 8 (1): 115–30.

Connolly, Norma. 2020. "$350 Million Hospital Planned for Grand Cayman: No Construction Concessions included in Agreement" *Cayman Compass*, 21 December 2020. https://www.caymancompass.com/2020/12/21/350-million-hospital-planned-for-grand-cayman.

Cordina, Jenny, Elizabeth P. Jones, Rohit Kumar, and Carlos Pardo Martin. 2018. "Healthcare Consumerism 2018: An Update on the Journey." *McKinsey & Company*, 9 July 2018. https://www.mckinsey.com/industries/healthcare-systems-and-services/our-insights/healthcare-consumerism-2018.

Criollo Oquero, A. 2021. "Puerto Rico Medical Tourism Stuck in the Sand: Private Sector Says Government is Hindering Potential." *Caribbean Business* 7 (13): 8–10.

Crooks, Valorie A., Rebecca Whitmore, Jeremy Snyder, and Leigh Turner. 2017. "'Ensure That You Are Well Aware of the Risks You Are Taking...': Actions and Activities Medical Tourists' Informal Caregivers Can Undertake to Protect Their Health and Safety." *BMC Public Health* 17 (487): 1–10. doi:10.1186/s12889-017-4442-1.

Ehrbeck, Tilman, Ceani Guevara, and Paul D. Mango. 2008. "Mapping the Market for Medical Travel." *The McKinsey Quarterly*, May 2008. https://www.researchgate.net/publication/265184262_Mapping_the_market_for_medical_ravel.

Goodman, J. C. 2016. "Better Care at a Fraction of The Cost – Only A Plane Ride Away." Last accessed 26 September 2021. https://www.forbes.com/sites/johngoodman/2016/04/11/better-care-at-a-fraction-of-the-cost-only-a-plane-ride-away/?sh=14d53d7147a2.

Govindarajan, Vijay and Ravi Ramamurti. 2018. "Is This the Hospital That Will Finally Push the Expensive U.S. Health Care System to Innovate?" *Harvard Business Review*, 22 June 2018. https://hbr.org/2018/06/is-this-the-hospital-that-will-finally-push-the-expensive-u-s-health-care-system-to-innovate.

Harkins, Joe. 2014. "Cayman Islands Health City: At Heart of Medical Tourism in Caribbean." *Medical Tourism*, December 5, 2014. https://www.magazine.medicaltourism.com/article/cayman-islands-heart-medical-tourism-caribbean.

Hart, Dana L., Robert Slater, and C. Bruce Kavan. 2018. "Considering the Tax Benefits of Medical Tourism." *CPA Journal* 88 (3): 48–52.

Holzer, Felicitas, and Ignacio Mastroleo. 2019. "Innovative Practice in Latin America: Medical Tourism and the Crowding Out of Research." *American Journal of Bioethics* 19 (6): 42–44. doi:10.1080/15265161.2019.1602189.

Johnston, R., and V. A. Crooks. 2013. "Medical Tourism in the Caribbean Region: A Call to Consider Environmental Health Equity." *West Indian Medical Journal* 62 (3): 250–53.

Kelley, Edward. 2013. "WHO Patient Safety Programme – Medical Tourism." World Health Organization. Accessed 26 September 2021. https://fliphtml5.com/sbxk/uprism.pdf.

Klijs, Jeroen, Meghann Ormond, Tomas Mainil, Jack Peerlings, and Wim Heijman. 2016. "A State-Level Analysis of the Economic Impacts of Medical Tourism in Malaysia." *Asian-Pacific Economic Literature* 30 (1): 3–29. doi:10.1111/apel.12132.

Lunt, Neil, Richard Smith, Mark Exworthy, Stephen T. Green, Daniel Horsfall and Russell Mannion. n.d. "Medical Tourism: Treatments, Markets and Health System Implications: A Scoping Review." OECD. Accessed 14 September 2021. https://www.oecd.org/els/health-systems/48723982.pdf.

Medical Tourism Index (MTI). 2020. "Medical Tourism Index 2020–2021." Medical Tourism. Accessed 26 September 2021. https://www.medicaltourism.com/mti/home.

Mittal, Monika. 2017. "Medical Tourism – Role of Insurance as a Catalyst for Growth." *Journal of the Insurance Institute of India* 4 (4): 21–27.

Pollard, Keith, Jenny Jenkins, and Ian Youngman. 2015. "Government Acted Unlawfully on Health City Cayman Islands Deal." *LaingBuisson*, 15 September 2015. https://www.laingbuissonnews.com/imtj/news-imtj/overnment-acted-unlawfully-on-health-city-cayman-islands-deal/.

Precy, M. R., and D. H. Malini. 2016. "Medical Tourism Insurance." *Journal of the Insurance Institute of India* 3 (4): 6–9.

Sanjivan, Gill, and Sahil Sinha. 2020. "Medical Tourism Market." Allied Market Research. Accessed 26 September 2021. https://www.alliedmarketresearch.com/medical-tourism-market.

Sharma, Bhawna, J. K. Sharma, and Sudir Padroo. 2016. "Medical Tourism in India: Growth or Dilemma." *Management Dynamics in the Knowledge Economy* 4 (2): 277–90.

Spencer, Andrew, and Peter Tarlow. 2021. "Health in the Caribbean." In *Tourism Safety and Security for the Caribbean*, edited by Andrew Spencer and Peter Tarlow, 61–84. Bingley: Emerald Publishing. https://doi.org/10.1108/978-1-80071-318-520211007.

Šuligoj, Metod. 2020. "Characterization of Health-Related Hotel Products on the Slovenian Coast." *Geoadria* 25 (1): 39–52. doi:10.15291/geoadria.3158.

The Global Wellness Institute. n.d.a. "2018 Global Wellness Tourism Economy." Accessed 26 September 2021. https://globalwellnessinstitute.org/industry-research/global-wellness-tourism-Economy/.

———. n.d.b. "What is Wellness." Accessed 26 September 2021. https://globalwellnessinstitute.org/what-is-wellness/what-is-wellness-tourism/.

Veselova, E.Sh. 2017. "Medical Tourism." *Problems of Economic Transition* 59 (6): 480–500. doi:10.1080/10611991.2017.1352363.

Xu, Qing, Vidya Purushothaman, Raphael E. Cuomo, and Tim K. Mackey. 2021. "A Bilingual Systematic Review of South Korean Medical Tourism: A Need to Rethink Policy and Priorities for Public Health?" *BMC Public Health* 21 (1): 1–17. doi:10.1186/s12889-021-10642-x.

11.
Cruise Tourism in the Caribbean Island of Cozumel: Challenges and Opportunities for Sustainability in the Post-COVID-19 Era

Kennedy Obombo Magio

Introduction

Cruise tourism in the Mexican Caribbean is experiencing major challenges as a result of the COVID-19 pandemic: cancellations or temporary suspension of cruise tourism activities by cruise lines and port destinations and loss of jobs and income for host communities. Many small island nations rely heavily on the jobs and cash flow from the industry. Other issues like climate change, increasing concerns about socio-economic and environmental impacts, insecurity and so on existed before the pandemic. Therefore, it is important to analyse and understand the depth of these issues in each port destination and identify the potential opportunities for cruise lines to make a positive difference in the host communities, especially as it relates to the local culture, environment, and sustainable on-shore excursions.

This analysis is well aligned with the new transformative post-COVID-19 vision proposed by different scholars for a steady and faster economic, environmental and social recovery in the tourism sector based on principles of sustainability (Băndoi et al. 2020, 10–12; Everingham and Chassagne 2020, 559–62; Galvany, Lew and Sotelo Perez 2020; OECD 2020; Lew 2018, 745–48) and prioritizing the local community and the environment. At the very least, tourism also involves communities (for example, residents), the natural environment and the lived environment (for example, overtourism issues). The main focus in this recovery process is to make sure that tourism does not return to its former state, where economic bottom line and the pressure to meet the needs of the visitor override real aspirations and concerns for the local people (and for the natural environment, for that matter). According to Galvany, Lew and Sotelo Perez (2020), tourism must consider inclusive social participation in order to democratize decisions and assume the responsibilities that the conservation of the natural and cultural heritage of a locality or region entails.

Focusing on Cozumel, the present study examines key issues facing cruise tourism on the island and how the destination is trying to cope with or manage change, both positive and negative. This analysis is based on desk research and local stakeholder feedback and the following questions are addressed:

1. What are the local attitudes towards cruise tourism?
2. What government policies are currently in place or in consideration that may impact cruise tourism?
3. Have any cruise competitors done community project work in the host destination in the past, and do they currently have any ongoing projects?
4. Who are some local community organizations that the cruise lines currently work with or support?
5. Who are some local tour operators and tourism businesses that the cruise lines currently work with?
6. What would local stakeholders identify as being the most important social or environmental projects that cruise companies should support in or around the host destination?
7. Who are some sustainable tour operators in the community that cruise lines could potentially work with to improve the sustainability of their land excursions?

It was found that stakeholders in both public and private sectors (residents, opinion leaders and tourism operators, among others) are supportive of cruise tourism. However, there were issues related to the excessive number of cruise tourists before the pandemic and diminishing recreational opportunities for the locals. Those who are critical of cruise tourism include: environmental groups that are critical of the rapid expansion and the impacts of cruise tourism on the environment because of how strong the environmental footprint of the cruise industry is; hotel operators who argue that the local government is more focused on cruise tourism than stay-over tourism, their main source of business; and the small enterprises who do not have direct access to do business with cruise lines.

Cruise Tourism and Sustainability in the Post-COVID-19 Era

The COVID-19 pandemic abruptly halted the mobility on which industries like mass cruise tourism rely. First, port destinations began to refuse to receive stopover vessels that were still at sea when COVID-19 numbers of infections and deaths began to grow at an alarming rate. Then travelling was halted when most Western countries closed their borders to non-essential transit. In Mexico, during the first three months of the COVID-19 pandemic, the industry came to a standstill, almost 2 million cruise passengers and revenues of US$134.4 million were lost, with the greatest impact in the Mexican Caribbean (Secretaría de Turismo–SEDETUR 2021). Experts estimate that it will take at least a couple of years for the sector to recover (Expansión 2020). In popular destinations like Cozumel, which are dependent on cruise tourism, the COVID-19 crisis puts not only visitors at great risk but also the livelihood of the local population.

A number of authors (Crossley 2020, 538–40; Everingham and Chassagne 2020, 556–59; Higgins-Desbiolles 2020, 612–21; Gössling, Scott and Hall 2020, 11–20; Sharma and Nicolau 2020, 1–3; Jones and Comfort 2020, 77–83; Jamal and Budke 2020, 183–85; Galvani, Lew and Perez 2020, 567–72) have questioned the hopes of returning to the pre-COVID-19 mass tourism, which was characterized by excessive mobility. Mass cruise tourism is not an exception, as observed by Renaud (2020, 680–85). This industry is one of the current emblematic manifestations of transnational capitalist tourism. It is an industry based on a complex and extraordinary tourist product that has often been criticized for creating collisions at the economic, environmental and socio-cultural levels, including socio-territorial exclusions, monopolies, inequality and precarious regional livelihood, deteriorated marine ecosystems, and increased air pollution (Vogel 2011, 230–35). These interrelations and spatial–temporal repercussions require renewed critical questioning as stakeholders try to restore normalcy after coronavirus shutdowns and to rebuild the industry in the post-COVID-19 era.

In this recovery process, it has been recognized that many acute shifts and turns lie ahead in terms of how tourism is conceptualized, understood, performed, governed and planned for, and topics related to sustainability and resilience of tourist destinations have never been so relevant. As well as presenting a range of new challenges which require informed and context-specific responses, the present moment is undoubtedly also an opportunity to build resilience and capacity and create positive transformation in destinations. This means that destinations should develop capacity for readiness, adaptability and resilience to achieve their own recovery, survival and prosperity and, in turn, to nurture versatility in how tourism activities can be employed to serve their host communities' needs in post-crisis recovery.

Methodology

The present assessment was carried out between December 2018 and August 2019, a few months before the start of COVID-19 pandemic, to assess key sustainability issues facing cruise tourism in Cozumel using a selected number of indicators from the Global Sustainable Tourism Council Destination criteria. The island of Cozumel, 30 miles long, is located off the eastern coast of Mexico's Yucatán Peninsula, opposite the coastal town of Playa del Carmen and near the Yucatán Channel. It has a population of about eighty-six thousand permanent residents and some five million visitors annually. The assessment steps included desk-based collection and analysis of destination policies; site visits, including an on-site workshop to brief stakeholders about the assessment purpose, method and criteria; focus groups and interviews to consult destination stakeholders on implementation of destination policies and practices; writing of a draft report; and a closing workshop to discuss and validate the researcher's key findings and recommendations. Some sixty stakeholders from government, tourism businesses, NGOs, civil society and academia were consulted during the focus groups and interviews, and some fifty participated in the final workshop.

This assessment builds on similar studies in the region, including the 2012 *Rapid Sustainable Cruise Destination Diagnostic* also known as the 2012 Rapid Assessment (Novedades Quintana Roo, 2013), and a growing recognition that properly planned tourism can contribute to healthy livelihoods and ecosystems based on multi-sectoral partnerships.

Overview of Tourism in Cozumel

Cozumel is Mexico's top tourism destination and host to a mix of several types of visitors, including cruse ship "daytrippers", who spend less than a day on the island; stay-over guests, mainly from the United States, who typically stay three to four days (some in all-inclusive resorts); domestic travellers; low-budget backpackers (both national and international); and long-stay expatriates and retirees with homes in Cozumel. There are three important tourism peaks in the year: Winter (December–March), Summer (June–August), and Holy Week (in March or April), when most people in Mexico have vacations. The slowest months are April and May (except for Holy Week) and September and October. According to González and Martínez (2021, 157–60), tourism and related commerce account for

78 per cent of the island's economic activities, with the remaining 22 per cent derived from fishing, agriculture, ranching, manufacturing and construction.

Cozumel's cruise infrastructure includes three piers, which receive about sixteen hundred ships a year (Secretaría de Turismo – SEDETUR 2021). There is no carrying capacity baseline (number of ships or passengers that Cozumel can accommodate in a day), however, stakeholders observed that the destination is usually overwhelmed when there are eight docked and four anchored ships. The average throughout the year is five docked and two anchored ships, which is still high. This happens once a year during the month of December. Nearly all (96 per cent) of Cozumel's cruise passengers come from the United States, the United Kingdom and Canada. Cruise ships arrive at the island early in the morning, and approximately 85 per cent of passengers disembark and spend from five to nine hours onshore. A 2014–15 cruise season study by Business Research and Economic Advisors (2012a; 2012b) found that many of the passengers did not venture beyond the cruise terminals, where they find restaurants, bars and souvenir stores; only 51 per cent of passengers tour the island and visit key tourist attractions.

In 2018, Cozumel set a record with 6,010,147 visitors, a 6.31 per cent increase over 2017, according to the Secretary of Tourism in Quintana Roo (Secretaría de Turismo – SEDETUR 2021). This included 5,070,611 cruise passengers, who spent an average of eight hours on the island, and 939,536 stay-over visitors, with an average stay of three days. Most stay-over visitors fly by plane to Cancún International Airport and then travel to Playa del Carmen by bus or car to take a ferry to Cozumel; a smaller number fly directly to Cozumel via scheduled or charter flights. Day visitors arrive via ferry from Riviera Maya. There is no official record of day travellers, though it is estimated that 12,500 passengers, including locals and workers, arrive by ferry every day. This number increases to about seventeen thousand during the high season.

Also, during 2018, cruise passengers and stay-over visitors generated a combined total spending of US$1,296.87 million, a 7.33 per cent increase over 2017. A 2016 Secretaría de Turismo study found that overnight visitors spent $538 for an average stay of three days, while cruise passengers spent an average of $120 per passenger (Secretaría de Turismo – SEDETUR 2021). The Business Research and Economic Advisors study commissioned by the Florida–Caribbean Cruise Association found comparable results on cruise passenger expenditures. In other Mexican ports, cruise passengers on average spent only US$75 (BREA 2012a; 2012b). The expenditures for Cozumel are higher, Secretaría de Turismo concludes, because of its natural attractions and the growing number of providers of tourist services (Secretaría de Turismo – SEDETUR 2021).

The Business Research and Economic Advisors study calculated that Cozumel generated US$366 million in direct cruise sector expenditures from passenger, crew and cruise line purchases, making it the third highest among the thirty-five destinations covered in the study (BREA 2012a; 2012b). The study identified three principal sources for the economic benefits Cozumel derives from cruise tourism: (1) on-shore expenditures by passengers, including shore excursions and retail purchases of clothing and jewellery; (2) on-shore spending by crew, which mainly comprises purchases of food and beverages, local transportation, and clothing and electronics; and (3) expenditures by the cruise lines for supplies, such as food and beverages, port services (navigation and utility services), and port fees and taxes, such as wharf and docking fees. The Business Research and Economic Advisors study also calculated that cruise tourism in Cozumel generated direct employment for 6,114 persons, paying US$37.9 million in annual wages, or just over US$6,000 per employee. These were the highest employment numbers among the thirty-five destinations Business Research and Economic Advisors studied.

Geography and Attractions

Cozumel, Mexico's longest island, lies about 12 miles off the mainland, surrounded by the Caribbean Sea. Edged with white sand beaches, the island is mostly flat and limestone based, with the highest point being only 20 meters above sea level. There are no aboveground aquifers (streams, rivers or lakes) in Cozumel because of its highly porous surface. Most of the fresh water comes from rainwater captured by water wells in the centre of the island, and its availability increases or decreases depending on rainfall. There are also several freshwater sink holes on the island.

Cozumel's fragile natural ecosystems include the Mesoamerican Barrier Reef, the western hemisphere's largest reef system, stretching from Isla Contoy at the tip of the Yucatán Peninsula down to Belize, Guatemala and the Bay Islands of Honduras. The island's wildlife includes more than seven hundred animal and plant species (both marine and terrestrial) and thirty-one endemic species and subspecies, including the Cozumel fox (nearly extinct), the Cozumel raccoon (critically endangered), the Cozumel coati (endangered) and the splendid toadfish (vulnerable). Cozumel Island has five protected areas and was recently designated as a UNESCO Biosphere Reserve.

Cozumel offers a mix of cultural and natural activities in locations such as Mayan archaeological sites, white sand beaches, coral reefs, mangrove swamps, wetlands and salt marshes. Cozumel has become recognized worldwide as a destination for scuba diving and snorkelling. The main tourism sites and activities include:

1. Arrecifes de Cozumel National Park, home of the world's second largest coral barrier reef (scuba diving tourism)
2. Punta Sur Ecological Beach Park, with unique biodiversity (eco and nature tourism)
3. Archaeological site of San Gervasio, with Mayan temples and the sanctuary of the Mayan goddess Ixchel (cultural and archaeological tourism)
4. Town of San Miguel, renowned for music, crafts, local restaurants and its small town vibe (cultural tourism)
5. Chankanaab National Park (ecotourism)
6. Beach clubs (sun and sand tourism)
7. Souvenir and jewellery stores (shopping tourism)
8. A visit to the eastern, wild side of the island, with breathtaking scenery
9. Other activities like sports tourism

Accommodations include forty-five hotels with 4,098 rooms, of which 18 per cent are 5-star, 24 per cent are 4-star, 26 per cent are 3-star, 20 per cent are 2-star and 9 per cent are 1-star. Overall occupancy is relatively high, with an annual average of 67.8 per cent. There is no carrying capacity baseline for accommodation establishments, and it is estimated that, in addition to hotels, Cozumel has about three hundred establishments (mainly houses and apartments) offering lodging, with Airbnb emerging as an increasingly popular option. There are an estimated eighty-six food and beverage establishments serving both Mexican and international cuisine, ten nightclubs and more than fourteen bars. Other tourism service providers include a museum, twenty travel agencies, 101 car and scooter rentals, sixty-five scuba dive operators, twenty-one beach recreational areas, twelve beach clubs, one golf course, one convention centre, one international airport, one tourism school (University of Quintana Roo), two marinas, three cruise ports, two ferry terminals, one for cars and the other for passengers, five tourist information modules, two tourist transportation companies, seven post offices (including parcel delivery services), 155 tour operators (45 land and 130 aquatic), as well as banks, souvenir shops, and taxis. The island can be reached by air, through commercial (including direct flights from eight North American cities) and charter flights, or by a forty-minute ferry ride, offered hourly, from Playa del Carmen.

Findings and Discussion

This section contains a summary of the key issues identified as crucial for Cozumel's sustainability during the assessment process. The discussion delves into local community involvement and perception of cruise tourism, public and private sector involvement and opportunities for the cruise lines.

Local Perception of Cruise Tourism

Generally, local stakeholders (for example, residents, opinion leaders, tourism operators) appreciate and have positive attitudes towards cruise tourism; they recognize the importance of cruise visits to the destination. The most supportive members of the private sector are transnational companies with businesses on the island, such as jewellery shops. This support is shaped by the benefits generated from cruise tourism; the government gets taxes while the transnational companies dominate the three terminals and the busiest street of the island, Avenida Melgar, frequented by cruise tourists; most have agreements with cruise lines to be promoted and get business from them.

However, there are feelings that there are already too many visitors and diminishing recreational opportunities for the locals. Those who are critical of cruise tourism include environmental groups, who are critical of the rapid expansion and the impacts of cruise tourism on the environment, hotel operators, who argue that the local government is more focused on cruise tourism than stay-over tourism (their main source of business), and small enterprises, who do not have direct access to do business with cruise lines. The academic community is also critical of cruise tourism, particularly towards the socio-environmental impact of the high visitations of cruise ships. Most of the articles reviewed for this study find that cruise tourism has a negative effect on the island (see González Damián, Macias Ramirez and Sepulveda Alcazar 2017, 40–45).

The local community is particularly critical of the economic spill, which they say is low, and that this spill should be distributed more equitably. Although there are adequate laws supporting equal opportunities in employment, occupational safety and fair wages for all including women, youth, disabled people, minorities and other vulnerable populations, the main challenge is in enforcement. For example, there is only one case where legislation and policies involving concession grants to communities who are engaged or willing to engage in natural resource management were implemented. There are training programs that provide equal access to women, youth, disabled people, minorities and other vulnerable populations; however, there is a need for increased support for people with disabilities.

The Rapid Assessment in 2012 identified local ownership and control as a high priority issue rated red and recommended creating an enabling environment for local ownership and control through federal and state incentives that ensure the continued and meaningful participation of native islanders and Mexican nationals in Cozumel's tourism sector. This issue remains a major challenge. It is thought that the biggest winners have been those who are directly involved in cruise tourism, in particular, tourism service providers on the main streets (Avenida Melgar and 5a Avenida Sur, also known as Calle 5 by locals); the cruise terminal operators, such as restaurants, bars and shops; foreign and local hotel chains; and diving operators. It has also been argued that most of the jobs are entry-level positions and temporary, in a destination where the cost of living has increased dramatically in recent years. Stakeholders from the private sector pointed to the high rate of job change, especially among young employees who do not keep an employment opportunity for long. Despite the available job opportunities, some have left the island in search of a more fulfilling life on the mainland, where they can interact more with people from other regions of the country.

Most of the respondents were unaware of specific negative media reports on cruise lines visiting Cozumel, however, they were aware of reports in international media about fines imposed on cruise lines for contaminating ports of entry by disposing of waste in the sea. Examples of negative reports about cruise tourism in Cozumel include: a) *Paradise Lost? Tourism in Cozumel* on DW TV (2018), where it is argued that cruise tourism is both a blessing and a curse for the island; b) *Cruise Ships that Dock in Cozumel Contaminate the Environment?* in Novedades Quintana Roo (2017), where potential environmental impacts such as pollution are highlighted; and c) *The Construction of a New Cruise Terminal Should be Analysed* in Novedades Quintana Roo (2018). In the last example, environmental groups are questioning the need to construct a fourth terminal, given the potential impact on the island's ecosystem. Two environmental groups (Conservación, Investigación y Manejo Ambiental de Cozumel – Cimac and Cielo, Tierra y Mar – Citymar) are pushing for public consultation to sensitize all stakeholders to the economic, social and environmental impacts of the project. It is said that Disney Cruise Line is interested in funding the building, but it is not clear what their stake is in the venture.

There have been other conflicts, key among them the issue of the environmental impact raised by several environmental groups through media reports. These include over-visitation of some sites leading to negative effects on the delicate ecosystem and the overall impact of cruise tourism activities on the reef system, particularly the white band disease, also known in Spanish as *síndrome Blanco*, an epidemic that completely destroys the coral tissue of the Caribbean acroporid corals, exhibiting a pronounced division between the remaining coral tissue and the exposed coral skeleton. The syndrome is relatively new and may be caused by a number of factors such as deterioration of coastal waters due to human activities or, according to preliminary findings presented by researchers such as Magio (2021, 89–107), bad tourism activities, including the absence or malfunctioning of waste treatment plants.

Another point of conflict arises from the perception that cruise tourism is a monopoly that only benefits a few in Cozumel and that the cruise lines hijack the cruise business by discouraging the tourists from leaving the terminals for security/safety reasons. A 2014–15 cruise season study by Business Research and Economic Advisors (BREA) found that many of the passengers did not venture beyond the cruise terminals, where they find restaurants, bars, and souvenir stores; only 51 per cent of passengers tour the island and visit key tourist attractions. Participants of more recent assessments think this figure is even higher (Magio 2021, 89–107).

Also, there is the issue of public transport and it is argued that the cruise lines have asked the local government to regulate the transport business – taxis, motorcycles, trucks, buses, freight vans and passenger vehicles – but their requests have not borne fruit. Respondents singled out the lack of regulation in the taxi business and noted that operators tend to charge much higher than expected.

They also think that the cruise lines are aware of this, but there is little they can do; in their opinion, the taxi union is strong and anchored on political ties, making any kind of reform difficult. Additionally, all the above-mentioned forms of transport depend on fossil fuels and contribute to the emission of greenhouse gases, global warming and noise and visual pollution. It is estimated that 50 per cent of these vehicles are more than five years old and therefore are less energy efficient. Interviewees identified the need for cheap, efficient and sustainable public transport services for the entire island.

Government Involvement with Cruise Tourism

The municipal government of Cozumel and the state government of Quintana Roo are highly involved in tourism activities and favour further growth of the cruise industry; this is evident in their long-term development plans as well as short-term strategies and actions. For example, the tourism promotion strategy at both municipal and state levels seeks to increase the number of visitors in Cozumel, including cruise tourists. The Riviera Maya Promotion Trust (Fideicomiso de Promoción Turística de la Riviera Maya) works on diversifying tourism offerings and marketing off-season events year-round. The Trust promotes Riviera Maya (including Cozumel) in national and international fairs, events, trade shows and road shows; it also produces printed and electronic materials to attract more visitors (Riviera Maya 2023). All Promotion Trusts in Quintana Roo will be dissolved by the end of 2021 to form the new Tourism Promotion Council, Quintana Roo, in which all municipalities will have a permanent seat. It will be necessary to approach the new council with a long-term marketing strategy for Cozumel that is guided by the principles of sustainability and based on the unique natural and cultural heritage characteristics of the destination and its recent designation as a biosphere reserve by UNESCO.

During the interviews, it was affirmed that the local municipal government favours the construction of a fourth terminal. This has been a thorny political issue pitting different political factions against environmental groups, with some favouring the idea and others critical of it. There is no official declaration from leaders in the current municipal administration, but their intentions are clear to many stakeholders. A fourth terminal will significantly increase the number of cruise lines and cruise tourists visiting the island.

Local Community and Private Sector Involvement

In relation to private sector involvement, the researcher sought to find out whether any cruise companies have done community project work in the host destination in the past, identify some local community organizations that the cruise lines currently work with or support, find out whether they currently have any ongoing projects and, finally, identify some local tour operators or tourism businesses in general that the cruise lines currently work with. Respondents agreed that most of the cruise lines have carried out or carry out donation activities for different groups in the Cozumel community; donations include toys, wheelchairs, prostheses, backpacks and so on. Some involve their crew members in social work, for example, painting schools. Royal Caribbean has funded marine conservation projects on the island and, as recently as 2018, was involved as a principal collaborator alongside the World Wide Fund for Nature US, the World Wide Fund for Nature México, the Global Sustainable Tourism Council, the Cozumel Municlity, GIZGerman Agency for International Cooperation, Royal Caribbean Cruises and local stakeholders in a study using the Global Sustainable Tourism Council Destination criteria and assessment methodology and World Wide Fund for Nature's Marine and Coastal Tourism Strategy. The project sought to identify issues that are undermining Cozumel's environmental, social and economic sustainability and to recommend improvements for responsible tourism practices on the island.

The following local community organizations frequently work with or receive support from cruise lines: Integral Family Development (Desarrollo Integral de la Familia – DIF) which benefits vulnerable families on the island, Red Cross (Cruz Roja), Rotary Club (Club Rotarios) and Humanitarian Society (Sociedad Humanitaria). Also, there are medium-sized companies, both national and international, that have agreements with the cruise lines and that have been lucky enough to be promoted inside the cruise lines as safe or recommended companies, including: a) Four Tuna and Chili Charters, who specialize in sports fishing (catch and release), bird watching and sunset tours, b) Explora Caribe, Aviomar, Sand Dollar Sports and Playa Mía, who have developed processes and actions in their excursions aimed at environmental care, and d) Tripping Cool Group, Promotora Isla Maya, Rancho integral Las Perlitas, Mercado orgánico de Cozumel and Temazcal Sweat Lodge, who specialize in low impact and high experience tours. Most of them have positioned themselves as sustainable tourism operators based on their conservation and corporate social responsibility activities in Cozumel, and cruise lines could potentially work with them to improve the sustainability of their land excursions.

Cozumel has mechanisms for involving public, private and community stakeholders in destination management planning and decision-making on an ongoing basis; however, this does not happen in a systematic manner. It is important to recognize that a plethora of stakeholders actively participate in the monitoring and management of tourism activities in Cozumel. They regularly participate in public meetings to discuss destination management issues; the majority of them have taken part in previous assessments or diagnostics, including the present Global Sustainable Tourism Council assessment. A non-governmental organization called Intersectorial Group Cozumel Island, with representatives from several sectors of the tourism industry, was formed to implement sustainable tourism strategies. The group's results have been minimal due to financial constraints. Several other groups are involved in the sustainable management of tourism, and the impact of their programmes, activities and initiatives is significant; however, the effort among different groups of stakeholders is not integrated. These groups include Businesses for European Tourism (Empresarios Por el Turismo Europeo), spearhed by GIZGerman Agency for International Cooperation and the Network of Civil Society Organizations of Cozumel Island (Red de Organizaciones de la Sociedad Civil de Isla Cozumel), which was formed in 2005 to unite stakeholders from the social sector in improving community well-being. There are more than forty non-governmental organizations on the island, many of which work toward cultural and environmental protection.

The Cozumel Hotels Association works on improving the tourist experience and contributes to increasing Cozumel's sustainability and competitiveness as a destination by, among other activities, promoting diving, ecotourism, sports and culture tourism. The municipal government has a technical secretariat and a tourism directorate that work in coordination with Fideicomiso de Promoción Turística de la Riviera Maya, the Secretariat of Tourism of Quintana Roo, the Parks and Museums Foundation, tour operators, food and beverage establishments, cruise companies, ferry companies and individual taxis, and airport operators to manage and promote tourism in Cozumel. The Secretariat of Tourism of Quintana Roo is particularly in charge of establishing, implementing and supervising tourism development and promotion of the state's destinations and serves as a link with other tourism-related organizations in the country. World Wide Fund for Nature México worked on a proposal with the Secretariat of Tourism of Quintana Roo to formally designate Cozumel as a Sustainable Tourism Zone (Zona de Desarrollo turístico sustentable), but the process did not start due to lack of financing.

Opportunities for the Cruise Lines

Respondents were asked to identify the most important social or environmental projects that cruise companies should support in or around the host destination and it was suggested that cruise lines should partner with the public sector (government), the civil society, including the academic community, and other stakeholders in the private sector to find crucial sustainability answers for the destination. There is an action plan that was developed from Cozumel's Global Sustainable Tourism Council assessment, and within these, there are five priority areas where cruise companies can have an influence See table 11.1 below.

Table 11.1: High-Risk Topics and Recommendations Based on Stakeholder Views

High-Risk Topics	Recommendations
1. Build solid-waste management and reduction programs: Only an estimated 7% of Cozumel's solid waste is recycled. Current facilities do not contain adequate record keeping nor do they have proper capacity in relation to the volume of solid waste generated in Cozumel.	• Develop integrated waste management system. • Develop waste reduction incentive programme for local enterprises. • Seek infrastructure investment projects.
2. Increase safe water management and conservation: Cozumel does not have a system to monitor its water resources to ensure that use by tourism enterprises is balanced with the water requirements of the host community. In addition, Cozumel does not have a management system to monitor drinking and recreational water quality using international quality standards.	• Develop a water distribution and use plan to balance present and future water consumption needs by residents and tourism enterprises. • Conduct study on quantity and quality of the island's aquifer. • Improve efficacy of aqueducts and water treatment plants and replace old pipes. • Create water conservation programme for local enterprises.

High-Risk Topics	Recommendations
3. **Develop a multi-year Strategic Plan and Vision for Sustainability:** Cozumel does not have an officially recognized multi-year destination strategy for sustainable tourism development.	• Hold consultative forums to communicate Global Sustainable Tourism Council Destination assessment results and action plans. • Begin to monitor resident and visitor satisfaction. • Update and integrate various local, state and national tourism plans.
4. **Create a destination management organization:** None exists at the moment in Cozumel.	• Identify and select the destination management organization model best suited for Cozumel to include balanced representation. • Consistently update management tools and plans. • Establish best practices in sensitive sites.
5. **Develop standards and training for tour operators and guides:** Tour guides do not receive periodic training on the use of interpretive information. Training on a local code of conduct would help to ensure proper tourism behaviour by visitors and guides.	• Establish, maintain and track tour operator permits and licences and make information publicly available. • Establish a programme to train tour guides in the techniques and content of effective interpretation. • Develop a local code of conduct for tour guides, tour operators and visitors and requirements for implementing it.

In addition, Cozumel, Roatán and Belize have formed a Cruise Ship Network of the Mesoamerican Reef Destinations and work on six priority issues common to the three destinations where cruise lines can contribute: water quality and its treatment, use and distribution of taxes and duties that cruise ship companies pay to national governments, adequate management of solid waste, establishment of carrying capacities in the destinations, long-term planning documents that give a vision of sustainability to the destinations as well as a management body that implements the plans and training of tour guides and educating cruise tourists about their environmental and cultural impact on destinations.

Environmental care is undoubtedly one of the priorities in the mind of the host community; cruise lines can contribute to this by financing projects and studies on the impact of tourism, particularly cruise tourism, on reefs and protected areas. Generally, joint studies where the private sector partners with the public sector and the civil society, including the academic community, in search of crucial sustainability answers for the destination are deemed to be objective, transparent and, above all, credible in the eyes of stakeholders. In the wake of environmental epidemics like the white band disease, which is aggravated by human activity, cruise lines should consider funding and implementing a communication campaign of good practices for visitors when approaching protected areas. They should also consider financing environmental conservation programmes – Royal Caribbean is an example of a cruise line that has been doing this – and focus on priority conservation areas like the arrival, monitoring and release of turtles and the arrival of sargassum at Mexico's Yucatan Peninsula.

Another area where cruise lines may have an impact is the creation of more space and opportunities for the local community to promote their products and crafts instead of restricting the benefits to transnational companies or companies with agreements. Support is required for cultural and musical events organized by non-governmental organizations such as the Cultural Autumn (Otoño cultural). Cruise lines may also support students through scholarships to be trained in tourism-related skills or entrepreneurship, allowing the destination to have a skilled workforce that meets the training needs of the cruise industry. As a basic start, they may allow and facilitate guided visits by students on the docked cruise ships to give them first-hand experience of how cruise businesses operate and an appreciation of how important they are to the destination.

Conclusion

This chapter presents a detailed overview of key issues facing cruise tourism in Cozumel, the most important port of entry and cruise destination in Mexico, and areas of opportunity to cope with and manage change, both positive and negative. In summary, both the public and private sectors are supportive of cruise tourism, particularly the former (both the local municipal government of Cozumel and the state government of Quintana Roo). Local attitudes vary with the degree of involvement in the cruise tourism business; those with links, businesses or work in the cruise industry have a moderately positive perception of the activity. Those whose work or businesses do not depend directly on cruise tourism perceive it negatively, with specific reference to the fact that little benefit accrues to the local population. Issues identified include the excessive number of cruise tourists (before the pandemic) and the diminishing recreational opportunities for locals. Those who are critical of cruise tourism include environmental groups, which are critical of the rapid expansion and impact of cruise tourism on the environment because of how signification the environmental footprint of the cruise industry is; hotel operators, who argue that the local government is more focused on cruise tourism than stay-over tourism, their main source of business; and the small enterprises who do not have direct access to do business with cruise lines.

The destination scores well in the regular and timely collection, monitoring, recording and public reporting of data on residents' aspirations, concerns and satisfaction with destination management. The municipal government has a designated office where members of the public can air their views and aspirations about the island's economic, environmental and social well-being. The municipal president periodically holds public forums to discuss various issues and seeks public opinion on the services offered by the government. These initiatives are not carried out as envisaged by the Global Sustainable Tourism Council criteria; however, their impact is significant. Some actions have been implemented as a result of these opinions to improve resident satisfaction.

The following is a summary of social or environmental projects that cruise companies should support in or around Cozumel as a host destination to foster sustainability after the pandemic and to improve their reputation as contributors to the well-being of the ports that host their activities:

1. Overall, they should seek to fund or participate in the implementation of the social or environmental projects identified in table 11.1 above.
2. They should prioritize and finance initiatives and projects that connect them with the local community through commercial, social and environmental activities.
3. They should eliminate barriers by including locals in cruise tourism business ventures and not dealing exclusively with transnational companies or a few national companies.
4. They should open economic linkages that facilitate sourcing products and services from local companies.

5. They should allow and facilitate guided academic visits by students on the cruise ships and contribute to the training of skilled human capital through scholarships.
6. They should also fund a programme to train tour guides in the techniques of effective interpretation.
7. They should fund studies on environmental issues like coral reef monitoring and the arrival of sargassum in partnership with local researchers and research centres like Centro de Investigación y Estudios Avanzados.
8. They should fund programmes and initiatives aimed at mitigating the impact of tourism on the reef, endemic species and mangroves and environmental regeneration programmes like reforestation.
9. They should facilitate programmes that foster travel philanthropy by the cruise lines and cruise tourists.
10. They should also work with the Civil Society Network to implement programmes that support and build the capacity of local, small- and medium-sized enterprises and encourage enterprises to purchase goods and services locally following fair trade principles. This would strengthen efforts by the municipal government and the Conservation for Sustainable Development Program (Programa de Conservación para el Desarrollo Sostenible) to promote the development of local sustainable products based on local nature and culture. Overall, the destination requires an entrepreneurship policy framework and implementation guidance to overcome obstacles faced by local artisans who are eager to grow their small businesses.

It is expected that the assessment results, which include important recommendations, will assist Cozumel to address the identified weaknesses and to implement key initiatives and projects through strategic partnerships and prioritized investments. The outcomes should be used to inform and shape policy and planning in other Mexican destinations as well as those throughout the Mesoamerican Barrier Reef. Broader and deeper collective action remains critical to achieving the three primary destination stewardship goals: (1) providing sustainable livelihoods; (2) conserving the resources for future generations; and (3) creating a high quality visitor experience.

References

Băndoi, Anca, Elena Jianu, Maria Enescu, Gheorghe Axinte, Sorin Tudor, and Daniela Firoiu. 2020. "The Relationship between Development of Tourism, Quality of Life and Sustainable Performance in EU Countries." *Sustainability* 12 (4): 1628. https://doi.org/10.3390/su12041628.

Business Research & Economic Advisors (BREA). 2012a. "Economic Contribution of Cruise Tourism to the Destination Economies Volume 1: Aggregate Analysis." Florida-Caribbean Cruise Association and Participating Destinations http://www.f-cca.com/downloads/2012-Cruise-Analysis-vol-1.pdf.

———. 2012b. *Economic Contribution of Cruise Tourism to the Destination Economies Volume 2: Destination Reports.* Florida-Caribbean Cruise Association http://www.f-cca.com/downloads/2012-Cruise-Analysis-vol-2.pdf.

Crossley, Émilie. 2020. "Ecological Grief Generates Desire for Environmental Healing in Tourism after COVID-19." *Tourism Geographies* 22 (3): 536–46. https://doi.org/10.1080/14616688.2020.1759133.

DW TV. 2018. "Paradise Lost? Tourism in Cozumel." Video. https://www.dw.com/en/paradise-lost-tourism-in-cozumel/av-43003000.

Everingham, Phoebe, and Natasha Chassagne. 2020. "Post COVID-19 Ecological and Social Reset: Moving Away from Capitalist Growth Models towards Tourism as Buen Vivir." *Tourism Geographies* 22 (3): 555–66. https://doi.org/10.1080/14616688.2020.1762119.

Expansión. 2020. "El COVID-19 le ha Costado a los Cruceros 2 Millones de Pasajeros y 134 MDD. Sección Empresas." Expansión, May 15. https://expansion.mx/empresas/2020/08/07/el-covid-19-le-ha-costado-cruceros-2-millones-de-passajeros.

Galvani, Adriana, Alan A. Lew, and Maria Sotelo Perez. 2020. "COVID-19 is Expanding Global Consciousness and the Sustainability of Travel and Tourism." *Tourism Geographies* 22 (3): 567–76. https://doi.org/10.1080/14616688.2020.1760924.

González, Erick David García, and Oscar Frausto Martínez. 2021. "Distribution and Socio-Spatial Segregation of Cruise Ship Workers in Cozumel, Mexico." *Regiones y Desarrollo Sustentable* 21 (40): 147–64. http://www.coltlax.edu.mx/openj/index.php/ReyDS/article/view/141/pdf.

González Damián, Alfonso, Alma Rosa Macias Ramirez, and Maria del Carmen Sepulveda Alcazar. 2017. "Cruise Tourism as Factor of Social Exclusion on Co"umel Island's Residents' Perception." *CULTUR: Revista de Cultura e Turismo* 11 (2): 29–53. https://dialnet.unirioja.es/servlet/articulo?codigo=6311568.

Gössling, Stefan, Daniel Scott, and C. Michael Hall. 2020. "Pandemics, Tourism and Global Change: A Rapid Assessment of COVID-19." *Journal of Sustainable Tourism* 29 (1): 1–20. https://doi.org/10.1080/09669582.2020.1758708.

Higgins-Desbiolles, Freya. 2020. "Socialising Tourism for Social and Ecological Justice after COVID-19." *Tourism Geographies* 22 (3): 610–23. https://doi.org/10.1080/14616688.2020.1757748.

Jamal, Tazim, and Christine Budke. 2020. "Tourism in a World with Pandemics: Local-Global Responsibility and Action." *Journal of Tourism Futures* 6 (2): 181–88. https://doi.org/10.1108/JTF-02-2020-0014.

Jones, Peter, and Daphne Comfort. 2020. "The COVID-19 Crisis, Tourism and Sustainable Development." *Athens Journal of Tourism* 7 (2): 75–86. https://www.athensjournals.gr/tourism/2"20-7-2-1-Jones.pdf.

Lew, Alan A. 2018. "Why Travel? – Travel, Tourism, and Global Consciousness." *Tourism Geographies* 20 (4): 742–49. https://doi.org/10.1080/14616688.2018.1490343.

Magio, Kennedy Obombo. 2021. "Tourism Resilience in the Caribbean Island of Cozumel: Best Practice and High-Risk Areas." In *Managing Crises in Tourism*, edited by Acolla Lewis-Cameron, Leslie-Ann Jordan, and Sherma Roberts, 89–107. New York City: Palgrave Macmillan.

Novedades Quintana Roo. 2017. "Cruceros que arriban a Cozumel... ¿Dañan el medio ambiente?" https://sipse.com/novedades/impacto-cruceros-arribo-cozumel-isla-de-las-golondrinas-turistas-medio-ambiente-dano-ecosistema-256611.html.

———. 2018. "Analizarán la Creación de un Nuevo Muelle en Cozumel". Novedades Quintana Roo, April 3. https://sipse.com/novedades/creacion-muelle-isla-cozumel-ambientalistas-apiqroo-impacto-ambiental-313373.html.

Organisation for Economic Conservation Development (OECD). 2020. "Rethinking Tourism Success for Sustainable Growth." In *OECD Tourism Trends and Policies 2020*. https://www.oecd-ilibrary.org/docserver/82b46508-en.pdf?expires=1599912610&id=id&accname=guest&checksum=6E3F44FE682E9F1D4417856A8AB17D56.

Renaud, Luc. 2020. "Reconsidering Global Mobility – Distancing from Mass Cruise Tourism in the Aftermath of COVID-19." *Tourism Geographies* 22 (3): 679–89. https://doi.org/10.1080/14616688.2020.1762116.

Secretaría de Turismo – SEDETUR. 2021. "Indicadores Turísticos." SEDETUR. June 16. http://qroo.gob.mx/sedetur/indicadores-turisticos.

Sharma, Abhinav, and Juan Luis Nicolau. 2020. "An Open Market Valuation of the Effects of COVID-19 on the Travel and Tourism Industry." *Annals of Tourism Research* 83:102990. https://doi.org/10.1016/j.annals.2020.102990.

Vogel, Michael P. 2011. "Critical Cruise Research in the Age of Performativity." In *Cruise Sector Challenges*, edited by Philip Gibson, Alexis Papathanassis, and Petra Milde, 227–44. New York City: Gabler Verlag Wiesbaden. https://link.springer.com/book/10.1007/978-3-8349-6871-5.

12.
Resident Attitude to Domestic Tourism in a Core-Periphery Island Context

Sherma Roberts

Introduction

One of the early outcomes of the adoption of sustainable tourism practice by the global tourism industry has been the vilification of mass tourism and the almost unquestioning acceptance of alternative forms of tourism as the holy grail for destinations (Bramwell and Lane 2017; Butler 1999). In this regard, all genres of small scale, locally owned, low density, environmentally sensitive developments and activities that potentially spread the benefits of tourism throughout the economy have been labelled alternative. The chapters in this book bear testament to what are now regarded as alternative or niche forms of tourism. Domestic tourism, which is antithetical to international tourism, has not exactly been embraced as a sustainability response to mass tourism or, more specifically, as an alternative tourism product (Douglas, Douglas and Derrett 2001). Perhaps the reason for this occlusion is that domestic tourism tends to use some of the same resources and reflect similar consumption patterns as international travel and tourism.

Additionally, unlike traditional alternative forms of tourism, domestic tourism does not generate foreign exchange, which is a primary reason for governments' pursuit of tourism development. Thus, domestic tourism is not acknowledged *a priori* as an alternative form of tourism in the conventional, sustainable tourism sense. This author suggests, however, that domestic tourism should be given consideration as a niche tourism product (as defined in chapter 1) given its intrinsic sustainable tourism elements such as promoting social cohesion, local empowerment through business ownership and enhancing sectoral linkages (Canavan 2013; Kabote, Mamimine and Muranda 2017; Robinson and Novelli 2005).

Beyond being peripheralized in the sustainable tourism literature, domestic tourism is also relatively under-researched in the extant tourism literature, especially when compared to published work on international tourism and its consequences for destinations, residents, policy and future knowledge (Scheyvens 2007). Canavan (2016) argues that the reasons for the relative neglect of domestic tourism research include ambiguities associated with distinguishing between tourism and leisure, motivations and behaviour, cultural proximity and distance travelled. In other words, there are uncertainties and blurring around whether domestic tourists can in fact indulge in specific tourist pursuits, take a holiday within driving distance of the home environment and be motivated by a need to escape and explore, given the familiarity of the culture and landscapes. Research on domestic tourism has to some extent implicitly tried to respond to these ambiguities by focusing on the role of domestic tourism in the local economy, understanding domestic visitor motivations and behaviours (Canavan 2013 and 2016; Carr 2002; Mustafa 2012; Wen 1997; Yap and Allen 2011) and, more recently, linking domestic tourism to sustainable tourism development (Pegas, Weaver and Castley 2015; Kabote, Mamimine, and Muranda 2017). These investigations have primarily taken place in larger countries, ignoring the fact that small islands can also be sites of domestic tourism experiences. Work on domestic tourism on the Isle of Man provides an exception (Canavan 2013; 2016). To date, no study has explored resident attitude in relation to domestic tourism, and where there is research on resident behaviour, the focus is in relation to mass tourism and in larger jurisdictions, particularly the United States (Gursoy et al. 2019; Hadinejad et al. 2019; Telfer and Sharpley 2008).

This chapter therefore fills this gap by examining resident attitude to domestic tourism in the context of the twin-island state of Trinidad and Tobago, with the site of study being Tobago. This analysis was further deemed important given the core periphery tropes that are often used to characterize the two islands; where Tobago, the periphery and more tourist-driven of the economies, is seen as the most proximate playground of residents from the core, Trinidad (Weaver 1998). The discussion draws on social exchange and integrated threat theories to examine resident attitude within this island context. The study's theoretical contribution is threefold. First, domestic tourism is examined from the perspective of the resident, not as an active or immersed domestic tourist participant

(Canavan 2013 and 2016; Carr 2012; Mustafa 2012) but as resident observer of domestic tourism's benefits and challenges. Second, the core-periphery context provides more nuanced insights into domestic tourism possibilities and the ways in which residents navigate domestic tourism within the sphere of economic and political dependence. Finally, the analysis is expanded using both social exchange and integrated threat theories given the limited explanatory powers of the widely employed social exchange theory (Gursoy et al. 2019; Hadinejad et al. 2019). The chapter begins with a discussion of the definition and role of domestic tourism, considers the relevant theories, explains the study setting and methods, and ends with the results and discussion of the findings. Summary reflections are also provided.

Towards an Understanding of Domestic Tourism

Notwithstanding the fact that domestic tourism is not a recent phenomenon, its definition remains contested. One of the earliest definitions suggest that domestic tourism is travel outside of the normal place of residence in other areas within the country (Burkhart and Medlik 1981). Similarly, the UNWTO (n.d) posits that domestic tourism comprises the activities of a resident visitor within the country of residence either as part of a domestic tourism trip or part of an outbound tourism trip. Other definitions consider distance travelled away from usual environment, some make the distinction between day trippers and overnight stays and neglect the visiting friends and relatives segment (Canavan 2016; Eijgelaar, Peeters and Piket 2008; Scheyvens 2007). For instance, Tourism Research Australia (cited in Yap and Allen 2011) differentiates between a domestic overnight visitor and a domestic day visitor, where the former stays one or more nights and the latter takes a round trip within a single day that is no less than 50 kilometres. Canavan (2013) proposes greater definitional flexibility that recognizes that the distance travelled criteria may be very context specific so that it ignores micro-domestic tourism, where island distances are generally shorter but where island residents are motivated to travel and to engage in tourist-specific activities (Chaperon and Bramwell 2013; Weaver 1998).

Despite these contestations around meaning, the significance of domestic tourism as a tool for advancing world peace was stated in the United Nations Manila Declaration on World Tourism (United Nations World Tourism Organization 1980). Pertinently, the declaration recognized that domestic tourism should be an equal partner alongside international tourism in accomplishing this goal and pronounced that:

> Within each country, domestic tourism contributes to an improved balance of the national economy through a redistribution of the national income. Domestic tourism also heightens the awareness of common interest and contributes to the development of activities favourable to the general economy of the country. Thus, the development of tourism from abroad should be accompanied by a similar effort to expand domestic tourism. The economic returns of tourism, however real and significant they may be, do not and cannot constitute the only criterion for the decision by States to encourage this activity. The right to holidays, the opportunity for the citizen to get to know his own environment, a deeper awareness of his national identity and of the solidarity that links him to his compatriots and the sense of belonging to a culture and to a people are all major reasons for stimulating the individual's participation in domestic and international tourism, through access to holidays and travel. (7–8)

Thus, domestic tourism has been advanced in the literature as playing an important role in the social and economic life of a destination. Notably, domestic tourism mitigates the seasonality effect, strengthens sectoral linkages and stimulates stronger multipliers through the use of small, often locally owned accommodation, increases local employment and investment and has a higher tendency to repeat visits than international tourists (Bui and Jolliffe 2011; Canavan 2013 and 2016; Rogerson and Lisa 2005; Scheyvens 2007; Telfer and Sharpley 2008). Further, while domestic tourists' spend might often be smaller than their international counterparts, purchases are done across a wide cross section of services such as accommodation, gifts for relatives, feast and religious events, excursions and recreational activities and shopping (Carr 2002; Mustafa 2012), with spending habits varying by demographic segments (Canavan 2016; Gardiner, Grace and King 2014).

Other studies have pointed to the possibilities of domestic tourism as an agent to slowing or even preventing a destination going into decline through the patronage of local tourists in all sectors of the industry (Canavan 2013; Mustafa 2012). The redistributive effect of domestic tourism has also been highlighted, where wealth from the core is spent in the periphery thereby improving regional inequalities (Haddad, Porsse and Rabahy 2013). In some respects, as intimated by Scheyvens (2007), domestic tourism is implicated in the sustainable goal of poverty alleviation. For instance, domestic tourists from the urban Jordanian capital of Amman spent substantially during their visits to attractions located 20km or more from their place of residence (Mustafa 2012).

Still, variations in findings and conclusions exist when it comes to determining domestic tourism's overall contribution to the economy. For example, Yap and Allen (2011) highlighted that Australia's domestic tourism consumption patterns are associated with higher multipliers than international visitors. In contrast, it was found that domestic tourism's contribution to Brazil's gross national output and income was negligible and a function of household incomes (Haddad et al. 2013). Wen (1997, 568) also suggested that one of the primary features of domestic tourism is its "low consumption level and individual travel focus", as a large number of domestic tourists stay with relatives and friends. Similarly, it has been argued that in small island economies, domestic tourism simply represents a recycling of money in the local economy and fails to consider that foreign exchange is being spent to satisfy even domestic tourists' tastes (Ayres 2000).

The reality is that the full extent of domestic tourism's contribution to the national economy might not ever be known given the failure by many Destination Management Organizations to capture the motivations, flows and activities related to domestic tourism (Mustafa 2012). Scheyvens (2007) avers that this is because domestic tourists are often relegated to the tacit nomenclature of "poor cousins" with the assumption that this segment does not generate the same level of economic benefits as international tourists. Reporting on her study in Samoa, she revealed that domestic tourists provide significant economic benefits to the Samoan economy since their spend goes beyond accommodation to attractions and other tourist sectors. Accordingly, she observed that "domestic and diaspora tourism has ensured the viability of a number of *beach fale* enterprises thus contributing to the economic rejuvenation of some villages, and it has also reduced rural–urban migration as young people feel they can now stay in their home village and have a viable future" (320). Data from Australia also showed that international tourists spend 10–36 per cent less than the average domestic tourist who engaged in traditional tourist activities such as sightseeing and water sports (Yap and Allen 2011). Indeed, these findings must take into consideration the size of sectoral linkages, level of economic development in the destination, the extent of local ownership and the level of importation, where the bigger and less import dependent the economy, the greater the economic multipliers (Mathieson and Wall 1992; Telfer and Sharpley 2008).

There are also non-economic reasons for encouraging destinations to pursue a domestic tourism strategy. These social reasons are often bound up in the motivations of domestic tourists and include a desire to connect with family and friends, to escape from routine, to explore new environments, to meet new people, and for pleasure and leisure (Adams 1998; Bui and Jolliffe 2011; Gardiner et al. 2014; Scheyvens 2007; Rogerson and Lisa 2005). These socio-psychological motivations are then reflected in the activities local tourists engage in and provide the basis for behaviours that lend to social cohesion, national pride, reinforced cultural identity and, to the other extreme, hedonism (Canavan 2013; Carr 2002; Mustafa 2012; Scheyvens 2007). Commenting on domestic tourism's role in strengthening national cultural identity, Canavan (2013, 348) noted that "research on the Isle of Man agrees with judgements that domestic tourism can be associated with deepening collective identity and understanding, rather than the more individualistic associations with international tourism". On the other hand, Carr (2002) found that domestic tourists were more engaged in active leisure pursuits, such as visiting places, walking around resorts and taking tours. This is in contrast to international visitors who spent more time in hedonistic activities such as bar hopping and night clubs. Carr's argument is that domestic tourists are less disruptive given their close proximity to the residual culture, which keeps them more aligned to familiar socio-cultural norms and values. Thus, while domestic tourism provides opportunities for leisure and learning, it also reflects a higher sense of cultural sensitivity and, as corollary, contributes to greater social cohesion in the destination. Consequently, tensions between hosts and guests are removed and there is local support for the industry (Canavan 2013; Telfer and Sharpley 2008).

Theorizing Resident Attitude

The cautionary phase of tourism's evolution has led to a plethora of research on the social, economic and environmental impacts of tourism. Informed implicitly by sustainable tourism thinking where it is argued that residents should not be asked to bear the costs while not partaking in the benefits, studies have also begun to pay attention to the attitude of residents to tourism development (cf. Davis, Allen and Cosenza 1988; Perdue, Long and Allen 1987;

Madrigal 1993; Ryan and Montgomery 1994; Weaver and Lawton 2001). These earlier works provided the foundation for understanding the heterogenous community and, by extension, the variability of attitudes to tourism that can exist within the same community. This notion of the heterogenous community has inspired a number of resident typologies. For example, Davis et al. (1988) characterized residents in a Florida community as "lovers, haters, cautious romantics, in betweeners and love 'em for a reason". In England, Ryan and Montgomery (1994) proposed resident typologies of "enthusiasts, somewhat irritated and the middle-of-the roaders". Arguably, the first work to move beyond typology building was Ap (1992) when he applied social exchange theory (SET) to examining resident attitude. SET sees social interactions as process transactions between individuals or groups based on expected benefits arising from the exchange. The primary motive for engagement is the maximization of benefits while minimizing the costs, where the perceived rewards go beyond economic to include social and psychological ones (Kayat 2002). Within the context of tourism, SET suggests that residents evaluate tourism based on the potential benefits to their social and economic well-being so that if the perceived benefits are higher, tourism is likely to receive their support.

In applying SET, studies have used socio-demographic variables to predict resident attitude to tourism (Long et al. 1990; McGhee and Anderek 2004; Mason and Cheyne 2000; Pappas 2008; Weaver and Lawton 2001). For instance, one study found that women are more supportive of tourism than men because of the perceived benefits that could be derived from the industry (Sinclair-Maragh 2017). In contrast, Mason and Cheyne (2000) reported a lack of support for the industry by women due to impacts related to traffic, noise and crime. Other researchers have reported conflicting results using age, education, affiliation with the industry and interactions between residents and tourists (Choi and Murray 2010; Long and Kyat 2011; Weaver and Lawton 2001). The nuanced nature of these findings has led some to conclude that socio-demographic variables are not foolproof predictors of perceptions of tourism (Perdue et al. 1987) but rather, that individuals and communities judge the industry based upon how it affects their lives (Lankford and Howard 1994; Mason and Cheyne 2000).

Even as it is criticized on the grounds that it lacks theoretical sophistication, emphasizes residents' rationality, ignores context and oversimplifies residents' decision-making process (Pearce, Moscardo and Ross 1996; Sharpley 2014), SET has been the most frequently used theoretical frame in residents' attitude studies (Gursoy et al. 2019). For theoretical comparison with previous research, this study also uses SET but focuses more on residents' perceptions of the impacts of domestic tourism rather than on socio-demographic variables. In order to compensate for SET's limitations, integrated threat theory is also being employed. This integration of theories recognizes that no one theory is sufficient to account for resident attitude (Ward and Berno 2011).

Borrowing from social psychology, integrated threat theory offers a framework for explaining how the perception of threats can affect relationships and attitudes between groups of persons (Stephan et al. 1998). This theoretical framework is pertinent here given the historically ambivalent and sometimes fractious relationship between polity and society in the two islands (Weaver 1998) coupled with the exponential increase in domestic tourism arrivals to the periphery over time (Tobago Tourism Agency 2021). Central to integrated threat theory is the presence of in-groups and out-groups, where the former occupies a particular space as a result of, *inter alia*, factors such birth right, longevity of residence, culture, language and familial connections and where the latter does not possess any of these. Threats therefore develop due to prejudices (negative beliefs and emotions) that were formed through contact experiences between the out-group and the in-group. According to Monterrubio (2016, 422), "contact plays a particular role in defining negative attitudes because contact provides more direct and immediate information about other groups. Consequently, integrated threat theory has been largely used for the analysis of possible tensions between interacting social groups".

The theory also identifies four sources of threats that inspire prejudice towards the out-group, namely, realistic threats, symbolic threats, intergroup anxiety and negative stereotypes – all of which influence attitudes (Stephan et al. 1998). Realistic threats arise when the in-group's material circumstances are perceptually or realistically threatened and are often tied to historical interactions between the two groups. Symbolic threats occur as a result of any challenge to the in-group's values, societal or cultural, and can be triggered because of visible differences in group culture and morals. Out-groups with a different moral code are therefore seen as threats. Intergroup anxiety refers to fears that the in-group has about interacting with the out-group, the basis of which is usually past experiences. Finally, negative stereotypes are associated with in-group expectations concerning the behaviour of the out-group where these stereotypes can lead to negative consequences for both (Stephan et al. 1998). While this theory has been applied to the study of migrants, only a few studies within tourism have applied it. For example, Monterrubio (2016) examined local attitudes towards backpackers in Cancun, Mexico, and found that realistic threats and intergroup anxiety were the dominant prejudices against this visitor segment. Application of the combined theoretical frameworks provides a contribution to understanding resident attitude to domestic tourism not simply within an island but within islands characterized by core-periphery relations of neglect, dominance, inequity and stereotypes (Chaperon and Bramwell 2013; Weaver 1998).

Overview of Core-Periphery Relations and Domestic Tourism in Tobago

As the smaller of the unitary state of Trinidad and Tobago, the island of Tobago is 116 square miles with an estimated population of sixty-one thousand inhabitants, approximately 4.6 per cent of the national population (Ministry of Planning and Sustainable Development Central Statistical Office n.d.). Where Trinidad's economy is dominated by oil and gas (contributing 45.3 per cent of gross domestic product), manufacturing and agriculture, Tobago's economy is underpinned by leisure tourism, which accounted for 36.9 per cent of the island's overall earnings and 47.6 per cent of total employment in 2017 (World Travel and Tourism Council 2018). Outside of government, tourism is Tobago's largest employer.

Analyses of the relationship between the two islands have either implicitly or explicitly alluded to the existence of core-periphery relations (Carrington 1995; Craig-James 2008; Luke 2007; Weaver 1998). The notion of core-periphery borrows from early theorist Andre Gunder Frank (1969) who argued that modernization theory was essentially a perpetuation of domination, inequality and exploitation as the richer northern countries continued to extract wealth from developing countries and advance at their expense. What resulted was not progress or development, but underdevelopment and dependency. Weaver (1998) suggests that these analytical lenses are also applicable to assess internal political configurations where there are spatial disparities of power and levels of development. Chaperon and Bramwell (2013) observed that there was a tendency to imbue core-periphery analysis with a certain level of determinism, in which the periphery cannot break free from its dependency. Their study of Gozo signals that residents of peripheral islands have and do exhibit strategic and selective actions that can create a shift in the dependency paradigm. Relatedly, Scheyvens and Momsen (2008) highlighted that there are advantages to peripherality that are often elided, such as these islands' coastal resource endowments, resonance with the preferences of the new tourists and their ability to be proactive in planning.

In the case of Tobago, periphery status was bestowed at the inception of the union of the islands in 1889 when the British Crown made Tobago a ward of Trinidad (Carrington 1985; Ottley 1973). For Tobagonians, this union meant a loss of autonomy and political identity, while for Trinidad, Tobago was regarded as a financial burden (Luke 2007). The union was therefore inorganic and the assigning of the term "ward of Trinidad" on Tobago did not engender positive sentiments toward Trinidad, exacerbated by the smaller island's lack of political autonomy (Carrington 1995). In post-independence Trinidad and Tobago, Tobagonians continue to allude to a legacy of neglect, domination and inequitable budgetary allocations on the part of the Trinidad-based central government, an allegation not without substance (PRDI 1998; Weaver 1998). Of note is the fact that Tobago's current development progress is highly dependent on budgetary allocations from Trinidad, a situation that was contrived a century ago but from which Tobago has been unable to free itself. Consequently, productive activity and development projects in Tobago, including tourism development, are financed by disbursements from Trinidad, which are not always dependable or equitable (Luke 2007). According to the Policy Research and Development Unit: "Cuts in government expenditure in Tobago amount to direct creation of a slump, business failure and unemployment, and will correspondingly retard the process by which Tobago will end its excessive dependence on the State's budget" (PRDI 1998, 9–10).

While the relationship between the two islands may not be regarded as inherently or classically exploitative, it does reflect acute imbalance and dependence in terms of decision-making, power, policy formulation and government expenditure (Roberts 1994; Weaver 1998). So that, despite the establishment of the Tobago House of Assembly through parliamentary majority and presidential proclamation in 1980, which granted some degree of self-government to Tobago, there continues to be persistent accusations of neglect, which have now accelerated into intentional actions towards full internal self-government and, possibly, secession of Tobago from Trinidad (Oxford Business Group 2017).

The strong feelings of neglect and inequity have undoubtedly transferred to the populace. Luke (2007) writes that complaints about unfair treatment of Tobagonians and characterizations of Tobago being rural, backward and inferior by Trinidadians have created an entrenched Tobago identity where, among other things, Trinidadians are treated with unveiled suspicion. Interestingly, this antipathy does not translate to Tobagonians' interactions with international visitors (Luke 2007). Other observations on society in Tobago include strong attachments to family, societal collectivism, communal production, respect for elders, unpretentious hospitality and a tradition of land ownership and entrepreneurship (Craig-James 2008). Of note is that there have been visible increases of serious crime in the last fifteen years, with visitors being the targets of some of the more serious offences (Lee-Tang 2011; Overseas Advisory Security Council 2020). While domestic murders are comparatively low, statistics on crimes committed against visitors to the island have fluctuated, with the most common being robberies, assault and battery, and house break-ins (Economic Management Research Unit 2020)

Notwithstanding the foregoing complexities, Tobago has always had a strong domestic tourism market supported by arrivals from Trinidad. The push factors for the growth in this niche are the high crime levels in Trinidad and improved inter-island transport, while the pull factors include the attractiveness of the beaches, the laid-back lifestyle and the tax-free movement of goods between the islands. Between 2000 and 2019, domestic arrivals to Tobago increased from 203,998 in 2000 to 497,675 in 2019, facilitated by more consistent air travel between the islands and the introduction of two fast ferries that reduced travel time from seven to two and a half hours (Tobago Tourism Agency 2021). Conversely, from 2000 to 2018, direct international tourism arrivals from the island's main source markets significantly declined, from 53,762 to 27,350, a phenomenon that the private sector has attributed to poor marketing and a decrease in direct airlift from the major source markets of the United Kingdom, the United States of America, Germany and Scandinavia (Williams 2016). Despite the increase in domestic tourism, total room stock has remained fairly stagnant (Tobago Tourism Agency 2018). The latest figures show that Tobago has a total of 578 rooms comprising 16 small hotels, 154 villas, 276 self-catering apartments with the remainder spread across bed and breakfast and guest houses (ibid.).

The sudden onset of the global pandemic resulted in the closure of the Trinidad and Tobago borders to international travel for over a year. Tobago became the only leisure option for Trinidad visitors, despite the decrease in scheduled domestic air and sea traffic due to social distancing restrictions. For the period March to September 2020, when compared with the same period in 2021, total domestic air arrivals increased by 5.9 per cent from 72,693 in 2020 to 77,000 in 2021. Similarly, total domestic ferry arrivals also increased, by 28.6 per cent from 103,858 in 2020 to 133,584 in 2021. In general, the propensity for domestic travel was also reflected in occupancy levels, as net occupancy increased by 2 per cent. To capitalize on the domestic market, the Tobago Tourism Agency, the local Destination Management Organization, ran a "Tobago Welcomes Your Return" campaign targeting residents from Trinidad (Tobago Tourism Agency 2020). To signal the importance of the industry to Tobago's economic development, the government of Trinidad and Tobago provided a TT$50 million (approximately US$714,000) grant facility to locally owned accommodation providers to undertake renovations and maintain their properties in readiness for the reopening of domestic and international tourism (Scott 2020).

Methodology

The data for this study was collected in 2018, using a self-administered questionnaire to residents over a period of three months. The surveyed population (1,049 individuals with a confidence interval of 95 per cent) included residents of the seven parishes in Tobago. Responses were garnered using a combination of quota and convenience sampling. Quota sampling, which is a form of non-probability sampling, allows respondents to be conveniently chosen from targeted groups (in this case the quota was residence by parish) according to some predetermined number or quota (Sekeran 2000). Quota sampling is therefore often regarded as a blend of purposive and stratified sampling in that it establishes certain categories which are considered vital for inclusion into the sample, but on a convenience basis (Denscombe 2010). The advantages of this method are that it is cost and time effective, and it ensures the representation of all crucial categories in the population. Its main disadvantage is that it does not contain a fully representative sample. The response rate was 47 per cent, or 491 residents.

The survey instrument consisted of four sections that covered resident attitudes to the economic and social dimension of domestic tourism, attitudes to the domestic tourist, and demographic data. The dependent variable was residents' attitudes to domestic tourism, while the independent variables included domestic tourism's effect on employment opportunities, land prices, prices for goods and services, business ownership, sectoral linkages, cultural conservation, identity and pride, improvements in leisure facilities, crime levels, moral standards and quality of life improvements. A Likert rating scale was used in sections A–C of the questionnaire and allowed for degrees of opinion to be collected. A weakness of this instrument, however, is that it is vulnerable to social desirability bias (Sekaran 2000). Data was analysed using SPSS software and, in this study, was limited to cross tabulations and frequencies.

Results

Demographic Analysis and General Attitude to Tourism Development in Tobago

Of the surveyed resident population, 22 per cent were employed in the tourism and hospitality industry, 26 per cent in the public sector, 8 per cent were students, 11 per cent were retired and the remainder (41 per cent) were employed in the private sector in areas such as agriculture, construction, finance, business, insurance and retail. Forty-one per cent of respondents indicated that immediate relatives were also employed in the industry. Millennials (aged 18–34) accounted for 41 per cent of the sampled population, Generation X (aged 35–54) were 43 per cent and baby boomers (aged over 54) were 16 per cent. The surveyed population was split equally between male and female respondents. Attitudes to overall tourism development in Tobago were positive, with 90 per cent of respondents stating that tourism was a significant driver in the overall development of the island and 63 per cent indicating that the pace of tourism development was acceptable. There was however some ambivalence on whether Tobago was attracting the right type of tourist. When asked this question, 36 per cent agreed that the current visitor segment (domestic tourists) was well aligned with the destination, 29 per cent were neutral and 35 per cent disagreed. Connected to this, 83 per cent of those surveyed felt that Tobago should pursue other niches such as eco, heritage, sports and adventure tourism.

Attitudes to the Economic Effects of Domestic Tourism

Respondents' perceptions of tourism were sought across a number of economic variables including employment, price inflation, entrepreneurship and sectoral linkages. Concerning employment, 86 per cent of respondents felt that domestic tourism created employment opportunities for local residents, although at the level of their community, the employment opportunities were less obvious for 58 per cent of the respondents. Those who worked in the industry (92 per cent) were marginally more inclined to agree with the provision of employment opportunities as a result of tourism, than those who were non-industry workers (85 per cent). All demographic groups felt that tourism positively contributed to employment. However, baby boomers (92 per cent) and men (89 per cent) were the most predisposed to this viewpoint. Notwithstanding these positive attitudes on employment, 81 per cent of respondents expressed that domestic tourism has led to a significant increase in the price of land in Tobago and in their specific communities, in particular (64 per cent). However, there were mixed views pertaining to domestic tourism's effects on the price of general goods and services, where 35 per cent disagreed with the view that domestic tourism had an inflationary effect, 17 per cent were neutral and 48 per cent thought that it increased prices. The older millennials (aged 26–34 – 81 per cent) and Generation X residents (85 per cent) showed greater concern about the impact of tourism on land prices than did baby boomers (63 per cent). In relation to whether domestic tourism strengthened other productive sectors, 26 per cent of respondents felt that it did not, while 57 per cent indicated that sectoral linkages were stimulated by domestic tourism activity and 17 per cent were neutral. Finally, 68 per cent of respondents felt that domestic tourism has created significant opportunities for local ownership of businesses, where 22 per cent of respondents were neutral and 10 per cent disagreed.

Attitudes to Socio-cultural Effects of Domestic Tourism

Respondents were asked whether domestic tourism led to improvements in their social well-being, specifically identity and pride, conservation and revitalization of culture, access to leisure facilities, crime levels, morals and overall quality of life. Sixty-nine per cent were of the view that domestic tourism strengthened the indigenous Tobagonian culture; 24 per cent were neutral and 7 per cent felt that there was cultural erosion. Similarly, 67 per cent of residents indicated that there was a stronger sense of cultural identity and pride as a consequence of domestic tourism, while 6 per cent stated that there was a loss of cultural identity and 27 per cent were neutral in their views. With respect to beach access, 48 per cent of respondents stated that this had improved; however, 33 per cent of respondents were neutral. There was greater consensus on whether domestic tourism had led to better leisure facilities both in terms of number and type, with 80 per cent of respondents affirming that this was the case. In terms of crime, 81 per cent of respondents felt that the number and type of crimes had worsened, and 63 per cent stated that there was decline in moral standards as a result of growth in domestic tourism. Baby boomers (76 per cent) and Generation X (75 per cent) were more inclined to believe that tourism was one of the triggers for the lowering of moral standards than millennials (50 per cent). Finally, respondents were asked whether domestic tourism improved the overall quality of life and sense of community. With respect to the former, 40 per cent felt that quality of life had improved, while 27 per cent felt that it had worsened and 33 per cent were neutral. Similar sentiments were expressed with respect to sense of community, where 36 per cent of respondents reported improvements and 43 per cent were neutral.

Attitudes to Domestic Tourists

Responding to whether real or perceived tensions between residents of Tobago and residents of Trinidad had improved or worsened, 24 per cent of those surveyed suggested that tensions had increased, while 43 per cent remained neutral and 33 per cent stated that tensions had lessened. Those with a longer historical memory, that is, the baby boomers (28 per cent) were less inclined to think that tensions had worsened, while millennials (37 per cent) and Generation X (31 per cent) respondents felt that they had. Respondents who worked in the industry (41 per cent) were also less inclined to think that inter-island tensions had increased, as opposed to 59 per cent of non-industry employees. Asked whether they felt that they were being overwhelmed by domestic tourists, 19 per cent reported that they did not, while 38 per cent indicated that they did, with 43 per cent remaining neutral. The perceived sense of domination was highest among millennials (43 per cent) and lower among the baby boomers (35 per cent). Thirty-nine per cent of those employed in the industry felt a greater sense of being overwhelmed by domestic tourists than those employed in other sectors (37 per cent).

Discussion

Tobagonians are very aware of the current benefits of tourism and its greater potential for economic development. Previous findings support the view that those who perceive greater benefits from tourism tend to have a more positive attitude to the industry. Notwithstanding that less than half of the respondents work in tourism, there is significant positivity about the economic benefits of tourism, a perception that might have derived from a combination of the employment of close relatives in the industry and the fact that the small size of the island allows residents to feel the industry's effects more keenly. The positive social exchange that is taking place in this context, then, seems to be less about the individual and more about the collective. This result contradicts those of Garau-Vadell et al. (2018), which point to an association between industry employment and support for tourism. The cultural norm in Tobago of collectivism and community allows for a different view. Still, while it is acknowledged that domestic tourism brings benefits, there is a sense that residents feel there are other niches more closely aligned to Tobago's comparative advantages that can provide even greater benefits.

From an economic perspective, residents thought that a number of benefits have accrued to them as a consequence of the growth of domestic tourism over the last twenty years, particularly in the areas of employment and business ownership. The redistributive effect of domestic tourism has also taken root in terms of business ownership and improved sectoral linkages in areas such as agriculture, fishing and construction (Haddad et al. 2013). Thus, domestic tourism has allowed, through tourist spending, for wealth to be reallocated from the core (Trinidad) to the periphery (Tobago), thereby improving the quality of life of the periphery's residents. In a sense, one can argue that reverse extraction is occurring as a result of domestic tourism. This supports the assertion that strategic calculation by residents can create a shift in the dependency discourse that might be more visible over time (Chaperon and Bramwell 2013). From a sustainable tourism perspective, business ownership is seen as creating a system of resident empowerment and a greater sense of self-reliance outside of government. Overton (1999) posited that local empowerment through business can also potentially reduce the level of antagonism directed towards tourists. These findings are similar to those of previous studies (Rogerson and Lisa 2005; Scheyvens 2011; Kabote et al. 2017). There are however concerns among segments of the

Tobago population about their inability to access land and goods and services at reasonable prices due to the inflationary effect of tourism-induced development. This result has not been found elsewhere and is often associated with international mass tourism (Telfer and Sharpley 2015). While this sentiment does not currently seem to colour the general attitude of residents, perhaps given the overall gains from tourism, it is a finding that should cause policymakers to pay attention, particularly as Tobagonians attach a high value to land ownership (Craig-James 2008; Luke 2007).

As the in-group, residents of Tobago appear to believe that domestic tourists (the out-group) pose a symbolic threat to their moral code, way of life and, perhaps, cultural traditions. The result is that, while there was general sense among Tobagonians that domestic tourism has strengthened and revitalized the distinctive Tobago culture and solidified their identity, as had been found in other studies (Canavan 2013; Carr 2002; Mustafa 2012), residents also generally believed that domestic tourism threatened traditional morals and led to increases in crime. Findings related to a reinforced sense of Tobagonian identity might be construed as a historical resistance mechanism to not acculturate into the culture of those whom they view as morally inferior. In the case of crime, the negative stereotypes and expectations that the in-group of Tobago residents hold about the out-group is reflected in the finding that respondents believed that the rise in domestic tourism is in some way responsible for increases in crime against visitors (Lee-Tang 2011). Luke (2007) reported that Tobagonians have always viewed their Trinidad neighbours with suspicion, often suggesting that they are tricksters and untrustworthy. These attitudes have been transposed onto the tourism landscape, and to some extent, has been laid at the doorstep of domestic tourism. Where other studies have reported that domestic tourism has improved social cohesion in communities (Carr 2002; Telfer and Sharpley 2015), this study's findings suggest otherwise since less than 50 per cent of residents demonstrated positive beliefs about domestic tourism improving their overall quality of life and strengthening their sense of community. Residents, while embracing the economic benefits of tourism, are ambivalent about trading their way of life and sense of collectivism for local tourism development. One possible reason for the quality of life position is that only 22 per cent of respondents were directly employed in the industry and, therefore, most respondents' material circumstances were not predicated upon its success or failure.

Notwithstanding the economic improvements from domestic tourism, underlying historic tensions continue to bedevil relations between the two islands. Exacerbating this situation is that the number of domestic tourists visiting the island on an annual basis is almost eight times the local population. This is likely to result in overcrowding of beaches and other shared spaces and contentions around resources at peak times. While there is no manifestation of overtourism sentiments, as seen in destinations like Venice and Barcelona (Alexis 2017), it is important that those who are charged with tourism responsibility closely monitor resident attitudes. Domestic overtourism has the potential to worsen existing prejudices and, by extension, both the in- and out-groups' realistic and symbolic threats.

Summary Reflections

This chapter has examined resident attitude to domestic tourism and within the context of core-periphery relations. Such a study has not been previously undertaken. Using social and integrated threat theories, the study found that while Tobagonians are happy to embrace the positive economic benefits of domestic tourism, they are very defensive in the face of what they perceive as symbolic and realistic threats to entrenched cultural mores that have defined them. Thus, they are unwilling to cede these as part of the process of tourism development. Relatedly, the study has challenged the notion that domestic tourism leads to greater social cohesion due to domestic tourists' tendency to be less disruptive and more aligned to the existing culture. In this case, the Tobago's culture is significantly different from Trinidad's culture, and this difference is worrying to residents. The study has therefore revealed new insights that can be useful in studying domestic tourism, such as perceptions of domestic tourism's inflationary effect, its gradual erosion of indigenous moral codes and its socially disruptive elements. Moreover, the study found that domestic tourism triggered a simultaneous deepening of cultural identity and a tendency towards cultural conservation, highlighting the complexity of the in-group. The reinforcing role that tourism plays in potentially increasing dependency and exacerbating tensions should prompt policymakers in Tobago to continuously monitor current and future resident attitudes to domestic tourism and its effects on prices, social cohesion and quality of life. Future research can revisit this topic post-COVID-19 to determine whether resident sentiment has changed. Research on domestic tourism should also explore the challenges of domestic tourism from a demand and supply perspective, as little is known about how this niche affects destination competitiveness. Within a core-periphery context, research insights are needed from the domestic visitor about their motivations for visiting and experiences while in the destination.

References

Adams, Kathleen M. 1998. "Domestic Tourism and Nation-Building in South Sulawesi." *Indonesia and the Malay World* 26 (75): 77–96.

Alexis, Papathanassis. 2017. "Over-Tourism and Anti-Tourist Sentiment: An Exploratory Analysis and Discussion." *Ovidius University Annals, Economic Sciences Series* 17 (2): 288–93.

Ap, John. 1992. "Residents' Perceptions on Tourism Impacts." *Annals of Tourism Research* 19 (4): 665–90.

Ayres, Ron. 2000. "Tourism as a Passport to Development in Small States: Reflections on Cyprus." *International Journal of Social Economics* 27 (2): 114–33.

Bierman, David. 2003. *Restoring Tourism Destinations in Crisis*. Wallingford: CABI Publishing.

Bui, Huong Thanh, and Lee Jolliffe. 2011. "Vietnamese Domestic Tourism: An Investigation of Travel Motivations." *Austrian Journal of South-East Asian Studies* 4 (1): 10–29.

Bramwell, Brian, John Highman, Bernard Lane, and Graham Miller. 2017. "Twenty-five Years of Sustainable Tourism and the Journal of Sustainable Tourism: Looking Back and Moving Forward." *Journal of Sustainable Tourism* 25 (1): 1–9.

Burkart, Arthur John, and Slavoj Medlik. 1981. *Tourism: Past, Present and Future*, 2nd ed. London: Heinemann.

Canavan, Brendan. 2013. "The Extent and Role of Domestic Tourism in a Small Island: The Case of the Isle of Man." *Journal of Travel Research* 5 (3): 340–52.

———. 2016. "Identification, Motivation and Facilitation of Domestic Tourism in a Small Island." *Scandinavian Journal of Hospitality and Tourism* 16 (4): 512–27.

Carr, Neil. 2002. "A Comparative Analysis of the Behaviour of Domestic and International Young Tourists." *Tourism Management* 23 (3): 321–25.

Carrington, S. 1985. "The Union of Tobago and Trinidad – The Emergence of Under-Development and Dependency." In *Forging a New Democracy – Beyond the Post-Colonial Era*, edited by R. Sebastien, 55–66. Trinidad and Tobago: Office of the Leader of the Opposition.

Chaperon, Samantha, and Bill Bramwell. 2013. "Dependency and Agency in Peripheral Tourism Development." *Annals of Tourism Research* 40:132–54.

Choi, Hwansuk Chris, and Iain Murray. 2010. "Resident Attitudes toward Sustainable Community Tourism." *Journal of Sustainable Tourism* 18 (4): 575–94.

Craig-James, S. E. 2008. *The Changing Society of Tobago, 1838–1938: A Fractured Whole Vol. 1: 1838–1900.* Arima, Trinidad and Tobago: Cornerstone.

Davis, Duane, Jeff Allen, and Robert M. Cosenza. 1988. "Segmenting Local Residents by their Attitudes, Interests, and Opinions toward Tourism." *Journal of Travel Research* 27 (2): 2–8.

Denscombe, Martyn. 2010. *The Good Research Guide: For Small-Scale Social Research Project*, 4th ed. Buckingham: Open University Press.

Douglas, Norman, Ngaire Douglas, and Ros Derrett. 2001. *Special Interest Tourism.* Sydney: John Wiley and Sons.

Economic Management Research Unit. 2020. *Tobago Social and Economic Statistical Digest, 2008–2018.* Scarborough, Tobago: Division of Finance and the Economy, Tobago House of Assembly.

Eijgelaar, E., P. M. Peeters, and P. C. Piket. 2008. "Domestic and International Tourism in a Globalized World." In International Conference *"Ever the Twain shall Meet – Relating International and Domestic Tourism"* of Research Committee RC50 International Tourism, International Sociological Association – Jaipur, Rajasthan, India – 24–26 November 2008. http://www.tourism-master.com/theses/Domestic_and_International_Tourism_in_a_Globalized_World.PDF.

Frank, A G. 1969. "The Development of Underdevelopment." *Monthly Review* 18 (4): 17–31.

Garau-Vadell, Joan B., Desiderio Gutierrez-Taño, and Ricardo Diaz-Armas. 2018. "Economic Crisis and Residents' Perception of the Impacts of Tourism in Mass Tourism Destinations." *Journal of Destination Marketing and Management* 7:68–75.

Gardiner, Sarah, Debra Grace, and Ceridwyn King. 2014. "The Generation Effect: The Future of Domestic Tourism in Australia." *Journal of Travel Research* 53 (6): 705–70.

Gursoy, Dogan, Zhe Ouyang, Robin Nunkoo, and Wei Wei. 2019. "Residents' Impact Perceptions of and Attitudes towards Tourism Development: A Meta-Analysis." *Journal of Hospitality Marketing and Management* 28 (3): 306–33.

Haddad, Eduardo Amaral, Alexandre Alves Porsse, and Wilson Rabahy. 2013. "Domestic Tourism and Regional Inequality in Brazil." *Tourism Economics* 19 (1): 173–86.

Hadinejad, Arghavan, Brent D. Moyle, Noel Scott, Anna Kralj, and Robin Nunkoo. 2019. "Residents' Attitudes to Tourism: A Review." *Tourism Review* 74 (2): 150–65.

Kabote, Forbes, Patrick Walter Mamimine, and Zororo Muranda. 2017. "Domestic Tourism for Sustainable Development in Developing Countries." *African Journal of Hospitality, Tourism and Leisure* 6 (2): 1–12.

Kayat, Kalsom. 2002. "Power, Social Exchanges and Tourism in Langkawi: Rethinking Resident Perceptions." *International Journal of Tourism Research* 4 (3): 171–91.

Lankford, Samuel V., and Dennis R. Howard. 1994. "Developing a Tourism Impact Attitude Scale." *Annals of Tourism Research* 21 (1): 121–39.

Lee-Tang, E. 2011. "Visitor Perceptions of Crime in Tobago." Unpublished master's thesis, University of the West Indies, Trinidad and Tobago.

Long, Pham, and Kalsom Kayat. 2011. "Residents' Perceptions of Tourism Impact and Their Support for Tourism Development: The Case Study of Cuc Phuong National Park, Ninh Binh Province, Vietnam." *European Journal of Tourism Research* 4 (2): 123–46.

Luke, L.B. 2007. *Identity and Secession in the Caribbean: Tobago versus Trinidad, 1889–1980.* Kingston: University of the West Indies Press.

Madrigal, Robert. 1993. "A Tale of Tourism in Two Cities." *Annals of Tourism Research* 20 (2): 336–53.

Mason, Peter, and Joanne Cheyne. 2000. "Residents' Attitudes to Proposed Tourism Development." *Annals of Tourism Research* 27 (2): 391–411.

Mathieson, Alister, and Geoffrey Wall. 1992. *Tourism, Economic, Physical and Social Impacts.* Harlow, UK: Longman.

McGehee, Nancy G., and Kathleen L. Andereck. 2004. "Factors Predicting Rural Residents' Support of Tourism." *Journal of Travel Research* 43 (2): 131–40.

Ministry of Planning and Sustainable Development Central Statistical Office. n.d. "Population." Accessed 14 October 2020. https://cso.gov.tt/subjects/population-and-vital-statistics/population/.

Monterrubio, Carlos. 2016. "The Impact of Spring Break Behaviour: An Integrated Threat Theory Analysis of Residents' Prejudice." *Tourism Management* 54:418–27.

Mustafa, Mairna H. 2012. "Improving the Contribution of Domestic Tourism to the Economy of Jordan." *Asian Social Science* 8 (2): 49.

Ottley, Carlton. R. 1973. *The Story of Tobago: Robinson Crusoe's Island in the Caribbean.* Trinidad: Longman.

Overseas Advisory Security Council. 2020. *Trinidad & Tobago 2020 Crime & Safety Report.* https://www.osac.gov/Country/TrinidadTobago/Content/Detail/Report/e71edbe1-3d87-4d1f-989d-18900d4002c6.

Overton, John. 1999. "Sustainable Development and the Pacific Islands." In *Strategies for Sustainable Development: Experiences from the Pacific*, edited by J. Overton and R. Scheyvens, 1–5. London: Zed.

Oxford Business Group. 2017. The Path to Self-Rule: A New Draft Bill could Increase Tobago's Autonomy. https://oxfordbusinessgroup.com/the-path-to-self-rule-a-new-draft-bill-could-increase-tobagos-autonomy/.

Pappas, Nikolaos V. 2008. "City of Rhodes: Residents' Attitudes toward Tourism Impacts and Development." *Anatolia* 19 (1): 51–70.

Pearce, Philip L., Gianna Moscardo, and Glenn F. Ross. 1996. *Tourism Community Relationships.* Oxford: Pergamon.

Pegas, Fernanda de Vasconcellos, David Weaver, and Guy Castley. 2015. "Domestic Tourism and Sustainability in an Emerging Economy: Brazil's Littoral Pleasure Periphery." *Journal of Sustainable Tourism* 23 (5): 748–69.

Perdue, Richard R., Patrick T. Long, and Lawrence Allen. 1987. "Rural Resident Tourism Perceptions and Attitudes." *Annals of Tourism Research* 14 (3): 420–29.

Policy Research and Development Institute (PRDI). 1998. *Tobago Development Plan, Report No. 2 – Medium-Term Policy Framework of Tobago, 1998–2000*. Tobago: Division of Finance and Planning, Office of the Chief Secretary, THA.

Roberts, S. 1994. "Tobago after Hurricane Flora: 1963–1973." Unpublished BA Caribbean Study Project. University of the West Indies, St Augustine Campus.

Robinson, Mike, and Marina Novelli. 2015. *Niche Tourism: An Introduction Niche Tourism in Contemporary Issues, Trends and Cases*, edited by Marina Novelli, 1–15. Oxford: Elsevier.

Rogerson, Christian M., and Zoleka Lisa. 2005. "'Sho't Left': Changing Domestic Tourism in South Africa." *Urban Forum* 16 (2): 88–111.

Ryan, Chris, and David Montgomery. 1994. "The Attitudes of Bakewell Residents to Tourism and Issues in Community Responsive Tourism." *Tourism Management* 15 (5): 358–69.

Scheyvens, Regina, and Janet Momsen. 2008. "Tourism in Small Island States: From Vulnerability to Strengths." *Journal of Sustainable Tourism* 16 (5): 491–510.

Scheyvens, Regina. 2007. "Poor Cousins No More: Valuing the Development Potential of Domestic and Diaspora Tourism." *Progress in Development Studies* 7 (4): 307–25.

Scheyvens Regina. 2011. The Challenge of Sustainable Tourism Development in the Maldives: Understanding the Social and Political Dimensions of Sustainability. *Asia Pacific Viewpoint* 52 (2): 148–64.

Sekeran, Uma. 2000. *Research Methods for Business – A Skill-Building Approach*, 3rd ed. New York: John Wiley.

Scott, J. 2020. "T&T Gov't Shores Up Hoteliers with TT$50 Million." *Caribbean Business Report*, 29 April 2020. https://caribbeanbusinessreport.com/news/tt-govt-shore-up-hoteliers-with-tt50-million/.

Sharpley, Richard. 2014. "Host Perceptions of Tourism: A Review of the Research." *Tourism Management* 42:37–49.

Sinclair-Maragh, Gaunette. 2017. "Demographic Analysis of Residents' Support for Tourism Development in Jamaica." *Journal of Destination Marketing and Management* 6 (1): 5–12.

Stephan, Walter G., Oscar Ybarra, Carmen Martnez Martnez, Joseph Schwarzwald, and Michal Tur-Kaspa. 1998. "Prejudice toward Immigrants to Spain and Israel: An Integrated Threat Theory Analysis." *Journal of Cross-Cultural Psychology* 29 (4): 559–76.

Telfer, David J., and Richard Sharpley. 2008. *Tourism and Development in the Developing World*. London, Routledge.

Tobago Tourism Agency. 2018. *Estimate of Room Stock in Tobago 2000–2018*. Scarborough, Tobago: Tobago Tourism Agency.

———. 2020. "Tobago Welcomes Your Return: TTAL Launches Domestic Tourism Campaign." *https://www.visittobago.gov.tt/tobago-welcomes-your-return-ttal-launches-domestic-tourism-campaign*.

Tobago Tourism Agency. 2021. *Research Reports on Domestic and International Arrivals 2000–2021*. Scarborough, Tobago: Tobago Tourism Agency.

United Nations World Tourism Organization. 1980. *Manila Declaration on World Tourism*. Madrid, Spain: UNWTO.
———. n.d. "Glossary of Tourism Terms." https://www.unwto.org/glossary-tourism-terms.
Ward, Colleen, and Tracy Berno. 2011. "Beyond Social Exchange Theory: Attitudes toward Tourists." *Annals of Tourism Research* 38 (4): 1556–69.
Weaver, David B. 1998. "Peripheries of the Periphery: Tourism in Tobago and Barbuda." *Annals of Tourism Research* 25 (2): 292–313.
———, and Laura J. Lawton. 2001. "Resident Perceptions in the Urban–Rural Fringe." *Annals of Tourism Research* 28 (2): 439–58.
Wen, Zhang. 1997. "China's Domestic Tourism: Impetus, Development and Trends." *Tourism Management* 18 (8): 565–71.
Williams, E. 2016. "Tobago Tourism Takes a Dive." *Trinidad Express*, 2 January 2016. http://www.trinidadexpress.com/20160102/news/tobago-tourism-takes-a-dive.
World Travel and Tourism Council. 2018. *Travel and Tourism: Global Economic & Impact Update*. London: World Travel and Tourism Council.
Yap, Ghialy, and David Allen. 2011. "Investigating Other Leading Indicators Influencing Australian Domestic Tourism Demand." *Mathematics and Computers in Simulation* 81 (7): 1365–74.

13.
Niche Marketing in the Caribbean: A Call for a Scorecard Approach in Tourism-Intensive SIDS

Narendra Ramgulam and Acolla Lewis-Cameron

Introduction

With the current global economic recession and other associated economic pressures affecting the gross domestic product of most countries, economic diversification has continued to be a front-burner topic for the past decade. Countries and regions are always seeking out new ways to generate revenue, increase employment and reduce poverty levels (World Bank 2015; Scheyvens and Momsen 2008). As such, countries should diversify their export capacity and become more economically sustainable if they are to cope with the volatility of global market conditions. According to Papatheodorou, Rosselló and Xiao (2010), times of economic downturn, where major source markets are affected, have resulted in ripple impacts particularly affecting tourism-dependent and small island developing countries, thereby making them socio-economically vulnerable, as discussed in chapter one. Economic diversification has been touted as an avenue that not only adds stability to a country's economy but also gives that country options to further its wealth generation (including foreign exchange earnings) and employment opportunities, generate new markets and, if managed properly, increase standard of living and quality of life for its citizens (Demas 2009).

In this regard, diversifying away from mainstream tourism (sun, sea and sand, as found in the majority of SIDS) and into other avenues can be a success route for SIDS that are overdependent on tourism (Holzner 2011; Chao et al. 2006). The previous chapters in this book highlighted the many success stories and challenges associated with developing specific niches in the region. This concluding chapter focuses on addressing the issue of how SIDS can select the best products to diversify into through the application of a scorecard model. This proposed scorecard model can offer a blueprint for SIDS to structure their development when selecting niche products. The model offers a quantitative dimension to a qualitative decision-making process. Having discussed the need for diversification in chapter two, this chapter will focus on an examination of product selection and development frameworks. This will be followed by a discussion on the development of the scorecard. Finally, the scorecard and its functionality will be shared and discussed.

Product Selection and Development

Since diversification and new product development can lead to economic development (Parrish, Cassill and Oxenham 2006; Benur and Bramwell 2015; Sakarya, Eckman and Hyllegard 2007), it is not surprising that it is a popular tool used in the marketing world today (Ansoff 1957; Ansoff and McDonnell 1988; and Kotler and Makens 1999). The product/market growth matrix developed by Ansoff and McDonnell (1988) is one theory that has emerged out of the product development and diversification literature, and it illustrates and guides the strategic direction for firms, companies and even countries. According to this matrix, several choices exist: penetrating further within existing markets with existing products; developing new products for existing markets; bringing existing products into new markets; or pursuing full diversification by combining the development of new products with entering new markets (Toften and Hammervoll 2011). Figure 13.1 displays the product/market growth matrix.

Figure 13.1: Product/Market Growth Matrix

	Products	
Markets	Existing	New
Existing	Market Penetration	Product Development
New	Market Development	Diversification

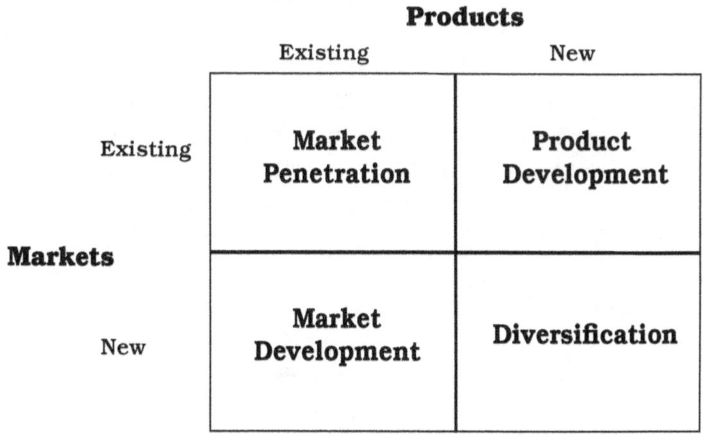

Source: Ansoff and McDonnell 1988

The strategic directions outlined in the matrix all depend on specific situations impacting the firm or country. There is no one correct option, and each strategic direction has its strengths and weaknesses. Market penetration into existing markets is used by firms with large market share wanting to remain dominant. Whereas diversification, new market development and product development are more popularly used today because they are considered more flexible and cater to emerging customer preferences (Toften and Hammervoll 2011).

Niche product development also satisfies the taste buds of varying customer product requirements. One way to diversify into different niche products is to be innovative with the existing and available resource base (Toften and Hammervoll 2011; Liao, Chen and Deng 2010; Nill and Kemp 2009; Schot and Geels 2008). Nill and Kemp (2009) and Schot and Geels (2008) stated that being innovative is a vital aspect of niche market development and that innovation adds an element of change via choice to an existing range of homogenous products. In this regard, countries seeking to diversify their products should be innovative in their outlook (Novelli, Schmitz and Spencer 2006; Sethi, Smith and Park 2001). According to the work of Lewis and Jordan (2008, 256), in order to carve a niche in a petroleum-based economy such as Trinidad and Tobago, it is important to foster a climate of innovation. The government can encourage tourism business expansion by providing awards for creativity and innovation in tourism product development.

Hassan (2000) outlined several areas that should be taken into consideration when diversifying in order to remain competitive. The external environment, which includes political, cultural, technological and socio-economic factors and trends, shapes and influences industry-specific variables (demand, industry structure, environmental commitment and comparative advantage), which then affect the competitiveness of the market. The supply and demand of certain niche tourism products are therefore determined by the external global competitive environment (Ansoff 1957; Murray and O'Neill 2012; Sakarya, Eckman and Hyllegard 2007). Figure 13.2 displays the factors in the external environment that shape market competitiveness.

Understanding the global competitive environment can help destinations to select the most appropriate niche products to invest in and develop, leading to competitive advantage (Dwyer et al. 2009; Dwyer and Edwards 2009; Bramwell 1998; Schilling and Hill 1998;

Figure 13.2: Factors Shaping Market Competitiveness

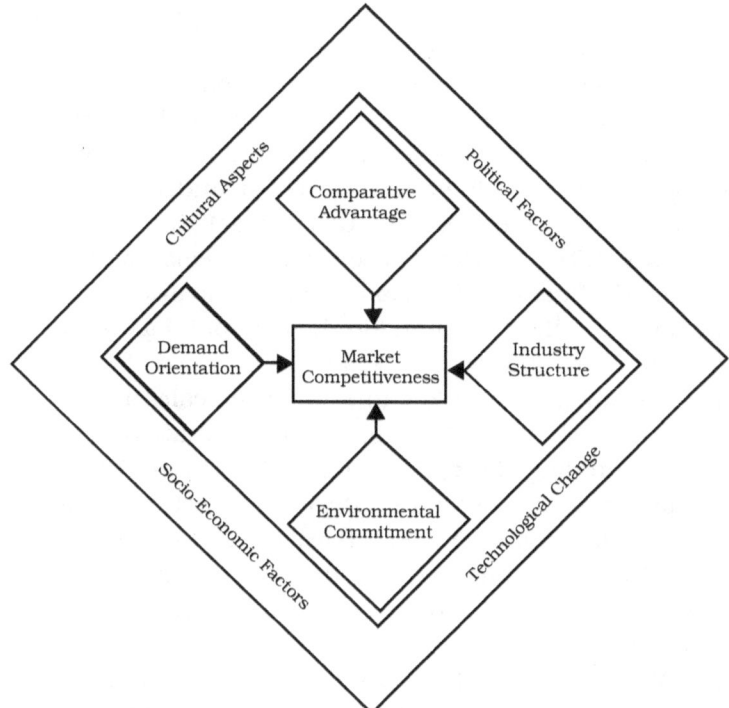

Source: Hassan (2000, 241)

Toften and Hammervoll 2011; Murray and O'Neill 2012; Page 1993; Novelli, Schmitz and Spencer 2006). Nill and Kemp (2009) addressed this as a key factor leading to Strategic Niche Management, which is an evolutionary approach aimed at fostering sustainability benefits by examining the external environment and being innovative in a competitive environment.

In the Caribbean context, by diversifying and proposing new products, destinations may not have to rely solely on their main source markets (United States of America and Canada) for revenue. By offering more choice, destinations can capture other markets in the global arena, making themselves attractive for new travellers (from other countries) seeking specific niche products. The choice to diversifying into tourism, away from tourism or through tourism linkages depends on the destination, its vision, external source market conditions and its available resource base. Regardless of choice, it opens the gate for other avenues to be developed and posits a sustainable solution of addressing overdependence on one major export product.

Schilling and Hill (1998, 67) stated that new product development has caught on as a strategic tool and grown over the last few decades and "is now the dominant driver of competition in many industries". As already discussed in chapter two, Benur and Bramwell (2015) added to the literature on tourism product development and diversification by proposing a framework for understanding tourism product development options. In their model, the authors (Benur and Bramwell 2015) conceptualized the strategic options available for tourism destinations by examining two features, namely: the extent of product diversification (on the horizontal axis) and tourism product intensification (on the vertical axis). Both of these features have a scale ranging from low to high. The scales help to identify broad options for tourism development at destinations.

By understanding the options available, destinations can make better informed decisions and strategically chart their way forward based on their unique context (Weaver 2000; and Benur and Bramwell 2015). For example, some destinations may choose to offer concentrated mass tourism because it works for them, such as in the case of Benidorm in Spain (Claver-Cortés, Molina-Azorín and Pereira-Moliner 2007), Yugoslavia (Hall 2002), South Africa (Rogerson 2004), Peru (Divino and McAleer 2010), and Mexico (Clancy 1999). Other destinations may have the resources available to develop and diversify into many niche tourism products because their context depends on that strategy, such as in the case of Dominica (Weaver 2000), New Zealand (Morgan and Pritchard 2006), Italy (Trunfio, Petruzzellis and Nigro 2006), and Central and Eastern Europe (Hall 1999). Tourism product diversification into many niche tourism products does present the benefit of offering many products to a varied group of customers, which allows the destination itself to be more competitive and economically sustainable leading to development (Ritchie and Crouch 2003). Due to this major advantage, destinations that traditionally provided mass tourism products can now examine broader options by also integrating niche product offerings as part of their strategy in moving forward (Benur and Bramwell 2015).

The development of niche tourism products allows countries to not only be competitive (Buhalis and Licata 2002; Dwyer et al. 2009) with their offering but also innovative and tap into new products and probable new sources of travellers with particular interests, as well as boost arrivals of those travellers likely to generate increased foreign exchange earnings (Guerreiro and Guerreiro 2017; Vanegas and Croes 2003; Page et al. 2017). When selecting niche products to develop for competitive advantage, one strategy identified by Lewis (1950) is that countries should look internally, analyse their resource base and develop products that complement what is available within its borders. This is not only a cost-saving measure, but promotes and develops other areas, thereby spreading development (Novelli, Schmitz and Spencer 2006; Smith 1994). Another strategy proposed by Hassan (2000) is to monitor the market situation and develop products that align with market changes. Hassan (2000, 242) further stated that some market indicators include "decreasing arrivals from traditional markets, reduced length of stay, lower per tourist spending rates, slowdown in new business development, lower repeat visit rates, increasing seasonality, safety and security breakdowns, bankruptcy or failure of business establishments, negative community attitudes, and leadership that focuses on short-term fixes rather than on long-term solutions".

When individual countries and destinations start observing these indicators becoming more ubiquitous as it relates to their contexts, they need to start shifting their pendulum towards other niches and areas of development by employing new destination plans and development strategies.

Poon (1993) and Vainikka (2013) advised that some destinations may need to consider niche tourism product development because the old mass tourism products are no longer sustainable, fashionable or in trend with what new (alternative) tourists are seeking. Therefore, destinations need to be flexible in their orientation if they are to attract new pockets of travellers. The new tourist seeks unconventional products and is a higher end spenders who is willing to pay for quality over quantity. Farmaki (2012) added to the discussion by postulating that diversifying into new niches is important economically because it is the decision that makes the most financial sense. Diversifying and taking advantage of developing new niche products is especially useful when old products or services stop yielding profits. Benur and Bramwell (2015) and Farmaki (2012) further stated that new product development also addresses the issue of seasonality in tourism planning.

The theoretical models and theories outlined earlier – specifically, niche marketing, the product/market growth matrix, factors shaping market competitiveness and the framework of tourism product development options – all provide an understanding of niche product development and diversification. And if these theories are given due consideration when diversifying into niche tourism products, it can lead to more informed planning that has positive social and economic development implications in the long term for destinations (Bramwell 1998; Parrish, Cassill and Oxenham 2006; McElroy and De Albuquerque 1998; Liao, Chen and Deng 2010).

Ansoff and McDonnell's (1988) product/market growth matrix stated that there was no single route that should be taken to guarantee success. Instead, every company, destination and country has unique factors and situations that should be evaluated based on their own context and that can become a platform for taking a specific strategic approach forward. In other words, it does not automatically fully support developing new products, stating that there may be some situations where market penetration might be the better option to follow instead of developing a new product, which may be costly. However, it does acknowledge that diversification strategy is best when various customer tastes exist (Toften and Hammervoll 2011). The work of Hassan (2000) compliments the logic of diversification and product development in order to seek competitive advantage, but adds that any strategy should carefully survey the macro environment before crafting a way forward. The external environment comprising social, cultural and political factors, among others, can influence and shape market competitiveness, and this then influences what products to develop. For example, Jamaica: while it has potential for offering many different tourism products and niches, its cultural environment does not allow for the development and promotion of some products such as LGBT tourism.

Dwyer et al. (2009) agreed with the rationale postulated by Hassan (2000) and stated that not only should the external environment be examined but there should also be a focus on the current trends in the industry because current trends can impact visitor flows. By understanding visitors, destinations can develop products to suit their needs. Benur and Bramwell (2015) provided the most comprehensive model for tourism product diversification and development options by combining the logic of all other models and proposing a framework from which different products (niche or even mass products) can be developed depending on a destination's strategy and what it wants to achieve. Contextual analysis is important and destinations' strategies will vary depending on their macro and micro environments.

Scorecard Development

According to Kaplan and Norton (1995), the balanced scorecard was created to help make better strategic decisions by looking at a range of variable measures, which include financials, the customer, learning and growth, and internal business processes. These four categories consist of scaled items used to rate business performance. In the past, business decisions were made solely on financial measures and, while this worked for some time, today the business and operating environment is considered to be very fast-paced, turbulent and sometimes unstable, and therefore requires comprehensive strategic decisions moving forward (Al-Zwyalif 2017; Khairat 2017; Chaker, Idrissi and Manouar 2017; Giannopoulos et al. 2013; Qin, Atkins and Yu 2013; Sainaghi, Phillips, and Corti 2013; Mooraj, Oyon and Hostettler 1999).

According to the literature (Halmi and Severović 2016; Vila, Costa and Rovira 2010; Banchieri et al. 2012; Rahman and Chin 2013; Qin, Atkins and Yu 2013), destinations are always seeking new ways of enhancing themselves in order to become successful. One kind of enhancement is the use of strategic decisions to move the destination forward. This can take the form of taking tools found in one branch or area of studies and applying them to other areas to enhance decision-making in those areas. For example, Rahman and Chin (2013) took note of the use of the balanced scorecard in business and applied it to the evaluation of sustainable urban transport in civil and environmental engineering in Singapore. Braam, Benders and Heusinkveld (2007) used the balanced scorecard approach in the Netherlands to assess the evolution of print media indicators. Greasley (2004) looked at improving human resource processes in a UK police force. Qin, Atkins and Yu (2013) used a balanced scorecard approach to evaluate performance in e-tourism. Qin, Atkins and Yu (2013, 822) stated that: "The search for knowledge base and selection of the most suitable web tool technological solutions and supporting infrastructure is a remarkable challenge to e-Tourism. The Balanced Scorecard (BSC) approach can then be employed to provide performance assessment and logical actions to facilitate strategic decision making for ICTs integration".

Qin, Atkins and Yu (2013) did not modify the scorecard's original measures. They used its original variables and measures to evaluate and assess one existing marketing tool, e-tourism. Therefore, the use of the balanced scorecard approach was not limited to its practicality via strategic decision-making; it could also be used to assess performance and guide firms to take action where necessary. While its practicality has been outlined by many, including Khairat (2017), Giannopoulos et al. (2013), Qin, Atkins and Yu (2013), Sen, Bingol and Vayvay (2017), and Banchieri et al. (2012), the authors suggested that the model is not flawless and therefore should not be applied to a situation without modifying it to suit the individual environment. Other critiques of the balanced scorecard model include:

- The lack of discussion of its political dimension. Politics internal and external to the organization has a huge role to play when making decisions on the way forward (Khairat 2017; Banchieri et al. 2012);
- The contradiction in its formation: In their seminal work, the creators of the model stated that its main objective was to maximize profit for shareholders, but they later cited customer satisfaction as the main objective instead (Kaplan and Norton 1996; Banchieri et al. 2012);
- The structure of the model, which is composed of only four perspectives, which can lead to key factors being omitted in some instances (Chaker, Idrissi and Manouar 2017; Giannopoulos et al. 2013);
- The fact that the model does not consider a time dimension or what may be important or critical at a given point in time (Chaker, Idrissi and Manouar 2017; Banchieri et al. 2012);
- The fact that the correlation between non-financial measures and future benefits has not been demonstrated (Vila, Costa and Rovira 2010).

Voelpel, Leibold and Eckhoff (2006) proposed an alternative model to the scorecard called the "systemic scorecard". This model examined more than just the four variables found on the balanced scorecard. Banchieri et al. (2012) cited the work of Othman (2008), which proposed adding external variables to the balanced scorecard. However, these alternative models were never empirically tested (Banchieri et al. 2012).

In the area of tourism, Evans (2005) applied the balanced scorecard as a management tool for hotels. Evans (2005) noted that strategy literature as it pertains to hospitality and tourism is somewhat weakly developed and that further strategy-oriented literature on models needs to be developed to take the industry forward. Notarstefano and Volo (2012) used the balanced scorecard in a tourism impact study to foster an integrated approach to tourism planning. Within their study, the four perspectives of the scorecard were used as measurement variables without modification. The results allowed for better decision-making and holistic planning by taking wider measures into consideration, not only economic and financial ones. Chang et al. (2008) examined travel agencies in Taiwan and the use of the balanced scorecard as a performance management model. The study revealed that the scorecard's performance indicators helped to improve efficiency.

Similarly, the balanced scorecard was also used successfully in a study evaluating and managing hot spring hotels in Taiwan (Chen, Hsu and Tzeng 2011). Karatzoglou and Spilanis (2010) focused on sustainable tourism in the Greek islands, taking an integration of activity-based environmental management to formulate a scorecard resource management paradigm. In this study, environmental factors were included in a scorecard to assist with decision-making. However, it was an environmental study and variables were biased towards sustainable tourism measurement variables. Khairat (2017) applied it to evaluate performance in the airline industry. That case study revealed that the four measures were not treated equally. The financial measure was regarded as the most important consideration when making decisions.

Yilmaz and Bititci (2006) stated that the balanced scorecard can be a very important tool for tourism diversification. It can help overcome seasonality problems by allowing other products to be selected for development. This is key to extending the tourism season year-round and making the destination more strategic and competitive. However, not much work has been done building a model for tourism or a scorecard that can be used to select the most appropriate niche products for development. It also broadens the scope for those countries and encourages them to be innovative (Sainaghi, Phillips and Corti 2013). In this regard, Chaker, Idrissi and Manouar (2017) stressed the importance of developing the balanced scorecard further and including other variables, such as ethics, which has an impact on business success and is more holistic because it increases the number of variables in the model. Giannopoulos et al. (2013) stated that the balanced scorecard ignores technological and competitive developments and expressed that these are important for companies nowadays.

Vila, Costa and Rovira (2010) proposed in their study a preliminary model for a balanced scorecard that can be used for tourism destinations. They stated that the balanced scorecard is critical to the value creation process and they advised that companies and even destinations can adapt the variables to suit their situations. Halmi and Severović (2016) built on and cited the work of Vila, Costa and Rovira (2010) and further examined how the balanced scorecard can be developed by expanding it to include social and environmental dimensions, thus creating sustainability balanced scorecards. Avci, Madanoglu and Okumus (2011) accepted this notion and stated that it was the best way forward for tourism firms, as there was a correlation between the use of scorecards and performance. Tourism firms that used scorecards were more strategic and performed better because they were able to assess different variables and then make decisions about the way forward. Maccarrone et al. (2014) demonstrated how action-oriented and practical scorecards can be and applied it in a coastal zone scenario to make action-oriented decisions.

Building on the literature, this study also proposes the use of scorecards, with specific emphasis on selecting the most appropriate niche products for development. It will examine the use of existing variables that have been used by different destinations to make decisions about the way forward. Combining the variables used by different countries and espoused in the literature into one rating sheet has not been done before and makes this study unique because it builds on the idea of creating scorecards to enhance tourism product development, which is important for increasing destination competitiveness (Goranczewski and Puciato 2010; Benur and Bramwell 2015).

Tourism product development in the Committee for Economic and Cultural Cooperation of the Organization of Islamic Cooperation (COMCEC) region follows a process of five steps when establishing the best product development opportunities. These five steps are (COMCEC 2013, 20):

1. Establishing the present situation,
2. Identifying the opportunities,
3. Prioritizing the tourism sector's objectives around niche products,
4. Supporting the prioritized forms of product development through facilitation and marketing,
5. Ongoing management and coordination.

The third step in the process prioritizes the niche products. This process of selecting the niches for diversification is sometimes biased. For example, government officials and tourism tour operators might select the ones that they feel have the most potential. Alternatively, niche products may be selected based on partisan bias, for example, an eco-tourism operator would support eco-tourism because they would benefit from its development the most. COMCEC (2013) reported that some of their member countries (Turkey, Malaysia, Saudi Arabia, Egypt, United Arab Emirates, Indonesia, Tunisia, Kazakhstan and Lebanon) select priority niches for development by examining niches that are compatible to the destination. Correspondingly, they also look at whether market data trends support the niche, the support systems already in place to sustain it, such as the existing human resources, and destination marketing.

Apart from the above factors used by COMCEC, the literature purports many other considerations that should be taken into account when deciding what products to diversify into. Some of the considerations identified by Manente (2008) include:
- Resources (human, capital, and so on)
- Territory
- Capacity and supporting infrastructure
- Services that support a particular niche
- Challenges posed by competition
- The extent of investment required for development of the niche
- Whether the product can be developed easily
- The environmental footprint and its sustainability
- Whether motivations, triggers and buying habits are already established
- The relevance of the consumption of the overall economic activity

Other considerations noted in the literature include:
- Current and potential linkages (Ritchie and Crouch 2003)
- Global industry trends (Pizam and Smith 2000)
- Transportation, airlift and local transport (PATA 2017)
- Government support (COMCEC 2013)
- Economic leakage (COMCEC 2013)
- Local society acceptance (COMCEC 2013)
- Image and perception – is the niche compatible to the destination? (COMCEC 2013)
- Funding and development costs (UNCTD 2010; COMCEC 2013)
- Whether people in this segment would realistically consider the destination (COMCEC 2013; PATA 2017)

Figure 13.3 illustrates an example of how the scorecard can be used to make decisions on which tourism niche area to develop and invest in. This model was developed for a Trinidad and Tobago context. Figure 13.3 displays the variables and the potential markets. A rating score will be applied to the selected variables for evaluating the identified niche products. The rating will range from zero to ten (lowest to highest) for each variable as it applies to a particular tourism niche product. Based on the tabulated scores, an evaluation will be conducted and used to select the most appropriate tourism markets and products to diversify into. Using these scores and ranking the products is new to this model. Furthermore, most filtering procedures for determining product development do not have a scoring system.

Against this background, this scorecard has the unique feature of adding a quantitative dimension to a qualitative process of niche selection, with the improved functional aspect of considering new measures by drawing from comprehensive case studies and the literature. The scorecard can be helpful in identifying the best niche products. Take, for example, a country that has limited financial resources and has only enough money to develop three products from the top five ranked products. This process allows for selecting the most appropriate niche products to invest in, even if one scored higher than the rest. The proposed scorecard acts as a filtering mechanism through which identified niches can be evaluated across a range of variables. The niche products that score the highest can then be prioritized in order and diversification can take effect in those specially selected niche tourism products. In summary, this scorecard is useful for breaking deadlocks on what products to select, develop and invest.

Personal bias is a real issue with the scoring and rating of products, so in order to get the scorecard to work more efficiently and remove the bias, owners and operators who belong to a particular niche (for example, a company that specializes in bird watching) should be asked to score and evaluate other niche areas but refrain from scoring the niche areas of their own business (eco-tourism). This is one way of removing personal bias while still receiving feedback on other products.

Figure 13.3: Sample of a Scorecard Model

Sample of Scorecard Model

			Niche Products →							
			Eco	Sport	Health	Weddings	Business	Culture	Soft Adventure	Cruise
	a	This niche's values are compatible to the destination								
	b	Market data trends support development of this niche								
	c	This niche and its products can be easily developed								
Extracted variables from case studies and the literature	d	In terms of competition, this niche and its products cannot be easily replicated by other destinations								
	e	Development of this niche has strong potential linkages to other sectors								
	f	Human capital already exists for this niche								
	g	This niche has existing infrastructure that can be easily upgraded or expanded								
	h	Development of this niche has a low carbon footprint on the environment								
	i	Development of this niche has a high level of financial return								

Figure 13.3: Sample of a Scorecard Model (contd)

		Niche Products →								
			Eco	Sport	Health	Weddings	Business	Culture	Soft Adventure	Cruise
Extracted variables from case studies and the literature	j	Development of this niche can assist with the current supply of tourism-related assets within a destination								
	k	Development of this niche offers benefits for rural communities								
	l	Development of this niche can lead to increased understanding and awareness of tourism's benefits, which can enable the host population to provide realistic support to maximize potential tourism opportunities								
	m	This niche product can generate employment for unskilled and semi-skilled workers								
	n	Development of this niche can boost the skill levels and enrich the capacity of employees operating in this niche								
	o	Development of this niche can foster economic growth								
	p	This niche can be developed responsibly and while following sustainable industry best practices								

Niche Marketing in the Caribbean

		Niche Products →							
		Eco	Sport	Health	Weddings	Business	Culture	Soft Adventure	Cruise
Extracted variables from case studies and the literature	q	Development of this niche can accelerate growth and transform the economy to create decent work and sustainable livelihoods							
	r	Development of this niche can build cohesive, caring communities and foster national pride							
	s	Development of this niche can lead to improvement of public services and strengthen democratic institutions							
	t	This niche has the potential to deliver a world-class visitor experience							
		TOTAL (sum of extracted variable scores) [a+b+c....+t]							

How it works:

Decision-makers would place a score ranging from 0 to 10 (zero representing a low rating of agreement, and ten representing the highest rating) as it applies for each variable relating to a particular niche. Each niche should be assessed and a score assigned vertically (moving downwards from one variable to the next), after the last variable is assessed, the total would be calculated by summing all the individual variable scores for that niche product.

> The next niche would then be assessed similarly following this same pattern, and after the last niche's total is scored, the comparisons can then be made. The niche with the highest score should be considered priority, and in terms of selecting niche products, it can be considered the best possible niche product for this destination.
>
> *Variable extraction sources*
>
> The selection of these variables emerged out of case studies, journals and country-specific studies where they have been successfully used. The criteria for adoption of variables must also match with broader international plans outlined by the World Tourism Organization such as Millennium Development Goals and sustainable tourism development criteria.

Conclusion

The tourism economy in most SIDS contributes heavily to their gross domestic product and earnings and, as a result of this, many SIDS are overdependent on tourism. When the main source markets for these SIDS are affected, it sends economic and social ripple effects throughout these small island economies, making them vulnerable to external conditions. However, the literature proposes a solution: diversifying the product offering. This is extremely beneficial since it reduces risk and spreads development across a range of assets, resulting in sustainable development of other areas if done well. This chapter builds on the question of how SIDS can diversify their product range by examining a scorecard model approach. This approach proposes a quantitative mechanism that can be applied to qualitative decision-making processes. It can be used to break deadlocks on what products to select and invest in. SIDS can use this model to give weight the options resulting in a ranking of the best possible areas for diversification as a way forward, thereby advancing options for diversification into other product areas and avoiding overdependence on one main product option.

References

Al-Zwyalif, Inaam M. 2017. "Using a Balanced Scorecard Approach to Measure Environmental Performance: A Proposed Model." *International Journal of Economics and Finance* 9 (8): 118–26.

Ansoff, H. Igor. 1957. "Strategies for Diversification." *Harvard Business Review* 35 (5): 113–24.

———, and Edward J. McDonnell. 1988. *The New Corporate Strategy.* New York: J. Wiley.

Avci, Umut, Melih Madanoglu, and Fevzi Okumus. 2011. "Strategic Orientation and Performance of Tourism Firms: Evidence from a Developing Country." *Tourism Management* 32 (1): 147–57.

Banchieri, Lucia Clara, Fernando Campa-Planas, Rosalia Cascón, Maria Belen Guercio, Ana Beatriz Hernández-Lara, and Maria Victoria Sánchez-Rebull. 2012. "Spanish Business Investment in China from the Perspective of the Consulting Firm Garrigues." *Measuring Business Excellence* 16 (2): 35–40.

Benur, Abdelati M., and Bill Bramwell. 2015. "Tourism Product Development and Product Diversification in Destinations." *Tourism Management* 50:213–24.

Braam, Geert J.M., Jos Benders, and Stefan Heusinkveld. 2007. "The Balanced Scorecard in the Netherlands: An Analysis of its Evolution using Print-Media Indicators." *Journal of Organizational Change Management* 20 (6): 866–79.

Bramwell, Bill. 1998. "User Satisfaction and Product Development in Urban Tourism." *Tourism Management* 19 (1): 35–47.

Buhalis, Dimitrios, and Maria Cristina Licata. 2002. "The Future eTourism Intermediaries." *Tourism Management* 23 (3): 207–20.

Chaker, Fadwa, Mohammed Abdou Janati Idrissi, and Abdellah El Manouar. 2017. "A Critical Evaluation of the Sustainability Balanced Scorecard as a Decision Aid Framework." *International Journal of Applied Engineering Research* 12 (14): 4221–37.

Chang, Wen-Cheng, Yu-Chi Tung, Chun-Hsiung Huang, and Ming-Chin Yang. 2008. "Performance Improvement after Implementing the Balanced Scorecard: A Large Hospital's Experience in Taiwan." *Total Quality Management* 19 (11): 1143–54.

Chao, Chi-Chur, Bharat R. Hazari, Jean-Pierre Laffargue, Pasquale M. Sgro, and Eden SH Yu. 2006. "Tourism, Dutch Disease and Welfare in an Open Dynamic Economy." *The Japanese Economic Review* 57 (4): 501–15.

Chen, Fu-Hsiang, Tsung-Shin Hsu, and Gwo-Hshiung Tzeng. 2011. "A Balanced Scorecard Approach to Establish a Performance Evaluation and Relationship Model for Hot Spring Hotels based on a Hybrid MCDM Model Combining DEMATEL and ANP." *International Journal of Hospitality Management* 30 (4): 908–32.

Clancy, Michael J. 1999. "Tourism and Development Evidence from Mexico." *Annals of Tourism Research* 26 (1): 1–20.

Claver-Cortés, Enrique, José F. Molina-Azorín, and Jorge Pereira-Moliner. 2007. "Competitiveness in Mass Tourism." *Annals of Tourism Research* 34 (3): 727–45.

Committee for Economic and Cultural Cooperation of the Organization of Islamic Cooperation (COMCEC). 2013. "Tourism Product Development and Marketing Strategies." COMCEC Member Countries 2013 Report. 30FC-D-15-eng-TOURISM.pdf (comcec.org).

Demas, William G. 2009. *The Economics of Development in Small Countries: With Special Reference to the Caribbean.* Kingston: University of the West Indies Press.

Divino, Jose Angelo, and Michael McAleer. 2010. "Modelling and Forecasting Daily International Mass Tourism to Peru." *Tourism Management* 31 (6): 846–54.

Dwyer, Larry, and Deborah Edwards. 2009. "Tourism Product and Service Innovation to Avoid 'Strategic Drift'." *International Journal of Tourism Research* 11 (4): 321–35.

Dwyer, Larry, Deborah Edwards, Nina Mistilis, Carolina Roman, and Noel Scott. 2009. "Destination and Enterprise Management for a Tourism Future." *Tourism Management* 30 (1): 63–74.

Evans, Nigel. 2005. "Assessing the Balanced Scorecard as a Management Tool for Hotels." *International Journal of Contemporary Hospitality Management* 17 (5): 376–90.

Farmaki, Anna. 2012. "A Supply-side Evaluation of Coastal Tourism Diversification: The Case of Cyprus." *Tourism Planning and Development* 9 (2): 183–203.

Giannopoulos, George, Andrew Holt, Ehsan Khansalar, and Stephanie Cleanthous. 2013. "The Use of the Balanced Scorecard in Small Companies." *International Journal of Business and Management* 8 (14): 1–22.

Goranczewski, Bolesław, and Daniel Puciato. 2010. "SWOT Analysis in the Formulation of Tourism Development Strategies for Destinations." *Turyzm* 20 (2): 45–53.

Greasley, Andrew. 2004. "Process Improvement within a HR division at a UK Police Force." *International Journal of Operations and Production Management* 24 (3): 230–40.

Guerreiro, Marta, and Marta Guerreiro. 2017. "Azores: More Than a Tourist Destination." *Worldwide Hospitality and Tourism Themes* 9 (6): 653–58.

———. 1999. "Destination Branding, Niche Marketing and National Image Projection in Central and Eastern Europe." *Journal of Vacation Marketing* 5 (3): 227–37.

Hall, Derek. 2002. "Brand Development, Tourism and National Identity: The Re-imaging of Former Yugoslavia." *Journal of Brand Management* 9 (4): 323–34.

Halmi, Lahorka, and Kornelija Severović. 2016. "Strategic Approach to Tourism Destination Management." *Zeszyty Naukowe Małopolskiej Wyższej Szkoły Ekonomicznej w Tarnowie* 4 (32): 77–86.

Hassan, Salah S. 2000. "Determinants of Market Competitiveness in an Environmentally Sustainable Tourism Industry." *Journal of Travel Research* 38 (3): 239–45.

Holzner, Mario. 2011. "Tourism and Economic Development: The Beach Disease?" *Tourism Management* 32 (4): 922–33.

Kaplan, Robert S., and David P. Norton. 1995. "Putting the Balanced Scorecard." *Performance Measurement, Management, and Appraisal Sourcebook* 66:66–74.

Karatzoglou, Benjamin, and Ioannis Spilanis. 2010. "Sustainable Tourism in Greek Islands: The Integration of Activity-based Environmental Management with a Destination Environmental Scorecard Based on the Adaptive Resource Management Paradigm." *Business Strategy and the Environment* 19 (1): 26–38.

Khairat, Ghada Mohamed. 2017. "The Balanced Scorecard Approach as a Tool for Performance Evaluation in the Airline Companies." *International Journal of Heritage, Tourism, and Hospitality* 10: n. pg.

Kotler, Phillip, and James Makens. 1999. *Marketing for Hospitality and Tourism*, 5th ed. Uttar Pradesh: Nodia Pearson Education India.

Lewis, William Arthur. 1950. *The Industrialisation of the British West Indies*. Washington, DC: US Government Printing Office.

Lewis, Acolla, and Leslie-Ann Jordan. 2008. "Tourism in Trinidad and Tobago: Carving a Niche in a Petroleum-based Economy." *International Journal of Tourism Research* 10 (3): 247–57.

Liao, Shu-hsien, Yin-Ju Chen, and Min-yi Deng. 2010. "Mining Customer Knowledge for Tourism New Product Development and Customer Relationship Management." *Expert Systems with Applications* 37 (6): 4212–23.

Maccarrone, Vincenzo, Francesco Filiciotto, Gaspare Buffa, Salvatore Mazzola, and Giuseppa Buscaino. 2014. "The ICZM Balanced Scorecard: A Tool for Putting Integrated Coastal Zone Management into Action." *Marine Policy* 44:321–34.

Manente, Mara. 2008. "Destination Management and Economic Background: Defining and Monitoring Local Tourist Destinations." In *International Conference on Measuring Tourism Economic Contribution at Sub-National Levels*, 29–31. October, Málaga, Spain.

McElroy, Jerome L., and Klaus De Albuquerque. 1998. "Tourism Penetration Index in Small Caribbean Islands." *Annals of Tourism Research* 25 (1): 145–68.

Mooraj, Stella, Daniel Oyon, and Didier Hostettler. 1999. "The Balanced Scorecard: A Necessary Good or an Unnecessary Evil?" *European Management Journal* 17 (5): 481–91.

Morgan, Nigel J., and Annette Pritchard. 2006. "Promoting Niche Tourism Destination Brands: Case Studies of New Zealand and Wales." *Journal of Promotion Management* 12 (1): 17–33.

Murray, Douglas W., and Martin A. O'Neill. 2012. "Craft Beer: Penetrating a Niche Market." *British Food Journal* 114 (7): 899–909.

Nill, Jan, and René Kemp. 2009. "Evolutionary Approaches for Sustainable Innovation Policies: From Niche to Paradigm?" *Research Policy* 38 (4): 668–80.

Notarstefano, G., and S. Volo. 2012. "A Balanced Score Card Approach to Measuring the Impact of Tourism." In *Riunione Scientifica della Società Italiana di Scienze del Turismo (SISTUR)* 6:551–61.

Novelli, Marina, Birte Schmitz, and Trisha Spencer. 2006. "Networks, Clusters and Innovation in Tourism: A UK Experience." *Tourism Management* 27 (6): 1141–52.

Othman, Rozhan. 2008. "Enhancing the Effectiveness of the Balanced Scorecard with Scenario Planning." *International Journal of Productivity and Performance Management* 57 (3): 259–66.

Page, Albert L. 1993. "Assessing New Product Development Practices and Performance: Establishing Crucial Norms." *Journal of Product Innovation Management* 10 (4): 273–90.

Page, Stephen J., Heather Hartwell, Nick Johns, Alan Fyall, Adele Ladkin, and Ann Hemingway. 2017. "Case Study: Wellness, Tourism and Small Business Development in a UK Coastal Resort: Public Engagement in Practice." *Tourism Management* 60:466–77.

Papatheodorou, Andreas, Jaume Rosselló, and Honggen Xiao. 2010. "Global Economic Crisis and Tourism: Consequences and Perspectives." *Journal of Travel Research* 49 (1): 39–45.

Parrish, Erin D., Nancy L. Cassill, and William Oxenham. 2006. "Niche Market Strategy for a Mature Marketplace." *Marketing Intelligence and Planning* 24 (7): 694–707.

Pacific Asia Travel Association (PATA). 2017. Sustainable Tourism Online: Destinations and Communities. http://sustain.pata.org/sustainable-tourism-online/destinations-andcommunities/implementation/destination-development/destination-products-and-experiences/.

Pizam, A., and Smith, G. 2000. "Tourism and Terrorism: A Quantitative Analysis of Major Terrorist Acts and Their Impact on Tourism Destinations." *Tourism Economics* 6 (2): 123–38.

Poon, Auliana. 1993. *Tourism, Technology and Competitive Strategies*. Wallingford: CAB International.

Qin, S.Y., A.S. Atkins, and H. Yu. 2013. "Balanced Scorecard Approach to Evaluate Business Performance Measurement using Web Tools in e-Tourism." *International Journal of Computing Science and Communication Technologies* 5 (2): 822–28.

Rahman, H., and Hoong Chor Chin. 2013. "A Balanced Scorecard for Performance Evaluation of Sustainable Urban Transport." *International Journal of Development and Sustainability* 2 (3): 1671–1702.

Ritchie, J.R. Brent, and Geoffrey Ian Crouch. 2003. *The Competitive Destination: A Sustainable Tourism Perspective*. Wallingford: CABI Publishing.

Rogerson, Christian M. 2004. "Regional Tourism in South Africa: A Case of 'Mass Tourism of the South'." *GeoJournal* 60 (3): 229–37.

Sainaghi, Ruggero, Paul Phillips, and Valentina Corti. 2013. "Measuring Hotel Performance: Using a Balanced Scorecard Perspectives' Approach." *International Journal of Hospitality Management* 34: 150–59.

Sakarya, Sema, Molly Eckman, and Karen H. Hyllegard. 2007. "Market Selection for International Expansion: Assessing Opportunities in Emerging Markets." *International Marketing Review* 24 (2): 208–38.

Scheyvens, Regina, and Janet H. Momsen. 2008. "Tourism and Poverty Reduction: Issues for Small Island States." *Tourism Geographies* 10 (1): 22–41.

Schilling, Melissa A., and Charles W.L. Hill. 1998. "Managing the New Product Development Process: Strategic Imperatives." *Academy of Management Perspectives* 12 (3): 67–81.

Schot, Johan, and Frank W. Geels. 2008. "Strategic Niche Management and Sustainable Innovation Journeys: Theory, Findings, Research Agenda, and Policy." *Technology Analysis and Strategic Management* 20 (5): 537–54.

Sen, Doruk, Sakir Bingol, and Ozalp Vayvay. 2017. "Strategic Enterprise Management for Innovative Companies: The Last Decade of the Balanced Scorecard." *International Journal of Asian Social Science* 7 (1): 97–109.

Sethi, Rajesh, Daniel C. Smith, and C. Whan Park. 2001. "Cross-Functional Product Development Teams, Creativity, and the Innovativeness of New Consumer Products." *Journal of Marketing Research* 38 (1): 73–85.

Smith, S.L. 1994. "The Tourism Product." *Annals of Tourism Research* 21 (3): 582–95.

Toften, Kjell, and Trond Hammervoll. 2011. "International Market Selection and Growth Strategies for Niche Firms." *International Journal of Entrepreneurship and Innovation Management* 13 (3–4): 282–95.

Trunfio, Mariapina, Luca Petruzzellis, and Claudio Nigro. 2006. "Tour Operators and Alternative Tourism in Italy: Exploiting Niche Markets to Increase International Competitiveness." *International Journal of Contemporary Hospitality Management* 18 (5): 426–38.

World Bank. *Global Economic Prospects. June 2015: The Global Economy in Transition.* Washington, DC: The World Bank.

United Nations Conference on Trade and Development (UNCTD). 2010. "Promoting Foreign Investment in Tourism." Investment Advisory Series. Series A, number 5. http://unctad.org/en/docs/diaepcb200916_en.pdf.

United Nations World Tourism Organization (UNWTO). 2014. *Tourism in Small Island Developing States: Building a More Sustainable Future for the People of the Islands.* Madrid: UNWTO. https://doi.org/10.18111/9789284416257.

Vainikka, Vilhelmiina. 2013. "Rethinking Mass Tourism." *Tourist Studies* 13 (3): 268–86.

Vanegas Sr, Manuel, and Robertico R. Croes. 2003. "Growth, Development and Tourism in a Small Economy: Evidence from Aruba." *International Journal of Tourism Research* 5 (5): 315–330.

Vila, Mar, Gerard Costa, and Xari Rovira. 2010. "The Creation and Use of Scorecards in Tourism Planning: A Spanish Example." *Tourism Management* 31 (2): 232–39.

Voelpel, Sven C., Marius Leibold, and Robert A. Eckhoff. 2006. "The Tyranny of the Balanced Scorecard in the Innovation Economy." *Journal of Intellectual Capital* 7 (1): 43–60.

Weaver, David B. 2000. "A Broad Context Model of Destination Development Scenarios." *Tourism Management* 21 (3): 217–24.

Yilmaz, Yildirim, and Umit Bititci. 2006. "Performance Measurement in the Value Chain: Manufacturing v. Tourism." *International Journal of Productivity and Performance Management* 55 (5): 371–89.

Concluding Remarks

Acolla Lewis-Cameron

"For island states that have very few resources, virtually the only resources where there may be some comparative advantage in favour of [island microstates] are clean beaches, unpolluted seas and warm weather and water, and at least vestiges of distinctive cultures." (Connell 1988, cited in Hall and Page 1996, 2)

It is this perception of Caribbean small island developing states (SIDS) that has informed the mass tourism model of tourism development adopted by the majority of tourism-dependent SIDS. Over the last four decades, Caribbean SIDS have exploited these few natural resources primarily for economic gain. Upon reflection and current examination of the state of these SIDS, some may argue that the overdependence on mass tourism was worth it, as focus is placed on the levels of infrastructural development, employment opportunities and tourism's contribution to gross domestic product. Conversely, others lament that the irreparable damage to the islands' ecosystems is a cost too high to bear for both current and future generations. As was aptly captured in the opening chapter, Caribbean SIDS find themselves in the unenviable position of being inherently vulnerable to external shocks and highly dependent on an extremely volatile tourism industry. According to Lewis-Cameron, Jordan and Roberts (2021, 6), "SIDS vulnerability is exaggerated and resilience diminished because of not only its dependency on tourism but also its development of tourism solely on demand factors and specifically, its dependency on particular types of tourism products, type of tourists and particular source markets".

Contemplation of the future of Caribbean SIDS brings to the fore the issue of its vulnerability and concomitant resilience in the face of inevitable crises and reliance on a volatile industry. At the time of writing, the region is reeling from the economic fallout of the COVID-19 pandemic, where the islands experienced over 70 per cent decline in growth over the last two years, the worst ever recorded economic shock. This pandemic follows a succession of destructive hurricanes that have wreaked havoc on the islands year after year. The lesson to be learned as the region looks past COVID-19 is the fact that the traditional 3S (sun, sand and sea) mass tourism development model can no longer sustain Caribbean SIDS. The future of Caribbean tourism relies on the adoption of a sun plus approach to development that is anchored in the region's range of resources and not solely on the 3S resources. The success of this approach requires a radical shift in the thinking purported by Connell (1988, cited in Hall and Page 1996) that the 3S resources are the only resources that can define a future Caribbean state. Undeniably, while the 3S resources remain the most ubiquitous and well known, the development of the region over the last two decades, in particular, has shown that there is much untapped potential, including the "vestiges of distinctive cultures". The smorgasbord of existing and potential niche tourism experiences detailed in the chapters of this book is testament to the rethinking of a Caribbean tourism that can be anchored on the bountiful natural resources, the creativity of the people and the rich cultural heritage. A sun plus approach to tourism development presents myriad possibilities for island destinations as consideration is given to complementary tourism experiences that enhance the overall tourism offering of the destination. The Balance Scorecard Model in chapter 13 provides Caribbean SIDS with a practical tool for the identification and development of competitive niche tourism products. As Caribbean SIDS look towards 2030 and beyond, the onus is on national governments, the private sector and civil society to work together to create opportunities for diverse tourism experiences, build capacity in local communities and protect all the resources upon which the industry must be anchored.

References

Hall, M, and S. Page, eds. 1996. *Tourism in the Pacific: Issues and Cases*. London: International Thomson Business Press.

Lewis-Cameron, A., L. Jordan, and S. Roberts, eds. 2021. *Managing Crises in Tourism: Resilience Strategies from the Caribbean*. Cham: Palgrave McMillan.

About the Contributors

Belinda Blessitt Vincent, EdD, has over twenty-five years of experience working in both the private and public sectors. She has a broad spectrum of expertise in the areas of strategic human resources management and development, organizational leadership, tourism and research. She is dean of business and finance at the University College of the Cayman Islands. Along with administration, she conducts leadership workshops and seminars, presents at conferences and is a dissertation advisor for students pursuing graduate studies in human resource management. She received the Stingray Award for her work in tourism and the Hon. W. McKeeva Bush Award in Recognition of Outstanding Dedication to the Tourism Apprenticeship Training Advisory Council in the Cayman Islands. Dr Blessitt Vincent is married to Nestor and has a son, Matthew.

Jovari Hagley was born and raised in the beautiful island of Grenada. He is a graduate of the University of the West Indies, St Augustine, and holds a MSc in tourism development and management and a BSc in tourism and hospitality management. He received both the Caribbean Tourism Organization and the Caribbean Hotel and Tourism Association educational scholarship awards. Jovari's academic accomplishments are also complemented by his wealth of experience within the hospitality and tourism industry. He has held positions ranging from tour guide to lecturer to hotel manager. To date, Jovari continues to work in the industry as a learning and development manager with one of the world's leading cruise lines.

Elizabeth Ince-Peters holds a BSc in economics and a MSc in tourism development and management. She has a passion for the development of alternative tourism in the Caribbean and has focused her research on the same. Ince-Peters worked as a research assistant at the University of the West Indies for over five years, first within the Trade and Economic Development Unit of the Department of Economics and then with the Department of Management Studies under the Sport and Tourism Unit. She has co-authored articles within multiple journals, including the peer-reviewed journal *Social and Economic Studies*.

Leslie-Ann Jordan, PhD, is a senior lecturer, hospitality and tourism management at the University of the West Indies (the UWI), Department of Management Studies, St Augustine, Trinidad, with more than eighteen years of teaching experience. She holds a BSc in tourism management (first class honours) from the UWI and a post-graduate diploma in tourism management (with distinction) and PhD in tourism policy and planning from the University of Otago, New Zealand. Her research interests include tourism development in small island developing states (SIDS) with special reference to the Anglophone Caribbean; tourism planning and development and tourism policy and decision-making. More recent research focuses on cruise tourism, heritage tourism, festival and event management and service management. Dr Jordan is the lead editor of the text *Sports Event Management: The Caribbean Experience* (Ashgate, 2011) and co-editor of the text *Managing Crises in Tourism: Resilience Strategies from the Caribbean* (Palgrave Macmillan, 2021).

Acolla Lewis-Cameron, PhD is currently dean of the Faculty of Social Sciences at the University of the West Indies (UWI), St Augustine, Trinidad. Her educational achievements include a MSc in hospitality and tourism education from the University of Surrey, UK and a PhD in tourism from Brunel University in the UK. Acolla's teaching experience in tourism planning and policy and marketing, and her research and consultancy in the above areas have provided an all-round understanding of the industry. She is the lead editor of the texts *Marketing Island Destinations: Concepts and Cases* and *Managing Crises in Tourism: Resilience Strategies from the Caribbean* and co-author of the text *Caribbean Tourism: Concepts and Cases*.

Kennedy Obombo Magio holds a PhD in tourism management from Universidad Autónoma de Occidente, México. He is a distinguished member of the National System of Researchers in México and his research is largely focused on tourism sustainability in the Mexican Caribbean. With over thirty publications, Kennedy has been awarded several scholarships and grants to contribute to tourism knowledge, including his current research fellowship and an Excellence Award by the Mexican Academy for Tourism Research. He has undertaken a number of consultancies for public and private sector tourism organizations within México and for international agencies.

Andre Phillips, DBA, is a Caribbean professional with experience in development consulting, entrepreneurship and civil society engagement. As an academic, his research concentration spans heritage preservation, tourism and diaspora studies. He holds a doctor of business administration degree from the University of the West Indies, St Augustine, and previously earned a master's in business administration (marketing) from Washington International University. His doctoral research examined the nexus between diaspora tourism and sustainable development. In 2018, his first academic publication, "Diaspora Engagement: New Imperatives for Tourism Growth in Trinidad and Tobago", was published in *Dynamics of Diaspora Engagement in the Caribbean*. He leads a non-profit organization dedicated to fostering social partnerships between Trinidad and Tobago diasporic groups and community organizations in their homeland.

Narendra Ramgulam was formerly the director of tourism product development and destination management at the Tobago Tourism Agency. Prior to this, Narendra was the MSc programme coordinator at the University of the West Indies. He is also a PhD economic development policy candidate at the University of the West Indies. Narendra has published several research articles in peer-reviewed academic journals across a range of topics. His research interests include sustainable development in Caribbean small island developing states, tourism anthropology, tourism impacts and niche tourism product development. Narendra has worked both in academia, lecturing tourism courses and in the tourism industry, allowing for a good understanding of the links between theory and practice.

Sherma Roberts, PhD, is a senior lecturer in tourism at the University of the West Indies, Cave Hill Campus. In addition to teaching, she contributes to the public discourse on regional tourism through service on boards, panel discussions and keynote addresses. From 2017 to 2021, she served as chairperson of the Tobago Tourism Agency, the first of its kind on the island. Sherma has co-edited four books and has written and presented papers in areas pertaining to community participation, corporate social responsibility, sustainable tourism, diaspora tourism, e-marketing and tourism entrepreneurship. In 2019, she chaired the fourth Caribbean Tourism International Conference in Barbados themed *Navigating the Destination of the Future*, hosted jointly by three of the campuses of the University of the West Indies. Sherma is an alumnus of Brunel University, University of Surrey and the University of the West Indies.

Leandra Simon-Richards conducted her research on music tourism development as a postgraduate student at the University of the West Indies while pursuing her MSc in tourism development and management. Her interests, training and experience extend over a wide variety of fields, including military leadership and management, politics, communications, digital content creation, sales, marketing, administration, customer service and procurement. An avid music lover, songwriter and performer, she is ever hopeful that her work can contribute to sustainable tourism development and increase its consideration and inclusion of marginalized communities.

Therez B. Walker, PhD, is a lecturer in tourism management. Her research focuses on sustainable tourism development in small island developing states and how islands can maximize linkages between tourism and other sectors of the local economy. In addition to her academic activities, she has a background in consultancy, working with destination management organizations and non-governmental organizations.

Ineta Rosetta West-Gerald is the director of tourism at the Montserrat Tourism Division. She has been involved in all aspects of tourism development on the island and was instrumental in the island's transition following the Soufrière Hills volcanic eruptions. Ineta graduated from Loughborough College, UK, with a Higher National Diploma in tourism in 2000 and from the University of Derby, UK, with a BA Hons. in tourism management in 2001. She is keen on sustainable tourism development and co-wrote an article on COVID-19 called "Paving the Way for a more Sustainable World – A Post COVID-19 Blueprint for Sustainable Tourism in Small Island Developing States". Ineta is married with two children.

Index

A

Accessible tourism, 5, 12, 13, 53–55, 57, 59, 61, 62-69, 71–76
Adventure tourism, 146, 151,152,165, 243
Agritourism, 122, 131, 132, 137–39, 143, 144
Alternative tourism, 18, 24–26, 32, 34, 35, 37, 139, 145, 231, 275, 279
Antigua and Barbuda, 5

B

Balanced scorecard approach, vi, 17, 254, 261, 270, 271, 273, 274, 277
Barbados, 5, 13, 14, 33, 101, 103, 105, 107, 109, 111–17, 119, 124, 127, 144, 162, 164, 184, 188, 190, 202, 282
Barbados Jazz Festival, 13, 14, 101, 103, 108, 109, 111–15, 117, 118, 119
Barbados Tourism Authority (BTA), 112, 117
Barrier-free tourism, vii, 53, 55, 64, 70, 74

C

Caribbean Community (CARICOM), 33, 74, 117, 119, 141
Caribbean Festival of the Arts (CARIFESTA), 106
Caribbean tourism, vii, xiii, xiv, 8, 11, 18, 19, 22, 30, 50–52, 55, 75, 106, 117, 118, 131, 142, 164, 169, 173, 184, 189, 191, 277, 279, 280, 282
Caribbean Tourism Organization (CTO), 8, 18, 19, 106, 164, 169, 173, 184, 279
Carnival, 77, 78, 86, 87, 95, 99, 103–5, 111, 114, 177–79
Cayman Islands, 9, 15, 103, 188, 189–91, 196-199, 202, 203, 205–10, 279
Caymankind, vi, 15, 187, 189, 191, 193, 195, 197, 199, 201, 203, 205–9
Collaboration, 12, 13, 38, 43, 46, 48, 49, 65, 66, 69–71, 73, 80, 89, 92, 94, 108, 113, 115, 125, 134, 135, 138, 141, 184, 189
Community participation, ix, 14, 51, 81, 82, 89, 99, 111, 135, 281
Core-periphery, vi, 231, 233, 239, 240, 248, 249
COVID-19, vi, 8, 9–11, 16, 18, 19, 20, 25, 26, 30, 38, 62, 85, 94, 108, 115, 159, 163, 189, 190, 197, 203, 206, 211, 212–14, 229, 230, 248, 276, 277, 282
Cozumel, vi, 15, 211–30
Cruise industry, 212, 221, 226, 227
Cruise lines, 16, 199, 211, 212, 216, 218-228, 279
Cruise tourism, vi, 15, 16, 33, 211–21, 223, 225, 226, 227, 229, 230, 280
Cruise tourists, 16, 212, 218, 221, 225, 227, 228
Cuba, 27, 80, 98, 103, 188, 191, 200, 217

D

Dependency, 8, 77, 98, 239, 240, 246, 248, 249, 276
Destination Health Care, 206, 207, 208
Diaspora, v, 15, 20, 115, 167–69, 171–86, 235, 252, 281, 282
Diaspora tourism, v, 15, 20, 167–69, 171–77, 179, 181–86, 235, 252, 281, 282

Disasters, 2, 3, 55, 151, 153, 165, 166
Diversification, 2, 8, 12, 23, 24, 28, 30–32, 41, 42, 51, 129, 176, 254, 255, 256, 258, 260, 263, 264, 266, 270, 271, 272
Domestic Tourism, vi, 16, 94, 231–41, 243–53
Domestic tourists, 16, 232, 234–36, 243, 245, 247, 248
Dominica, 27, 103, 149, 188, 200, 258
Dominican Republic, 103, 188, 200

E
Economic development, 1, 2, 8, 18, 24, 25, 52, 81, 96, 107, 111, 155, 156, 158, 165, 193, 200, 201, 235, 242, 246, 255, 260, 272, 280, 281
Economic diversification, 8, 23, 31, 32, 51, 254
Educational tourism, v, xiii, 12, 33–35, 37, 39, 41, 43, 45, 47, 49–51
Events, 3, 14, 43, 45, 46, 75, 77, 80, 96, 98, 101–4, 106, 108, 110, 112, 114–16, 118, 119, 124, 126, 132, 145, 154, 165, 172, 174, 175, 221, 226, 234
External shocks, 2, 4, 276

F
Festival management, 14, 105, 106, 107, 113, 117, 118
Festival product, 107, 114, 115
Festival tourism, v, 13, 27, 77, 101–3, 105, 107, 109, 111, 113, 115, 117–20, 183
Florida-Caribbean Cruise Association (FCCA), 215, 229
Food tourism, v, vii, 14, 121, 122, 125, 127–43, 145

G
Grand Anse Beach, 63–66, 74
Grand E'tang National Park & Forest Reserve, 63–65

Grenada, v, xiv, 5, 9, 12, 13, 34, 40–49, 51, 53–55, 61–67, 69–75, 149, 279
Grenada Tourism Authority (GTA), 41, 42, 45, 46, 63, 66, 69, 71, 72, 74
Grenadines, 27, 74, 162, 165
Guyana, 9, 10, 74, 174, 185, 186

H
Homeland visits, 168, 173, 174, 178, 180, 181, 182, 183
Hurricanes, 1, 9, 277

I
Institutional arrangements, 12, 39, 46, 49, 95, 98, 106, 113
International Convention on the Rights of Persons with Disabilities, 59, 60, 67
International Monetary Fund (IMF), 10, 19
Island economies, 8, 30, 133, 139, 235, 270

J
Jamaica, 5, 27, 87, 103, 112, 118, 143, 173, 174, 185, 188, 252, 260
Jazz festivals, v, ix, 13, 14, 101–4, 107, 109, 114, 115, 117

L
Linkages, 4, 5, 8, 14, 17, 23, 24, 42, 92, 101, 122, 131, 134, 136, 138, 143, 173, 175, 182, 185, 190, 194, 227, 231, 234, 235, 243, 244, 246, 257, 265, 267, 282

M
Mass tourism, 7, 8, 9, 11, 22, 24, 25, 27–30, 34, 167, 188, 213, 231, 232, 247, 250, 258, 259, 271, 272, 274, 275, 276, 277
Mass tourism products, 27, 29, 258, 259
Medical tourism, vi, 15, 27, 167, 176, 187–210
Mexico, 184, 213, 214, 216, 222,

224, 226, 229, 239, 258, 271, 280, 281
Montserrat, 160–62, 164–66, 282
Montserrat Volcano Observatory (MVO), 149, 153, 154, 155, 160, 165
Music tourism, vii, ix, 13, 77–81, 83–86, 88–90, 92–94, 97, 98, 100, 101, 103, 282
Music Tourism Participation (MTP), vii, 85, 88, 92–94

N
Natural disasters, 2, 3, 55, 151, 166
New tourist, 2, 24, 26, 34, 175, 240, 259
Niche market, 13, 17, 29, 71, 73, 101, 117, 133, 143, 256, 273, 274, 275
Niche marketing, vi, 254, 255, 257, 259, 261, 263, 265, 267, 269, 271–73, 275
Niche product development, 17, 29, 256
Niche tourism, iii, v, xi, xiii, xiv, 11–14, 17, 22-25, 27–29, 31, 41, 49–52, 98, 117, 231, 252, 256, 258-260, 266, 273, 277, 281
Niche tourism in the Caribbean, iii, xi, xiii
Niche tourism products, 11, 17, 27, 28, 31, 256, 258, 260, 266, 277

O
Overdependence on tourism, 8, 12

P
Participatory Tourism Development (PTD), 13, 79, 81
Partnerships, 14, 76, 109, 114, 115, 116, 202, 214, 228, 281
Port destination, 16, 211, 212
Product development, vii, 17, 25, 27–30, 32, 176, 182, 255, 256, 258–60, 264, 266, 271, 273, 274, 281

R
Risk management, 151, 165
Rural tourism, 51, 144

S
Seasonality, 5, 37, 41, 78, 175, 176, 179, 234, 259, 263
Seismic Research Centre, 160
SIDS. *See* Small Island Developing States, vi, ix, 1–6, 8, 12, 14, 17, 101, 122–25, 127, 128, 130, 132, 133, 135, 137, 143, 254, 270, 276, 277, 280
Slow food, v, vii, 14, 121–30, 132–45
Slow city, 124, 126, 130, 135, 142
Small island states (SIS), 3, 4, 5, 6, 18–20, 144, 252, 274
Social exchange theory (SET) 81, 233, 237, 253
Special interest tourism, 33, 34, 82, 87, 98, 100, 117, 140, 150, 250
St George's University, 34, 40, 46, 51
St Kitts and Nevis, 119, 200
St Lucia, 5, 13, 27, 33, 103, 106–10, 112–16
St Lucia Jazz Festival, v, 13, 14, 101, 103, 105, 107–11, 114, 118, 119
St Lucia Jazz and Arts Festival, 107, 11, 113
St Lucia Tourist Board (SLTB), 108, 110, 112, 119
St Vincent, 18, 147, 149, 162, 163, 165
Stakeholder participation, 88, 90, 122, 130, 138
Sustainability, vi, 6, 14, 16, 17, 22, 50, 61, 74, 93, 113–17, 122, 126, 128, 129, 132, 133, 137, 139, 141, 143, 145, 172, 211–14, 218, 221, 222–27, 229, 231, 251, 252, 257, 264, 265, 271, 274, 280
Sustainable development, 17, 18, 20, 42, 50, 98, 117, 126, 139–

41, 145, 159, 165, 168, 172, 173, 228, 230, 239, 250, 251
Sustainable development goals (SDGs), 17, 20, 140
Sustainable tourism, 1, 14, 15, 20, 24, 32, 51, 52, 68, 74, 81, 88, 99, 113, 119, 120, 125, 127, 131, 133, 135, 140–42, 144, 145, 168, 171, 172, 182–84, 214, 222–25, 227, 229, 231, 232, 236, 246, 249, 251, 252, 263, 270, 272, 274, 282

T

Tobago Tourism Agency, 16, 238, 241, 242, 252, 281
Tobago House of Assembly (THA), 240, 250
Tourism dependent islands, 22
Tourism development, v, vii, ix, 4, 6, 8, 9, 13, 16, 18–20, 22, 23, 25, 27, 29, 31, 37, 51, 77, 78, 81–84, 86, 87, 88, 89, 90, 93, 94, 97, 100, 106, 113, 119, 122, 131, 140–42, 164, 182, 186, 197, 223, 225, 231, 232, 236, 240, 243, 247–52, 258, 270, 272, 276, 277, 279, 280, 282
Tourism diversification, 12, 24, 41, 51, 263, 272
Tourism economic impacts, vii, 11
Tourism niche, xiii, 14, 67, 77, 78, 122, 128, 135, 136, 143, 144, 168, 182, 206, 266
Tourism product, 231, 256, 258, 259, 260, 264, 266, 271, 275, 276, 277, 281

Tourism product diversification, 28, 30, 258, 260
Trinidad and Tobago, v, ix, 5, 10, 15, 16, 30, 98, 99, 103, 105, 111, 114, 160, 167–72, 174, 176–86, 232, 239, 240, 242, 249, 251, 256, 266, 273, 281
Trinidad Carnival. *See* Carnival, 77
Training and education, 64, 67, 68, 70

U

United Nations World Tourism Organization (UNWTO), 4, 10, 20, 25, 32, 38, 39, 45, 46, 51, 73, 74, 76, 113, 120, 233, 253, 275
Universal design, 13, 57, 60–62, 68, 69, 75

V

Visiting Friends and Relatives (VFR), 48, 157, 174, 180, 233
Volcano tourism, v, 15, 146–51, 153, 155, 157, 158, 159, 161, 163, 165
Vulnerability, ix, 1, 2, 3, 7, 12, 18, 20, 144, 252, 276

W

Wellness tourism, 15, 190, 195, 196, 206, 207, 208, 210, 274
World Tourism and Travel Council (WTTC), 9, 21, 52, 106, 186, 239, 253

www.ingramcontent.com/pod-product-compliance
Lightning Source LLC
Chambersburg PA
CBHW021820300426
44114CB00009BA/252